BASKETBALL

DPH SPORTS SERIES

BASKETBALL

H. C. DUBEY

DISCOVERY PUBLISHING HOUSE
New Delhi-110002

First Published – 1999

Reprinted – 2015

ISBN: 978-81-7141-449-9

Basketball

Published by:

DISCOVERY PUBLISHING HOUSE PVT. LTD.
4383/4B, Ansari Road, Darya Ganj
New Delhi-110 002 (India)
Phone: +91-11-23279245, 43596064-65
Fax: +91-11-23253475
E-mail: discoverypublishinghouse@gmail.com
sales@discoverypublishinggroup.com
web: www.discoverypublishinggroup.com

Printed at:
Infinity Imaging Systems
Delhi

PREFACE

The need of having a sports series felt because today's situation of the world is not conducive to peace, all round there is destruction, despair, conflict and war; war if not between two nations then within the country itself. In a world where there are some 820 million people unemployed or under-employed, and where 86 million people are born every year, it is not surprising that one out of every four individuals lives in absolute poverty. The *Discovery Publishing House* by Publishing this series seeks to get positive response as—to means by which sports can promote and propagate peace and international cooperation. Sportsmen form a large identifiable cadre. We visualises a situation where a conscious efforts is made all over the world to train the sportspersons to spread the message of peace and international cooperation. Instead of peace keeping efforts through arms and army, the sportspersons may be used as soldiers of peace in a subtle manner. The effort is to make the realize the contribution of sports as a factor for sustainable development, peace keeping and international cooperation.

In developing countries, sports development cooperation is still in the need of justification and steadfast arguments. Many people ask the question "why invest in sports in developing countries for which water supply, health service and agriculture projects are much better suited? An apt reply to this question may be "for many of the people of a developing country,

Sports is the only 'Sweaty' Leisure-time activity. Sports represents a moment of joy in the midst of hard poverty-stricken and dirty everyday life. Doing sports even makes one's work go more smoothly the next day.

This series will be useful to the sports promoters, organisers, coaches and other persons related or interested in sports.

Editor

CONTENTS

1

HISTORY OF BASKETBALL

The basic idea of basketball-throwing at an elevated target is very old. According to documents by scientists writers and historians, the old civilized nations of Central America, the Aztecs, Mayas and Incas, used to play a game which can be regarded as the fore-runner of present-day basketball. The field consisted of two areas marked by different colours and separated by a groove. There were stone rings in the walls at the narrow ends through which a rubber ball had to be pushed either with the shoulder the hip or the knee. Also with the Normans in Brittany and Normandy some 1,000 years ago, in the ball game houses of the Middle ages, and later among the inhabitants of Florida a game was played where wicker baskets attached to high poles had to be hit.

Present day basketball, however, originated at Springfield College in the USA. Dr. James Naismith devised the basic form of the game in 1981 and it is believed that he was influenced by games played in antiquity. In his time, an interesting indoor game was required to fill the time between the American baseball and football seasons. The first match was played between students of Spring field College in a big hall in 1891 with a football. The target were peach baskets which were fitted at a height of 10 ft. (3.05 m). Each team consisted of about 40 players. In 1894 Naismith drew up the first rules which still from the basis of the modern basketball rules. The number of players was first reduced to nine and since 1896 to five players per team. From the very beginning the rules were such that mainly speed at passing and dexterity of actions should dominated; and the robust physical effort should be largely eliminated. In the beginning, a ladder was part of the equipment so that the ball could be taken out of the basket after a successful shot. Later the peach baskets were replaced by metal rings and nets. "Korbball" was introduced in Germany in 1896 by August Herrmann a gymnastics inspector from Braunschweig. It is believed that this development was influenced by information on basketball he obtained from his son who was a headmaster of a grammar school in Boston. However, "Korbball" never spread throughout the world as basketball did nor did it achieve its importance.

The game developed by Dr. Naismith was enthusiastically welcomed in Springfield and its environs and quickly spread in North, Central and South America. In Europe basketball was first played in France in 1896 and in Russia in 1906.

During the early stages many enthusiastically responding spectators tried from the gallery to direct the ball into the basket with their hands and walking sticks. Naismith then had a board fixed behind the baskets. Thus, more possibilities arose for the game the boards helped in aiming at the basket and they prevented the many out-of-bound throws. The game became more variable and quite different from

"Korbball". For a short period special rules had been introduced for women's basketball. But they were soon dropped after it had been realised that men and women can play according to the same rules. After 1918 basketball developed by leaps and bounds in South America, Asia, and several European countries. FIBA was founded in Geneva in 1932. In 1936 basketball was included in the Olympic Games programme. 21 nations took part in the first Olympic tournament. Since then basketball has had the highest number of entrants for the Olympic Games and many qualifying competitions had to be played.

Another great advance in basketball, partcularly in Europe occurred after 1945. The national teams of the Soviet Union and Yugoslavia took over the international lead from the USA who had previously dominated for many years. Not to be forgotten is the absolute top position occupied by the Soviet Union in women's basketball for many years. Other socialist countries have also done a great deal for the development of basketball; and at international championships countries like Bulgaria, Poland and Czechoslovakia performed admirably.

In the German Democratic Republic, basketball began to develop from around 1950. Some former and some younger players formed the first teams in Leipzig Halle, Berlin Jena Wurzen and Lauchhammer. In preparation for the 1951 World Youth Festival in Berlin, Soviet coaches helped form a national team which played numerous international friendlies and whose members officiated as judges and referees at the official tournament of the Academic Summer Games. A great deal of experience was gained and this motivated the development of further basketball centres in the GDR. Within a short period, several strong teams developed, particularly in Rostock, Dresden, Erfurt Ottendorf-Okrilla and Bitterfeld.

Since 1953 championships and cup competitions have been held in the various women's and divisions as well as for young people and school children. Since then GDR teams have also been participating in international competitions. In this connection the work put in by other coaches from the Soviet Union, Czechoslovakia and Bulgaria has to be mentioned. Thanks to their assistance our teams were able to match up to international level. The GDR's women's team, for example, won a bronze medal at the European Championships and were placed at the World Championships. The GDR's men team were placed sixth at the European championships. The main task of the "German Basketball association of the GDR", which in 1958 emerged from the "Basketball Section of the GDR" is not only to continually develop performance but also to improve mass sports, especially amongst women and youth. It is also important to recruit more citizens of all age groups to attend regular training sessions and to participate in basketball competitions. Although many thousands of citizens play basketball regularly at various levels of organisation, the value of basketball especially a recreational sport, has not yet been fully recognized in all parts of the country. As a game played on a small field with a small number of players, it can be played by anyone anywhere—both during the summer and winter.

2

BASKETBALL TACTICS

Characterization of playing tactics

Playing tactics is the systematic application of individual, group and team actions against the opponents in order to achieve victory or an optimum score. The main aim of tactics is to determine the means, methods and actions of play against a particular opponent. Thus, the players' tactical actions lie essentially in the continuous solving of tasks which unfold during the constantly changing situations of play in attack and defence. Nowadays, the tactics of the modern game of basketball comprises a large number of means, methods and elements. Its effective application is only possible if all factors that are characteristic of the particular match are taken into account. These factors result from the objective assessment of the possibilities of one's own team and those of the opponent (composition of the teams, moral disposition of the players, their technical and tactical abilities, the players' training conditions, etc.). But also to be considered are the concrete external conditions under which the match takes place (i.e. the weather in case of matches played in the open air, lighting, peculiarities of the court, spectators, etc.). If these factors are not taken into account a team will not be able to achieve an optimum score. Gaining effective control of these factors will only be possible if the tactics of basketball is mastered.

The tactics in basketball is constantly developing. But it also contains conservative elements. The struggle between attack and defence provides the impetus for the game's further tactical development. The use of new effective means and methods in attack necessarily forces the players and coaches to seek appropriate defensive countermeasures. Tactics cannot, however, provide formulae applicable to all situations that may occur in the course of a game. Tactics is not a rigid routine but a system of flexible response to the ever changing situations on the court. Inability to change one's own game according to the specific situations and the inability to give up the plan worked out in training is incompatible with the idea of playing tactics. Only when tactics is progressive and alive it can be continuously enhanced by new knowledge and enriched by new methods and means of conducting the game.

Certain tactical ways and forms of attack and defence-which are characterized by a high degree of effectiveness and the ability to convert opportunities develop from the wide range of theoretically possible tactical patterns of a game through playing practice and especially by analysing games played by the world's best teams at major international competitions. The most effective methods, measures and trends evident in present-day basketball tactics are described here.

The basic terms of playing tactics

The means of conducting game are the technical elements. A match cannot be carried out without mastering the technique. Whereas technical training is aimed at the players acquiring this or that technical element, it is the aim of tactical training to provide the players with the knowledge and ability required for the efficient and successful application of the elements and methods acquired in training in particular situations during the game.

By tactical methods one understands the actions of the players which they apply individually, in groups or as a tea against the opponent. The methods represent the qualitative side of the game and they have to be learnt and applied efficiently in the game. Actions of play are implemented individually, in groups and by the whole team.

Individual actions of play are independent actions by players. These actions are directed towards accomplishing various tactical tasks which have to be solved by the team but which are fulfilled without direct participation of the team-mates. Group actions are characterized by the cooperation between two or more players of a team to solve a tactical task. Team actions involve the cooperation of all players of the team who are out on the court. This is aimed at the implementation of a general tactical task by the whole team. Team actions are effected by various systems of play and combinations.

A system of play is the organization of the players' actions, in which the function and positioning on the court is determined in advance. Each system of play has its more or less constant pattern of array of players. This creates favourable conditions for the players to exercise their functions and to co-ordinate their actions with individual groups of players and with all players of the whole team.

Combinations are the player's actions which have been prepared and co-ordinated during training and which pursue the aim of creating favourable conditions for a team-make to successfully attack the basket. In competition it is often not possible to apply the combinations which have been practised. Besides, they must also be creatively developed in accordance with the particular situation. Each player must be able and ready to attack the basket directly during any combination when a suitable situation arises.

Combinations are applied during the match, during throw-in, during jump ball, during free throws and during other standard situations.

Nowadays, the typical style of play of the best teams in the world is characterized by a continuing increase in the tempo of play, in the activity and intensity of actions in attack and defence.

Classification of basketball tactics

It is necessary to classify and systematize the large number of tactical methods required for an effective organization of the game. On the one hand, in this way a general view can be given of the large number of tactical methods and actions and on the other hand, the relationship between the various parts of basketball tactics can be shown, which are of importance for the players' tactical training. Looking at it from this aspect and from the objective, which is to throw the ball into the opponent's basket and to prevent the opponent from throwing the ball into the basket being defended, basketball tactics can be subdivided into:

Offensive tactics and defensive tactics

These two classes of tactics can be further subdivided,

according to the organized actions of the players: into individual, group and team actions. Each of these groups can again be classified into several forms. For example, the individual actions in attack can be carried out by the player with and without the ball.

According to the contents of the actions of play, one distinguishes between different methods which can again be subdivided into different variations. Set play via the pivot player can, for example, take place via one or to or even three pivot players. The classification of basketball tactics.

Inductive tactical play is characterized by the fact that, based on the specific situation of the game, the means best suited for its solution is chosen by the player. This gives the instructor and coach good points to start from for effective tactical instruction. This aspect inevitably leads to alternative presentations of tactical methods, i.e. to tactical programmes for the solution of standard situations. The alternatives are (in a particular situation) effective tactical solutions which present the correct response to the opponent's tactical measures, i.e. solutions which point the way to achieving the attacking objectives or which maintain and improve defensive stability. These tactical programmes contain means and countermeasures (alternatives) for typical situations in the game. Thus, they apply equally to attackers and defenders. Thus, a tactical style of play is characterized by a systematic approach to creating favourable situations and to dealing with situations arising in the process of play. This should be borne in mind in tactical training.

The players' tactical functions

The assignment of functions to individual players is a

fundamental pre-requisite to co-ordinating the actions of the players. The distribution of functions is based on the two sides of the playing activity, attack and defence. Accordingly, in basketball the players are divided into forwards, pivot players and guards.

However, irrespective of his function, each player should have complete command of a wide range of technical tactical actions of both offensive and defensive character. These two essential directions in the players education and training are inseparably bound up with each other: continuous perfection both from an all round point of view and from the point of view of the player's specific function. This does not, however, mean that the distribution of functions among the players becomes meaningless, because this universality can never invalidate the players' use according to their tactical functions and because the players' biological performance pre-requisites (height, weight, reaction capacity, etc.), are taken into consideration in assigning the functions. The economic use of the players according to their abilities is, after all, in the interest of the whole team. The players all-round preparation is the basis for perfecting their specific functional and positional skills.

The fundamental tactical requirements made on the players according to their function and position in the team

In modern basketball, great importance is attacked to the pivot player. The performance of a team depends, to a large extent, on the abilities of pivot players. The pivot player should be tall and athletic. He should excel perseverance, coolness, boldness and quick reaction and he should have a distinct sense of play and a flair for combinations. In attack, he has to actively take part in both the fast break and in set play. During the fast break he has to fulfil, above all, the following tasks: to make a quick outlet pass after obtaining the ball in order to guarantee the well-timed initiation of the fast break; thereafter he has to join in the attack in order to be able to participate in the final phase of the fast break at the opponents' basket. Should the pivot player, for some reason, not be able to join in the fast break he is obliged to guard the rear court against possible counter-attacks by opponents.

During set play, the pivot takes up his position under the basket, in the midst of the opponents' defence. He is responsible for upsetting the defence of the opposing team and for attacking their basket. His actions happen mainly close to and in the free-throw lane and often from a starting position with his back to the basket.

The pivot player must be able to apply a large number of actions, both in the immediate vicinity of the basket, when his movement is restricted, when he is closely guarded by the opponent and also while moving very fast towards any place on the entire court.

In defence, he has to neutralize the opposing pivot player, to direct his own team's defence and, as the last man, to defend against any attacker making for the basket. He also has to follow rebounds after unsuccessful shots by the opponents. In the training of pivot players specific to their position, the emphasis is, on the one head, on continuously extending their radius of action and, on the other, on widening their all-round abilities.

The *forwards and utility players* are distinguished, above all, by the following qualities: tall built, speed and jumping power, distinct sense of time and space, good shooting ability, quick recognition of the playing situations and resolute action. Their main tasks are to join in the fast break timeously and to conclude it fearlessly. The must be able to shoot at the basket from various distances and to follow rebounds, i.e. to tip the ball into the basket. To accomplish these tasks, forwards and utility players must be able to execute their actions quickly, to shoot from medium and long distances while jumping, especially using the one handed shot, and open up the opponents' defence by means of individual break-throughs. In defence, they must be able to neutralize opposing forwards, pursue them successfully and form the second line of defence. To do this, these players must be able to counteract the opponents' typical offensive actions, i.e. to closely cover the attacker without the ball, to parry the jump shot and to prevent the attacker's baseline drive. The specific actions of the forwards determined by their position and function are extended and developed further in close connection with those of the guards. Nowadays, these players can be used with equally good results as utility players who can act as pivot players and as outside players.

The *guards* are mobile, persevering, circumspect, alert athletes who enjoy playing. Their main task in attack is to be the first to join the fast break and to conclude it without a moment's hesitation. They initiate the set play and the direct preparations for attacking the opposing basket, they master long distance shots and the individual breakthrough. At any time they are able to follow rebounding balls and to ward off counterattacks by the opposing team. The guards' main area of activity is the area around the semicircle of the free-throw lane. To perform their function efficiently, they must be excellent dribblers, have a comprehensive tactical knowledge, be able to lead a team and bring the ball into play. Therefore they are often called "playmakers". In defence, the guards are the first to disrupt the opponents' counterattacks, to neutralize the actions of the opposing team's guards and to assist the pivot players accordingly.

This requires specific skills, such as an excellent mastery of the technique of locomotion, of defending against the player in possession of the ball (intercepting knocking the ball out and wresting it from the opponent), the ability to fight successfully against attackers who outnumber the defenders and to cover an opponent directly.

The functions of the guards are developed and improved in close cooperation with those of the forwards. In modern basket-ball, the guards are also efficient attackers who score as many points for their teams as the forwards.

Offensive tactics

The attack is the fundamental function of the team during the game. Only by means of offensive actions is it possible to achieve a victory over the opponents. By active offensive play a team takes the initiative in the game, thus preventing the opposing team from implementing their plan. In order to achieve this aim, in such a sport period of only 30 seconds, it is necessary to use properly organized, previously thought out and well rehearsed tactical actions.

Attacking tactics gives the team-depending on the particular opponent and the various conditions of the competition-the possibility to choose and apply the most suitable means, forms and methods of carrying out a planned attack. All offensive actions can be subdivided into collective and individual actions. Collective actions can be further subdivided according to the number of players involved, into team and group actions.

Individual tactical methods of attack

Tactical principles of the individual attack

The absolute unit of team play is the duel between attacker and defender. The sum of the results of such duels largely decides between victory and defeat in the competition. In the end, each successful shot is the result of a duel won in the offensive action in question. In general, player and ball cannot get into favourable space and positions for shooting without struggling against the opponent successfully, i.e. in the end, successful individual actions of each attacker precede the effective teamwork. At the same time, however, each individual action must be in line with team tactical aspects and with the team's collective tactical actions and intentions. Decisive pre-requisites for individual offensive performances are, above all, the perfect mastery of the ball in receiving, passing, dribbling and shooting as well as high precision and a high degree of special co-ordinative and athletic qualities, such as body control, reaction capacity, starting speed, jumping power and endurance. The organization of the attack becomes, however, only then effective when the tactical principles and methods of individual attack which determine the performance and mastered and intelligently applied in the particular situation during the game. To do this, fundamental pre-requisites of successfully conducting duels, such as anticipation of movement and action, tactical thinking, tactical knowledge, abilities and skills as well as the necessary toughness, must be trained and developed continuously, systematically and according to plan.

The individual attacking manner is mainly determined by the situation on the court and the special function of each attacker. In addition, personality traits, such as preparedness to take chances, self-confidence, etc., play an important part.

In the following we shall explain the general tactical principles and how to act in typical situations in attack. For tactical actions in individual attack, above all, the following points should be borne in mind:

1. Each individual attacking action is embedded in an attacking system of the team. It demarcates the framework for the players' special tasks by restricting their playing areas and their manner of playing in order to guarantee optimum co-ordination of all players to secure a successful conclusion of the attack on the one hand and to bring to bear and utilize to the full the capacities of each individual attacker within the team's given functional framework.

2. An important tactical means of individual attack is cutting (moving free) without the ball in order to obtain, while tussling with the opponent, good possibilities to receive a pass in favourable playing or shooting positions.

Playing actions without the ball

Tactical rules for the attacker's cutting Playing actions without the ball include getting away from the closely marking defender and moving into an open space with the aim of receiving the ball from the team-mate who, at that particular moment, is in possession of the ball. Special observations have shown that, during a match of 40 minutes, any particular basketballer is effectively in possession of the ball for only 3.5 to 4.0 minutes. During the remaining period he participates in the game without having the ball, trying to obtain a favourable position for various tactical manoeuvres.

As regards the direction and the character of movement, we distinguish between two types of cutting:

Running towards the team-mate with the ball and cutting sideways towards the team-mate.

Both type of cutting have several variations:

1. Cutting behind the defender's back;

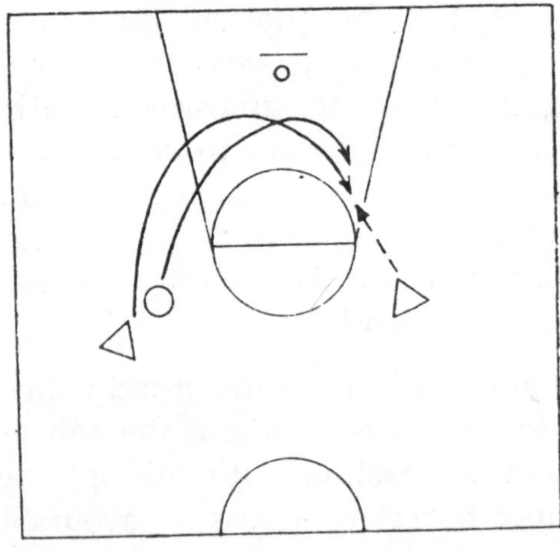

Cutting behind the defender

2. S-shaped cutting behind the defenders back;

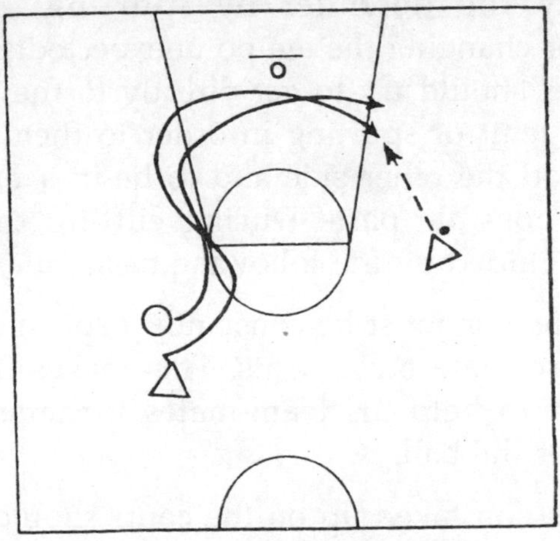

S-shaped cutting by the attacker

3. Cutting in the form of a loop in one corner of the court including stopping and forward turn round one's own axis;

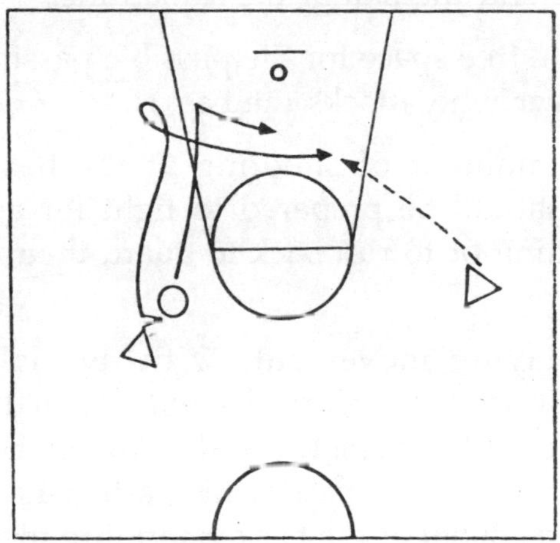

Cutting in the form of a loop

4. Cutting in the form of a U-turn in the semicircle of the free-throw area.

In executing any one of these variations, it is important to outplay the defender by spurting, changing direction or changing the tempo unexpectedly. Besides, the attacker should try to get directly to the defender, to make a feint of spurting in order to then get away from him on the other side and to be in a position to receive a possible pass. During cutting the player should be guided by the following basic rules:

1. The defender must be constantly kept under stress by appropriate movements. This makes it difficult for him to help his team-mates in defence or to intercept the ball.
2. The position taken up on the court should be such as to allow a good general view of the whole game and facilitate co-operation with the partner.
3. Furthermore a position should be chosen which makes it difficult for the defender to see the attacker and the ball at the same time.
4. To create free space for the possible passing line for the player who attacks the basket.
5. At the moment of shooting at the basket, each player should be prepared to fight for a place for rebounding or to run back to guard their own back court.

The playing movements with the ball are the efficient use of the technical elements in the game. Each player who gets the ball can overcome the opponent by a forceful pass to his partner he can drive for the basket shoot at the basket and lure the defender away from the shooting area by means of feints, etc. In the following we shall therefore concentrate mainly on describing the correct, appropriate and effective application of the technical elements, including feints.

The use of passes

Well executed passes give the players the possibility to bring the ball from their own basket to the opposite side very quickly and to provide a team-mate with a favourable position to attack the basket. Passes used in competition are distinguished between according to their tactical aim, their sharpness, direction and trajectory. The sharpness of a pass depends on the distance between the players and the speed at which the game proceeds, i.e. the longer the distance between the players, the more power must be transferred to the ball; and the shorter the moment during which the team-mate is able to get away from the opponent, the quicker and more powerfully the pass must be made.

We distinguish between long passes, cross-court passes and diagonal passes, each of which is used for special reasons. *Long passes* are chosen to execute fast breaks in order to get the ball to the forwards as quickly as possible. To do this, the ball is passed forcefully with a low trajectory. *Diagonal passes* are used to cover medium distances when executing the fast break in staggered stages and when throwing the ball in from the side lines.

Cross-court passes are made from one side of the court to the other in order to extend the attacking front and to find weak points i the opponents' defence (especially in zone defence). Cross-court passes are also used to distract the opponents and to give team-mates the opportunity to take up a free position and to prepare for the execution of a specific combination. With cross-court passes it must be borne in mind that they do not provide any advantage with regard to gaining ground and are often intercepted by the opponents. Therefore these passes should not be used too frequently, especially near the opponent's basket. During the game it is often difficult to pass the ball directly to the pivot player because he is closely covered. In such cases feints, concealed passes, bounce passes and other passes should be used. Peripheral rather than direct vision should be used for controlling the pass and co-ordinating it with one's team-mates. In general, these passes are made over short distances (approx. 2 to 6 m). If the pivot player is marked closely in front it is advisable to outmanoeuvre the opposing defender by a high pass so that the ball can be received by the pivot player on the jump. Frequently the pivot player *hands over* the balls to his team-mates running past him, the defender being distracted by feints before the ball is handed over. Timing is of special importance. Therefore a favourable starting position for the subsequent execution of a quick and accurate pass is to be taken very early during the reception of the ball.

The use of dribbling

Dribbling plays an important part in the individual attack. By means of the various types of dribbling and their combination with twists and turns, the attacker can free himself from the defender, to attack the basket or to attract a team-mate's defender towards him so that he can then pass the ball to the team-mate.

The dribbler can also screen his partner. The dribble is of special importance when attacking against press defence. An exaggerated use of the dribble may affect the pace of the game, complicate the development of the fast break and lead to frequent ball losses. However, nowadays, it can be observed that leading international teams too prefer dribbling to passing (especially in initiating the fast break) in order to create situations with a numerical advantage for the attackers by cleverly outplaying the defenders, and to prevent the defence from organizing themselves into a collective and compact defence.

The use of shots

When shooting at the basket, the players have to act with a great sense of responsibility by accurately assessing the situation and the defenders' area of influence. Each shot must be tactically justified and it must be performed under optimally favourable conditions. Otherwise the preceding efforts of the whole team are wasted. A shot at the basket should be made when there is a real chance for success or when the thrower or a team-mate have favourable opportunities for taking the rebound. In order to get away from the defender's close marking, passing feints or breakthrough feints should be applied before shooting.

Each attacker, including the thrower, must always try to go for the opponents' basket and to take up a favourable position for rebounds. By running up for the jump, they get the opportunity to tip the rebounding ball into the basket.

Against a close and flexible general and zone defence, the shots from medium and long distances must be prepared with special care. Only by means of accurate shooting from these distances is it possible to break up the defence and to make possible drives and short-distance shots. Fast breaks should be followed up mainly by short-distance shots because shots at the basket that have to be made at maximum speed are less likely to hit the mark from medium and long distances.

The use of feints and combinations of movements

Proficient players are able to combine various elements and feints. Proper use of shooting, breakthrough and passing feints gives the players the possibility to disguise their intended actions, to put the defender off balance, to undermine his defensive position and immediately then to attack the opposing basket by either a jump shot from a medium distance or by passing the ball to a team-mate who has cut into a favourable position.

A wealth of possible actions for the individual attack is created by combining the numerous elements of the playing technique (running, dribbling, catching, passing, shooting and feinting). Some of these actions are prominent for their effectiveness. They are combinations which facilitate the tactical solution of typical situations of play by one player, i.e. methods and variations of the tactical solution of standard one-one-one situations.

These tactical attacking methods should not only be mastered perfectly with regard to movement, but the players must also be able to apply them and their variations correctly as the situation demands.

The main method of the one-on-one situation is the individual drive for the basket. The player in possession of the ball uses the drive to outrun his opposing defender and, if possible, to achieve an unhindered shot at the basket from a very close distance.

Competition statistics show that the top rate teams are highly effective with this method (individual breakthrough of the outside player and pivot). In the course of game, time and again situations arise which are characterized by the fact that only the defender is in the way of the player with the ball, who is within shooting distance and who should otherwise have a free path to the basket. This fact is extraordinarily favourable for the individual breakthrough. Therefore, in preparation for an attack, the aim should be to consciously create such situations.

Basic solution of the one-on-one situation

— If still necessary, the attacker draws the defender closer by a shooting feint.

— Through a body feint (pivoting or passing feint), the defender is brought into an unfavourable position to the side.

— The opponent is out manoeuvred by a quick dribbling start.

Three typical one-on-one standard situations for utility players, their basic variations in solving them (individual breakthrough) and the tactical co-ordination of the team (securing and cutting for a possible pass). It can be seen very clearly that it is best to start from corners or at an angle when making individual breakthroughs and that one or two team-mates must cut in so that they can receive a pass if the breakthrough is not completed successfully.

Tactical variations of the one-on-one play from an outside position

In solving standard one-on-one situations the attacker must be able to adapt to the defender's individual tactics. For this purpose the attacker should master a number of routine variants of attack. Each offensive variant has a corresponding defensive variant against which it is used. Principal offensive variants should be developed in training, due consideration being given to tactical and motor aspects.

This does not restrict the range of variation of the play for once a player has mastered the main variants of the one-on-one play additional variations can be easily developed. These offensive combinations should be used as required by the situation at hand and according to the opponent's reaction, for in a one-on-one situation the defender can, for example,

— mark closely or loosely;

— have a stable or unstable stance;

— be in front of, on the side of or behind the attacker;

— create a new situation by a switch.

The correct tactical offensive variant is chosen with the aid of a programme of tactical solutions (algorithm). The tactical programme for solving the one-on-one situation shown gives a summary outline of offensive and defensive methods of play and shows the relations between defensive and attacking movements. Attacking sequences arise here from the attacker's constant adjustment to the situation. They are not fixed from the outset Only then is it possible to achieve a high tactical level. The programme shows the nature of tactical actions during play in an abstract form. The seven main variants are described by the pictures which follow.

Special tactical variations of the one-on-one play-from an inner position (pivot's one-on-one play)

In the main, the same tactical aspects apply to the specific one-on-one situation of the pivot or utility player who stands with his back towards the basket (typical one-on-one situation of the pivot player.

Tactical features of the one-on-one play of the pivot or utility player from inner positions (pivot breakthrough) with the back towards the basket:

— The one-on-one play of the pivot is a contest to acquire favourable shooting positions near the basket. An unfavourable defensive position (opponent on the side or he jumps when the attacker makes a shot feint) is sufficient for the pivot to successfully complete the attack (hook shots, jumps shots).

— Through good positional play and skilful cutting, the pivot or utility player can find himself in a receiving position close to the basket and can then get into an advantageous starting position for the one-on-one play.

— Breakthroughs by the pivot near the basket are executed after pivoting (main means to attain a favourable shooting position), but mostly without dribbling.

— It is difficult for the attacking player to know the defender's position behind his back. But this knowledge is essential for the success of offensive actions.

— The defender's active efforts to prevent a pass to the pivot very often result in an unstable position of the defender giving the pivot numerous possibilities to drive towards the basket or pivot to the free side immediately after receiving the ball.

— Breakthrough feints, without shifting the feet, are performed mainly by a short movement of the trunk and head to one side.

— In the case of loose defence-especially in distant positions from the basket (forward position-a frontal position towards the opponent should be assumed by turning. In this way the tactical possibilities for an individual breakthrough increase (see one-on-one play from an outside position).

— In positions close to the basket, with a close-marking defence, turns to the basket while jumping and then shooting from a frontal position (turn-jump shots) are an effective means of attack. Utility players and pivots should master the combination of receiving high balls passes or rebounds) while jumping and them immediately shooting after turning. This makes them considerably more dangerous (typical tactical variants of solving the one-on-one play of pivots.

— Because the pivot player is dangerous defensive assistance from other opponents must always be expected (double guarding, inner space is covered). This leads to one-on-one-play immediately after receiving the ball, but it also creates good opportunities for passing back to one of the outside players who is free.

Group attack tactics

Tactical group plays are important elements of collective play, i.e. they form the basis of systematic and well organized tactical actions of the whole team. The players' abilities and skills for creative team-play are developed and reflected by tactical group-actions. The most typical group techniques involve co-operation of two and three players. By means of co-ordinated passes and running movements, the players try to create favourable shooting opportunities for a team-mate. The wide variety of team play occurring in competition can be reduced to a certain number of tactical group techniques which are highly effective in solving frequently occurring situations during the game. At the same time they are the basis of all combinations. Smooth attacking plays are facilitated by combining these techniques. The use of these techniques is determined by the particular situation in the game, the actions of the team-mates, the defender, and the other opponents, i.e. they are interdependent. These tactical group techniques, as fundamental elements of combination play, should be mastered both theoretically and practically by all players. The ability to apply them during the game can only be acquired by playing practice matches involving two on two, three on three, four on four and, finally, five on five situations, with the aim of improving the players, tactical abilities under all circumstances.

The following tactical group techniques are basic combinations and are part of the tactical equipment of every player involved in offensive play with man-to-man cover:

— Give and go (cutting after passing)
— Brushing off onto a stationary team-mate (post play)
— Setting a front screen

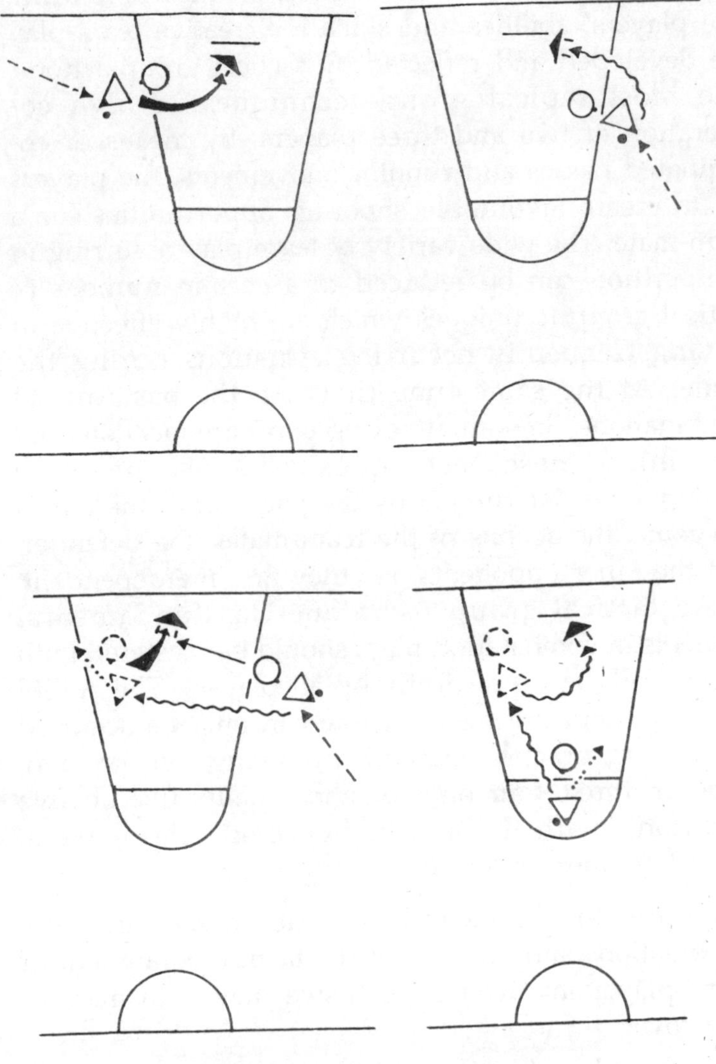

Variations of one on one play by the pivot

— Brushing off while two team-mates move towards each other
— Splitting the post (passing the ball to the post player and crossing in front of him)
— Screen play
— Pick and roll
— Change of positions
— Rebounding

Co-ordinated action between two players

Co-ordination between two players includes the tactical group actions of give and go, brushing off onto the stationary player, brushing off while running towards each other, screening and rebounding. Give and go means that the player with the ball puts the defender off balance by means of a breakthrough or passing feint; or he induces the defender to move towards the ball in order to then pass the ball to a team-mate and, taking advantage of the defender's bad positioning, he runs quickly to an open position and attacks the basket after receiving the ball back.

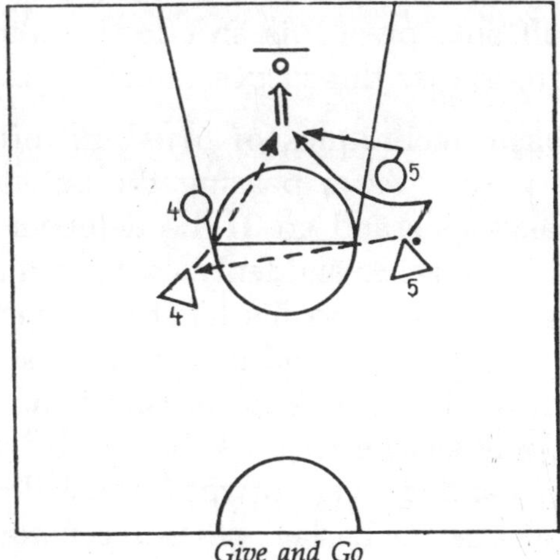

Give and Go

If the attacker carries out a feint before shooting, then the defender is forced to react by decreasing the distance between himself and the attacker. After having passed the ball the attacker can cut again to achieve a favourable position to shoot. Give and go is also (frequently applied during the fast break to overcome the distance to the opponents' basket as quickly as possible and to take maximum advantage of two-on-one situations.

Brushing off onto the stationary player

Formerly this type of brushing off was carried out on the player with the ball. But in modern basketball brushing off is applied, above all, by the dribbler. It is done between outside players and pivots and between outside players only. In this tactical action, the outside player leads his defender to his stationary pivot or some other team-mate, in such a way that the defensive player runs into a screen and is prevented from following the attacker. A typical situation clearly illustrating basic technique and its main variants. The starting position is identical to give and go. Thus, brushing off onto pivot 5 is an effective alternative to give and go, in case this tactics cannot be carried out.

The basic techniques of brushing off onto the stationary player. After passing the ball to pivot 5, player 1 fakes give and go. If the defender cannot be overtaken the attacker suddenly changes direction (by a vigorous push-off with his left foot), starts running towards the centre-field and then runs closely past the player with the ball, trying to brush off his opponent. At the same timely he receives the ball from the pivot (the ball is handed over forward and sideways) and dribbles towards the basket. When receiving the ball it is important that the pivot protect it with his body from the defensive player. To do this, the left shoulder is moved forward immediately after the player has received the ball and then begins dribbling with the right hand forward and sideways. The basket is attacked direct with a maximum of two dribbles and gaining space by the two-count rhythm.

Experience has shown that the defenders are aware of the attacker's intentions and they counter it with defensive tactics. Therefore the attackers have to master the main variants of brushing off and be able to adapt the plan to the situation, i.e. to the defender's movements.

For example, the brushing off manoeuvre, shown in cannot succeed because the defensive player is able to stay in front of the attacker and thus prevent his handing over the ball. Now the attacker has a chance of cutting to the left by a quick change of direction. Another typical variant. Although attacker 1 succeeds in brushing off his opponent he is taken on by the player covering the pivot. There is only one tactical countermeasure: Pivot 5 breaks away to the basket and attacker 1 passes the ball to him. The pivot should consider this possibility in advance and try to actively hinder the defensive player 1 when or after handing over the ball to attacker 1 so that the defender gets into an unfavourable position in relation to 5 in case he is taken on again by his defensive opponent 5.

Setting up a screen

In principle, this offensive method can be regarded as a variant of brushing off. It represents an alternative for attacker 1 if the direct opponent, defensive player 1, wants to avoid being brushed off by trying to catch the attacker by the shortest possible route behind the second pair of players 5 or, even better, between both of them. The position is characterized by the fact that the two attackers (player with ball 1 and pivot 5) stand in front of one another and 1 can shoot at the basket over the pivot unhindered. But this screen position can also be attained through other tactical manoeuvres. By the dribbler brushing off his opponent onto the stationary pivot player 5 or by brushing off while moving towards each other, the attackers achieve an identical position for a shot at the basket.

If the attackers master the technique of shooting over the screen, then the defenders are forced to apply countermeasures. The defender tries to actively hinder the shooter, despite the screen. To do this, the defender (in most cases that defender who is personal responsible for covering the attacker) usually steps out, thereby giving the attacker more options for attacking the basket. The situation defender 1 stepping out to the right. Attacker 1 dribbles on the left to the basket (left hand dribbles the ball) and shoots, using pivot 5 as a screen. In this situation, defender 5 will switch to attacker 1. Pivot 5 therefore takes advantage of this position and rolls to the basket to receive the pass from his team-mate.

If the attackers are very good at set shots then this group-tactical action is extremely effective. Every team should therefore have players who specialize in set shots because, with this method, one can also operate successfully against a very rigid man-to-man defence.

The screen by the pivot is so important because he can-in case of switching of the defence-roll towards the basket and offer his services by waiting for a pass in

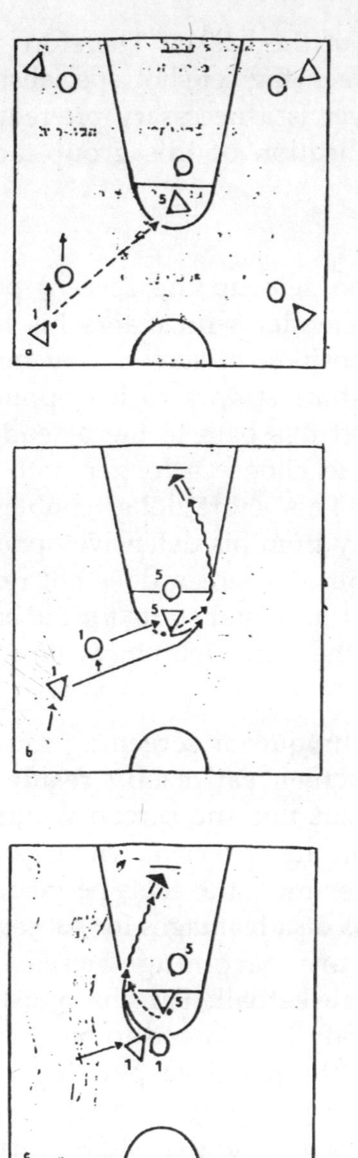

Brushing off onto the stationary player

the immediate vicinity of the basket. Therefore well-timed cooperation between the set-shot specialist and the pivot or utility player is a necessary pre-requisite for the successful application of this group-tactical action.

Screening

The screen (player who sets up the screen) places himself close by the defender who marks his team-mate and chooses his position in such a way that he blocks the defender's shortest way to his opponent. The screen either cuts off this path to the defender or he forces the defender to choose a longer path than that of his team-mate. This short delay enables his team-mate to break away from his defensive opponent and attack the basket. But the screen does not remain passive either. He turns round and starts for the basket in order to take part in the attack (cutting without ball or dribbling).

First of all the technique of screening must be mastered, because a screen can easily result in a personal foul. To prevent this the screen is applied about a metre away from the opponent. The legs must not be too wide apart nor must the arms be made use of. The frontal screen has disadvantages for subsequent actions (roll) which are becoming increasingly important in modern basketball. Far this reason, a lateral position of the body has proved to be effective. A slight slide position (the rear root pointing to the basket to facility turning round and starting for the basket when breaking away) and a slight forward bending of the trunk give the attacker high stability and freedom of movement as well as a relatively large screening area. In this position it is possible to visually

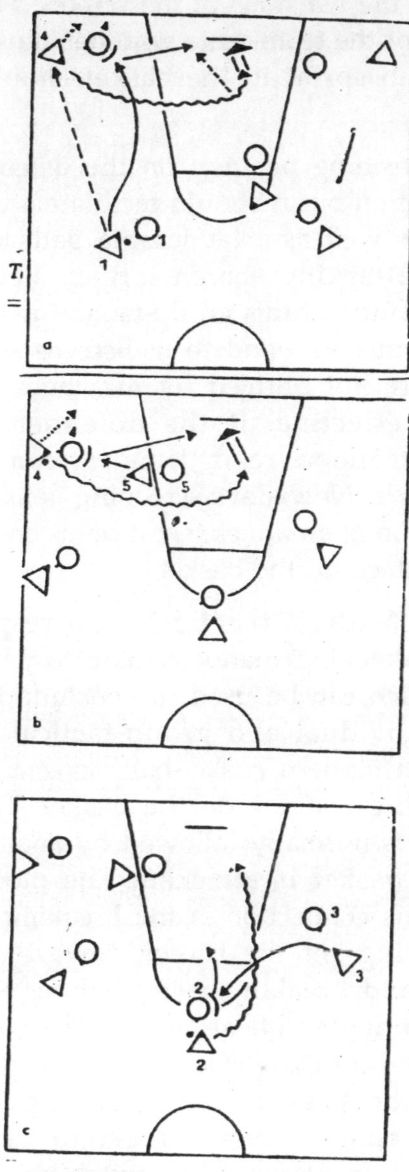

Pick and Roll

follow both the reactions of the screened defender and the actions of the team-mate who has thus become free as well as to sprint to the basket should it become necessary.

The screening position on the defender depends on the situation but it should facilitate a useful follow-up action as well as a favourable path to the basket. Thus, the attacking screen largely decides on the success or failure of this group-tactical manoeuvre. The team-mate must respond to it. Screens set behind the defender are not noticed by him and are therefore especially effective. If the defender discovers a screening manoeuvre in time he can avoid it by stepping aside. Nowadays screening is used, above all, in preparation of an attack, i.e. it helps create situations for direct attack on the basket.

The defenders' reactions-as a response to the attackers' screening manoeuvrable to gaps in a tight defence which can be used to conclude the attack by various individual and group-tactical movements. However, in modern basket-ball, screens very seldom lead to a direct attack on the basket. The screening manoeuvre is normally followed by another operation before the basket is attacked. The most important action in this connection is the breaking away of the player having set the screen towards the basket. Screening and breaking away belong together as a method of bringing off an attack. The combination of screening and breaking away allows the offensive team to attack the basket from close up because the defenders almost always react to the successful screening of an attacker by switching defence. This gives the screen a favourable starting position for a promising attack on the basket. This screening and breaking away combination (pick and roll) should be taken into consideration when learning how to screen so that rolling after screening becomes a habit.

Screen for the player in possession of the ball (direct screen;)

Typical situations of direct screening and breaking away in guard 1 obstructs the left forward 4. The second variant shows a screen by the pivot 5 applied behind the defender 4. The third variant shows a screen within the basic triangle.

These typical situations show that screening is particularly effective where there is free space for the player in possession of the ball and whose defender has been screened. It is also effective for the player breaking away from the screen to move towards the basket.

Co-ordinated action between three players

Three players co-operate on the same basis as described above. The temporary inclusion of a third player improves the team's tactical manoeuvring and passing chances.

The main tactical methods are:

— triangular play

— splitting the post

— brushing off while approaching each other (figure of eight)

— screening

— rebounding.

Triangular play

Many situation during the game can be effected through passes by three players in a triangle formation. The player in possession of the ball and forming the apex of the triangle, must be farther away from the opposing basket than his two team-mates, who should be within shooting distance of the basket and threatening to shoot. He passes the ball to the side. The defence now concentrates on the player with the ball who then passes the ball back immediately to the player in the middle. That player then passes the ball immediately to the other outside player who now has a chance to attack the basket with a set shot; or, if he is closely covered by a drive. This triangular play requires quick passes. It can, however, also involve a change of positions. In case of a three-on-two situation (with the attackers having numerical superiority) it can be successfully applied during the fast break.

Triangular play with change of positions

In this group-tactical measure, the middle player passes the ball to one wing and then applies a screen for the team-mate on the other side.

The player who consequently gets free starts for the middle, receives the ball inside the free-throw lane and can now attack the basket. If this is not successful the player can cut somewhere near the free-throw line and repeat the same action after receiving he ball. The player having applied the screen breaks away from his opponent and takes the wing position. Different variants can be developed from this basic formation. The triangular play is a successful tactical manoeuvre against man-to-man defence.

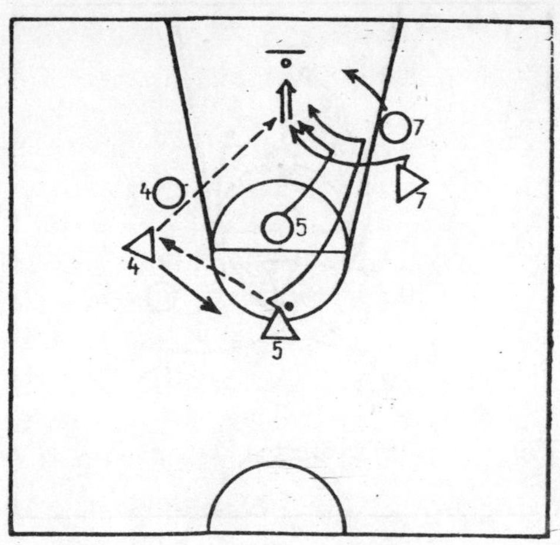

Triangular play with change of positions and 'pick and roll'

Splitting the post

With this manoeuvre, two players run almost simultaneously closely past a third team-mate who stands with his back towards the opponent's basket. The defenders 6 and 4 have a difficult task for they must neither obstruct one another nor get caught on attacker 5 or his defender. Splitting the post can also be carried out from the side of the free-throw lane. If this manoeuvre is not successful the ball goes to one of the forwards who calls for it. They can then start the manoeuvre again. The main variants of splitting the post which are the alternatives of attacking organization are Give and Go and "swerving out". Pivot 5, after pivoting towards the basket, can himself shoot from the free-throw line if his defender retreats after crossing of the outside players. In most cases the pivot takes a pass to one the crossing team-mates.

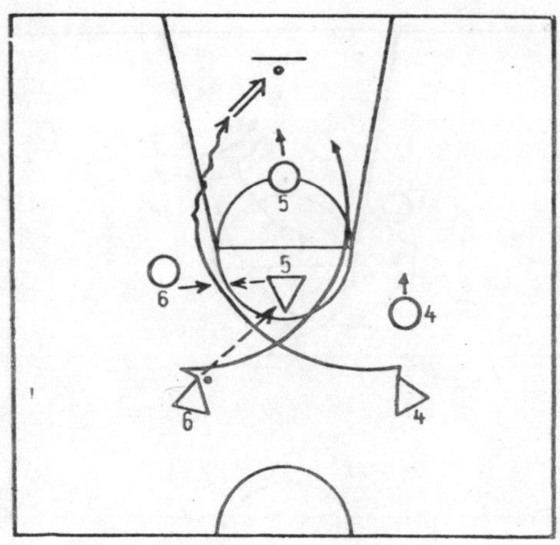

Splitting the post

Brushing off while approaching each other

Three players change their positions in a particular sequence using the dribble. The figure of eight bears a cyclic character and it can be applied several times in succession in the game until a favourable situation arises to attack the basket. In player 6 dribbles towards his team-mate 4 and when they meet 6 hands the ball over to 4. Player 4 then dribbles in the direction of the basket and

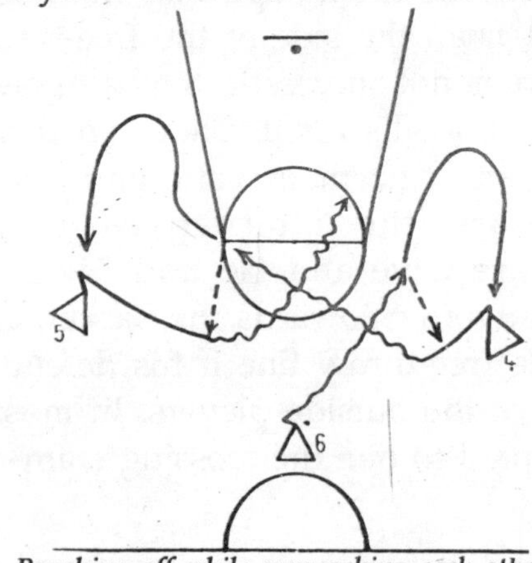

Brushing off while approaching each other

similarly hands the ball over to team-mate 5 who comes running towards him. Player 5 then dribbles towards player 6 who, after a short start towards the basket, stops and sprints towards the player in possession of the ball and takes over the ball and continues the manoeuvre in the opposite direction. To finish the attack from the figure of eight some variants result:

— the player in possession of the ball does not hand over the ball but dribbles towards the opponents' basket;

— the dribbler passes the ball to the team-mate who cuts towards the basket;

— the dribbler passes the ball to the team-mate who stops a faked spurt to the basket and, after receiving the ball, shoots at the basket;

— the player with the ball executes a jump shot from a medium distance if the defender retreats to foil the drive.

Screen off the ball screen for the player not in possession of the ball

Three players are involved in this screen: one who screens, one who is to be screened so that he can get free and the player with the ball. The purpose of the screen off the ball is to assist the cutting of a player without the ball to cut (mostly towards the basket). A pre-requisite for this is a favourable starting position of the player who is to cut. At the same time, the possibility of breaking away towards the basket must be taken into consideration:

— Attacker 2 passes to attacker 3 or 3 is already in possession of the ball;

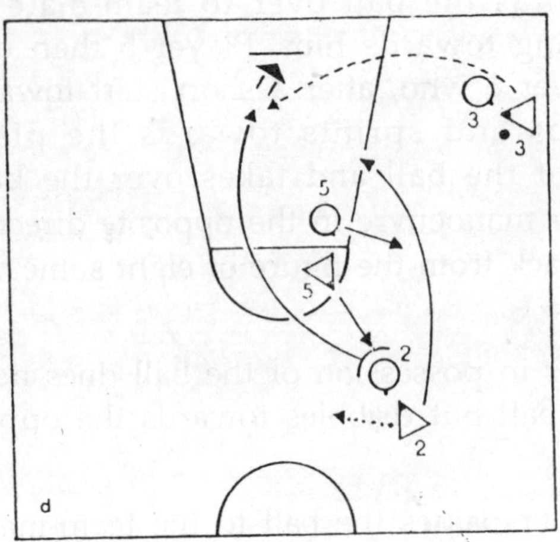

— Attacker 2 runs towards defender 1 to screen him. The first variant which presents itself is give and go with attacker 3. However, in the example illustrated the manoeuvre has been recognized by the defender in time and nipped in the bud;

— After a successful screen, attacker 1 runs towards the basket and receives a pass from team-mate 3.

If defender 2 switches to attacker 1, then attacker 2 breaks away from the screen and receives the ball from team-mate 3, and not from attacker 1. If attacker 1 is already in possession of the ball he passes it to player 2 after player 2 has broken away from the screen.

The subsequent further applications of this type of screening in typical playing situations. The attackers 1 and 4 use the screen in the left corner and create an outnumbering situation against the defence, caused by the breaking away of 1 from the screen After receiving the pass, player 4 shoots with a jump shot immediately or, if he is taken on by defender 1, he passes the ball to his team-mate 1.

Demonstrates the screen set by pivot 5 behind defender 2. With this variant, in most cases, switching is provoked by the pivot breaking away from the screen towards the basket and receiving a pass from attacker 3.

Screening against zone defence

The possibilities of applying the direct and indirect screen against zone defence. As switching is one of the

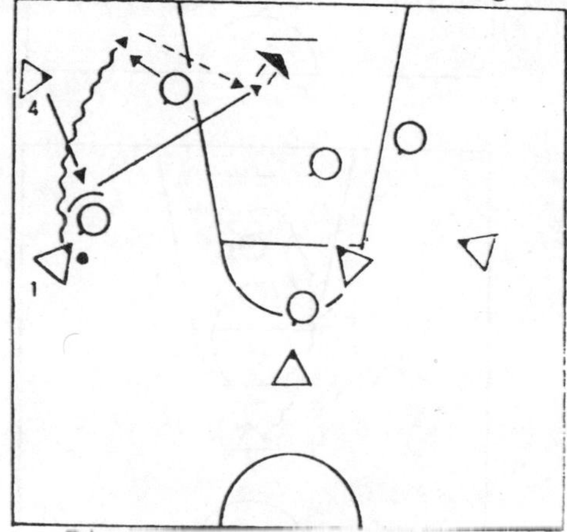

Direct screens against zone defence

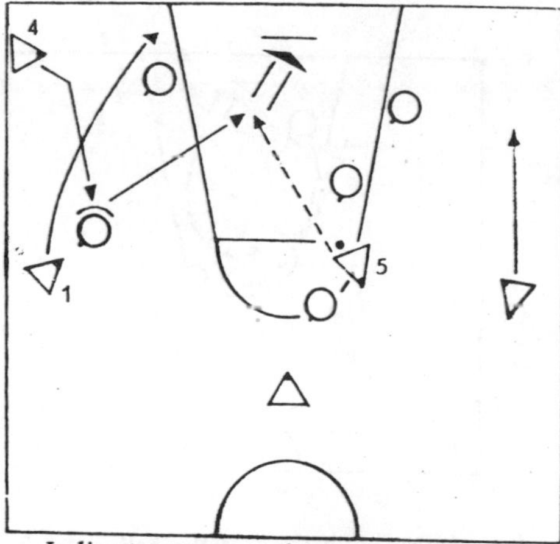

Indirect screens against zone defence

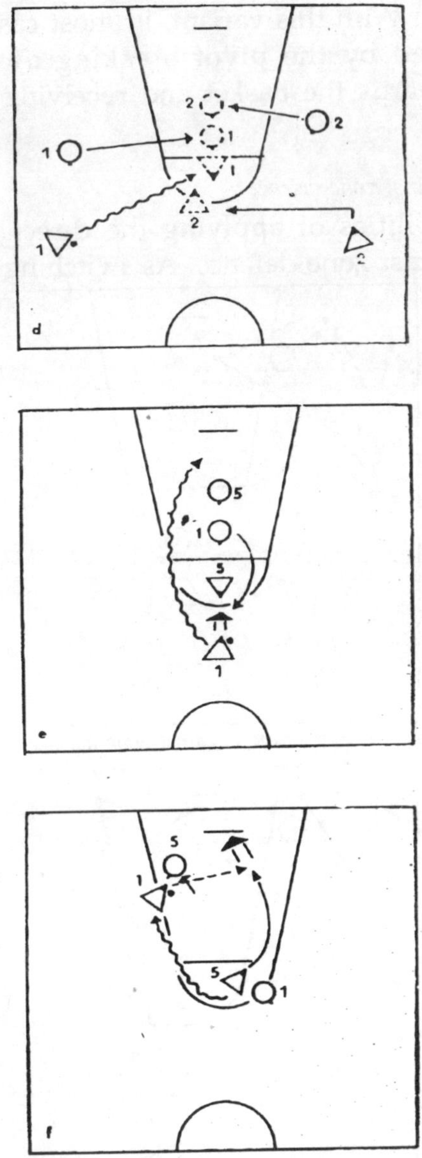

Screen off the ball

principles of zone defence, the roll becomes, in principle, the main offensive move. In both examples, player 4 completes the attack with a shot after having broken away from the screen and received a pass from dribbler 1 or from pivot 5. If attacker 4 remains guarded by the rear defender, then attacker 1 must continue dribbling and shoot at the basket himself or receive the pass from pivot 5 and attack the basket.

Combination screen

Further variants can be created by combining screening and brushing off. Screen off the ball is followed immediately by brushing off while running towards each other. After passing the ball to attacker 3, attacker 2 runs towards defender 1 to act as a screen. But as defender 1 falls back this screen is not successful and attacker 1 now runs towards the player with the ball, 3. He dribbles towards player 1 and both perform the brush-off as they approach each other. Now the different variants of brushing off can be performed.

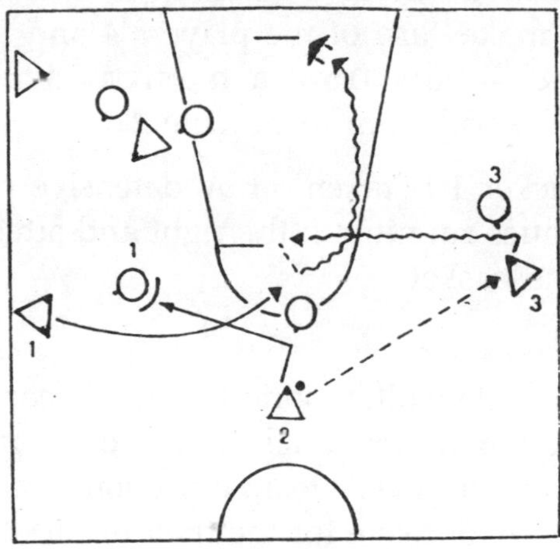

Combined screens

Double screen

The screening area and, consequently, the obstacle for the defender of the cutting attacker are increased by two attackers standing next to each other. This type of screen is frequently applied in throw-in combinations. A typical situation for the use of the double screen. Attacker 1 passes the ball to team-mate 2 (this can also happen from a throw-in). Meanwhile attacker 4 runs towards pivot 5 and creates the double screen. Attacker 1 runs, after a short running fake, towards team-mate 2 right through pivot 5 and the base line to the basket. If he loses his defender, who gets caught in the double screen, the attacker receives the ball from team-mates 2 or 3 in order to shoot. Top teams usually convey the ball immediately on to the basket for a team-mate to receive and shoot on the jump. This facilitates the exploitation of a slight advantage frequently presented with regard to space and time for an attack on the basket. The possibility is another variant. With defender 1 concentrating on attacker 4, attacker 1 makes use of the players 4 and 5 as double screen and shoots from a medium distance after receiving the ball from team-mate 2.

If attacker 1 is taken on by defensive players 4 or 5 he continues running to the right and attackers 4 and 5 roll to the basket.

Rebounding in attack

In modern basketball, rebounding has become a match-deciding element in attack. Superiority in offensive rebounding gives every team a preponderance of shots which is often decisive for the final result of the match. The following tactical rules should be observed in offensive rebounding:

— The attacker's less favourable outside position is somewhat mitigated by the fact that it is easier for the attacker to follow the flight of the ball because of his frontal position to the basket. The defender who takes the more favourable inside position and who is trying to hold that position must turn with his side or back to the attacker when he follows the flight of the ball. Thus, the defender is put in a difficult position because he cannot then keep his eye on the attacker. The attacker must make use of this advantage by anticipating the ball's possible rebound (e.g. angle of incidence equals angle of reflection in case of direct shots, etc.) and bring himself into a favourable position for rebounding.

— Rebounding from the outside position (in most cases from the corners of the court diagonal to the basket) provides the attacker with a longer run-up and, consequently, he has greater jumping/reaching height. This advantage is mainly utilized by utility players who are tall and can jump well and who, by means of immediate one-handed and two-handed tipping, can push the ball into the basket again. These players should therefore be specialized for rebounding.

— In most cases, the attackers' actions are co-ordinated by three attackers rebounding in general. They form a triangle in the area near the basket. Two attackers (pivot and utility player) occupy diagonal positions near the basket and he third attacker takes up a position at a medium distance (approximately on a level with the free-throw line) to catch the balls which rebound farther and which neither the defenders nor the two attackers under

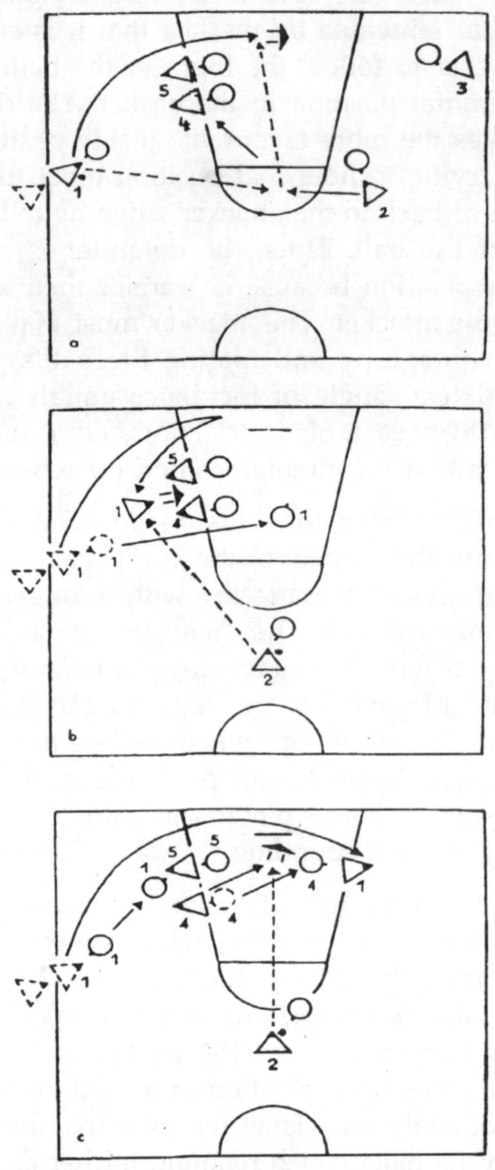

Typical situations for using double screens

the basket are able to get to. The third attacker must apply running takes to get free because the defenders generally occupy the position close to the basket (defensive triangle).

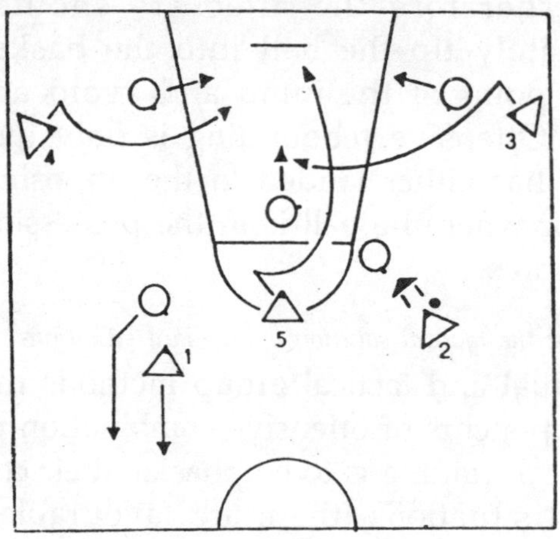

Rebound triangle in attack

— The tussle for the rebounding ball is decided by the correct position, the specific time for the take-off and, above all, by the jumping/reaching height. Nowadays, considering the intensive activity under the basket, it is desirable for the attacker to be able to tip the ball directly into the basket while jumping. In addition, there are the possibilities of outplaying the defenders after landing by means of feints and of attacking the basket again or of passing the ball to the guards. This has to be decided in each specific situation.

— If the defender gains the ball while rebounding, then the attacker must actively continue his tussle for the ball. He can either knock the ball out of the hand of the defender who is in a downward movement and tries to secure the ball, or he can gain a jump ball by grasping the ball with one or two hands. These possibilities are applied in rebounding mainly by players who are smaller in build. Therefore the attackers should try to immediately tip the ball into the basket at the highest point of the jump and avoid additional actions. Offensive rebounding is only over when the ball has either landed in the opposing team's basket or when the ball is in the possession of one of the teams.

Programmes for the tactical solution of standard situations

The individual and tactical group methods mentioned are the components of offensive combination play. The aim of tactical training is to emphasize their correct use in standard situations (these are favourable starting positions to be taken up before executing an attack.) The training for handling one-on-one, two-on-two and three-on-three situations, which are decisive during the game, form the main content of tactical training. Therefore, after dealing with the various group-tactical methods, we shall describe some tactical programmes for important two-on-two situations. The comparison between offensive and defensive play as encountered in real match situations is extremely important in theoretical and practical tactical training. This is the actual basis on which players develop their tactical proficiency. The programmes described here, more or less abstractly, illustrate the main methods of regulating the actions in tussles between attacker and defender.

Programmes for the tactical solution of the two-on-two situation (guard-pivot)

The tactical solutions for the two-on-two play of guard and pivot are illustrated in the programme in Diagram 18. Proceeding from the concrete two-on-two situation shown on the left, player 1 has three basic offensive options:

— The main tactical method-brushing off onto the pivot (with variants) after a pass to the pivot, as option

— One-on-one play of player 1 as option B

— Two-on-two play with attacker 4, especially give and go, as option C.

In the "programme of solutions", the main tactical method and the tactical alternatives after the pass to the pivot are pursued further. The tactics of brushing off, give and go, one on one play of the pivot, "swerving out", setting a front screen, breaking away after brushing off, and other variations are tactically and logically integrated into the defensive movements. The basic framework of tactical movements in this situation (and other similar ones) is illustrated here in sequence (from left to right). It shows the tactical methods and actions to be developed in their context. Players master tactical skills if they discover and apply the correct solutions during play with lightning-speed. This means that the solutions to such situations should be taught in such a way that players can skilfully apply them. The "programme of tactical solutions" is the best training programme for developing tactical skills.

Programme for the tactical solution of the two on two situation (utility player-pivot) Utility player 4

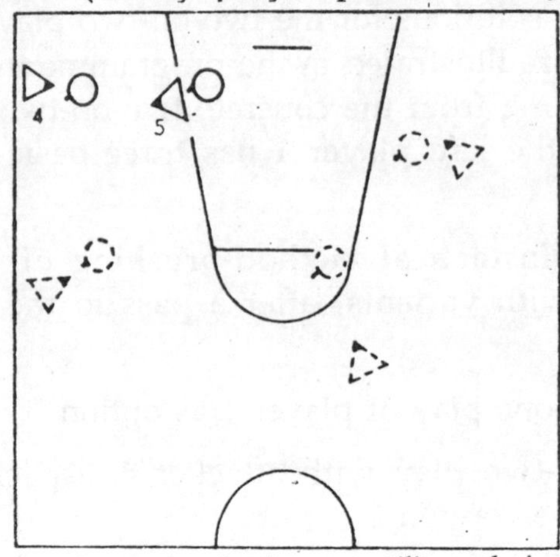

Basic set-up for co-operation between utility and pivot players

receives the ball in the left corner. Pivot 5 is in the left rear position. The "programme of solutions" lists 13 tactical offensive actions corresponding to the defender's 12 tactical options. Depending on the situation, the following systems of completing the attack can be used:

— set shot by player 4 from the corner;

— pass to the pivot and one on one play by the pivot;

— pass to the pivot, pass back to player 4 and set shot;

— pass to the pivot, brushing off on the pivot, close shot player 4;

— pass to the pivot by passing over the pivot's defender, close shot player 5;

— screen (direct) by the pivot;

— breaking away from the direct screen.

"Programmes of solution" should be developed for the most important standard situations. The higher the level of training, the greater is the number of variants. With beginners, one should start with two variations each. The "programmes of solutions' should take into consideration the special strengths of the team or individual players and at the same time they should include the most effective ways of solution. These programmes can serve to demonstrate the content and level of tactical training. The tactical solutions of certain situations mastered by a particular group of a team are listed and characterized. In this manner the "programme of solutions" is gradually extended.

The three programmes described reflect a high level of tactical proficiency. However, it has to be very clearly pointed out that the players' tactical initiative must not be restricted by the general programme of solutions. The players' creative tactical actions take place within the established regulation framework. Solutions which are generally correct can be wrong in certain situations (relative heights of the pairs of players, opponent is prepared for the action, etc.). However, if players master the "programmes of solution" they are better able to concentrate their attention more intensively on the tactical peculiarities of the specific situation and also on the overall tactical correlation of team play. This is the great, advantage of tactical skills.

Team tactics in attack

The successful conclusion of an attack is based on the players' collective actions which are aimed at creating a favourable position for one of their team-mates to effect a successful shot. Therefore an effective offensive play requires collective actions, mutual understanding and the sub-ordination and integration of individual interests and actions into those of the team.

In accordance with its tactical aims, we distinguish between fast break and set play.

The fast break

The fast break is subdivided into two main variants: Attack via the spearhead players and attack with players following up.

The fast break via the forwards

This offensive variant is extremely effective. It is the shortest way of achieving superiority over the opponent. The essence of this kind of attack is that the players of the team in possession of the ball try to cover the distance to the opposite basket in the shortest possible time, to outnumber the defence and to shoot from a very close distance. The aim to outnumber can only be achieved when the forwards start running towards the opposite basket as soon as their team gains possession of the ball. The fast break will succeed when the ball has been snatched from the opponent or gained while rebounding. However, there are also other possibilities to create the pre-requisites for a fast break and, consequently, to outnumber the opposing team. Throw-ins from the side lines and base lines as well as jump balls are ideal to start a fast break. It must also be pointed out that even with a numerical balance (1:1, 2:2, 3:3) favourable situations can arise for successfully attacking the opposite basket. The fast break can be subdivided into three phases: beginning, execution and finish. The success in the first phase is determined by the speed at which the players break away and by the timing of the initial pass. The players must break away from the opponent as soon as the team-mate prepares to take possession of the ball. It goes without saying that it must be highly probable that the ball will be brought under control. Usually the two or three players who take up a forward defensive position participate actively in the fast break. Their direction of running is determined by their particular position on the court and the point where their team-mate takes possession of the ball. The player in possession of the ball must pass the ball directly to his team-mate who has overtaken his opponent. Nowadays, top teams increasingly use the dribble to start the fast break. The player with the ball overcomes the midfield by a fast dribbling advance and, by outmanoeuvring his opponent, he tries to create an outnumbering situation or a jump shot from a medium distance.

A favourable situation for the fast break must be created collectively. The fastest players should be closet to the opponents' basket while they are still on the defensive (e.g. as "chasers" in zone defence) so that, when their own team gains possession of the ball, they can spurt to the opposite basket. With man-to-man defence it is advisable that the opponent who is farthest back be marked by the quickest player of the defending team.

The second phase of the fast break includes more players, dribbling and one or two passes between the attackers. This phase lasts longer than the first and comprises two to three seconds.

The final phase takes place within 1 to 1.5 seconds in the immediate vicinity of the basket. A shot at the basket is usually performed after a short dribble or pass to the team-mate who is cutting towards the basket.

A well-trained team requires a total of about three to six seconds to carry out a fast break and it does not make more than two to three passes. Currently, fast breaks are often concluded with jump shots from a medium distance, i.e. the aim of the fast break is not always a shot from a very close distance.

If, in the final phase of the fast break, a numerical advantage (two attackers against one defender) has been gained, several solutions are possible. Player 7 passes the ball to player 4 and runs towards the basket. If the defender switches to attacker 4 the ball goes back to player 7 who shoots. Should be defender try to guard attacker 7, the player 4 dribbles to the basket and shoots. Alternatively, attacker 7 begins running towards the basket and if the defender does not attempt to guard him he receives the ball from 4 and concludes the attack with a close shot. Should the defender try to prevent player 7 from shooting, the ball has to be passed to player 4 who can now attack the basket without hindrance. If the two attacking players are one the same side of the court the player without the ball runs behind the defender.

In case of a 3:2 outnumbering situation, the middle player dribbles towards the opposite basket. At the same time, the two team-mates run towards the basket at the side of the free-throw lines there by attracting the defenders. The player in possession of the ball can then dribble to the basket and shoot. But if he is attacked by a defender, which is usually the case, then he immediately passes the ball to the player who

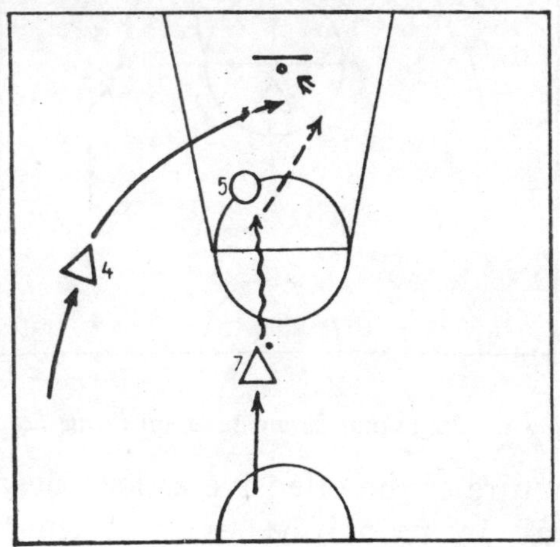

Solving the 2:1 outnumbering situation in the fast break

has become free. If the attack is started by one of the two players who run towards the basket on either side of the court, he has to dribble the ball until he is attacked by a defender. At that moment, attacker 6 passes the ball to team-mate 7 who has logged somewhat behind and who decides, depending on the actions of the second defender, whether to shoot or to pass the ball to attacker 5.

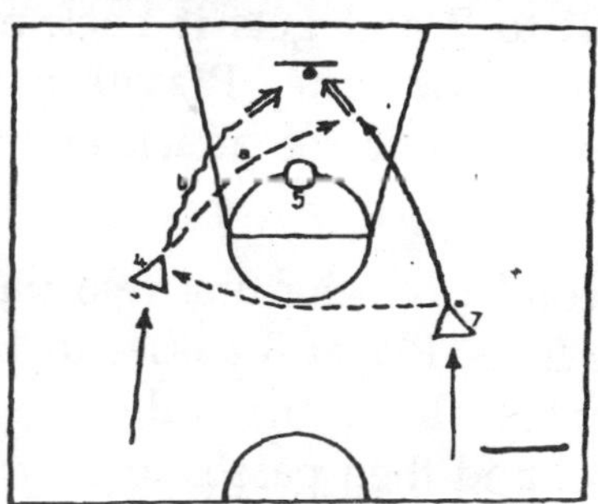

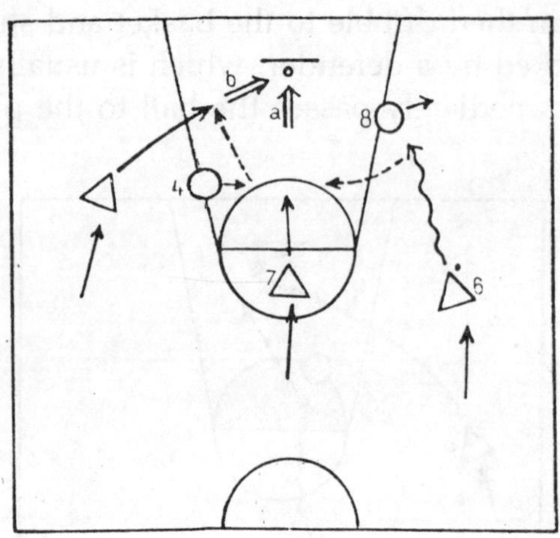

Solving the 3:2 outnumbering situation in the fast break

The nature of the offensive actions described does not change in principle, even if the numerical advantage is 4:3 or 5:4. The fast break can be carried out in a tandem position or with change of positions (crossing-over). However, it can also be performed along the middle of the court and along the side lines.

In the first case, attacker 8, who has gained the rebound, passes the ball immediately to 4. At the same time, players 6 and 7 star running towards the opposite basket in a straight line. Player 4 passes the ball to team-mate 6 who, with or without a dribble, passes the ball to 7 and gets it back in front of the opposite free-throw lane. Player 6 now has the opportunity to conclude the attack or to pass the ball to 4 or 7.

In the second case, the first two passes are made along the side lines. Player 8 passes to 12, 12 passes to 11 who dribbles along the side line towards the opposite basket and then passes to 10 who has cut in

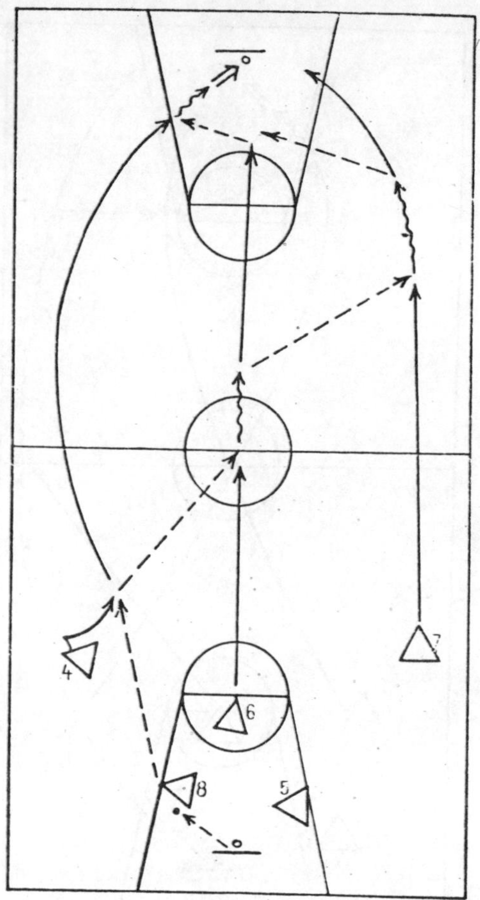

Fast break across the middle of the court

front of the free-throw lane. Now player 10 can either attack the basket or pass the ball to 12. Player 9 protects the rear court against possible counterattacks by the opponents.

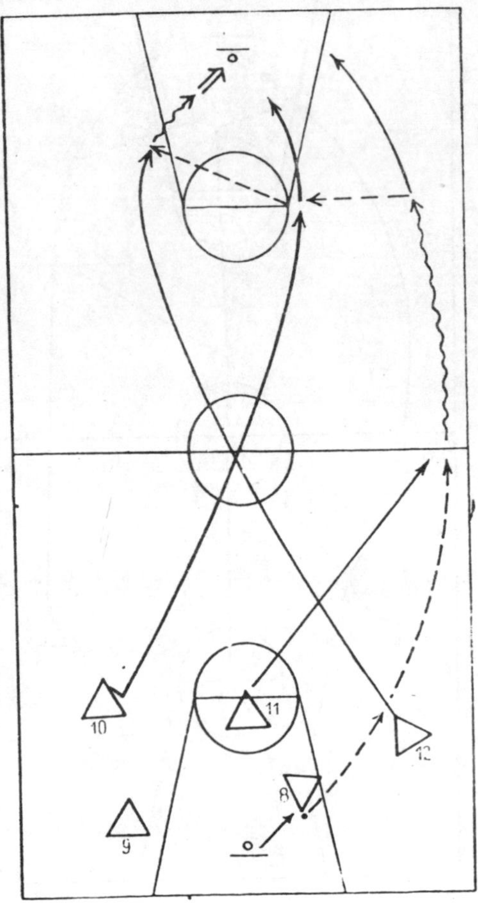

Fast break along the side lines of the court

Staggered fast break

This variant can be applied in almost any situation. It gives the attacking team the possibility to overcome the opponents' defence near one's own basket (first line) and near the opposing basket (second line). This attack takes place a bit more slowly than the one described above. In case of a numerical balance between attackers and defenders, change of pace, cutting, crossing over, etc. is applied. The involvement of almost all players (including the pivots) and the attack organized in two waves enable the team to outplay the defence and to successfully attack the basket from close or medium distances. This staggered attack can also be subdivided into three phases. During the first phase, when the attacking team gains possession of the ball, two players of the first line of attack start running towards the opposite basket so as to create free space for the team-mates' subsequent operations. The player who gathers the rebound must resist fierce pressure from the opponent who, on his part, tries to prevent the outlet pass (first pass) or to render it difficult. The player in possession of the ball gets rid of his opponent by a dribble to the side and he then passes the ball to a team-mate who cuts to one of the previously determined positions. He executes a direct pass to the players in the first line (or wave). This phase of the attack takes between 2.5 and 3 seconds.

In the second phase, two players of the second wave, who had rebounded at their own basket, come into play. The third player drops back a little as a safeguard against possible counterattacks. These players move into the free space and, in close co-operation with the players of the first line, try to outmanoeuvre the defence by cutting, crossing over, etc. Although the number of attackers and defenders is equal, the defenders find it difficult to orient themselves while moving backwards and to give each other the mutual assistance required. Consequently, the attacking team has an advantage and, with the organized attack of the second line (especially with the tall players), they an successfully overcome the defence. This phase lasts for about 3 seconds.

In the third phase, the attack is concluded by coordinated action of two or three players adapting their actions to the typical situations of play which have been developed in the preceding phase. If the defenders retreat towards the basket a player of the second line can finish the attack with a jump shot from medium distance. In general, this phase takes about 2 seconds.

This kind of fast break can be played in different ways. The co-operation of three players, based on the triangle principle. Player 4 who has gathered the rebound breaks away from his opponent by dribbling and passes the ball to team-mate 5 who signals, after a faked spurt, for the ball. At that moment, the two players of the first line (7 and 8) start running toward the opposite basket. Their paths cross and they call for a pass when they get to a favourable position. 5 passes to 8 and runs toward team-mate 6 as fast as he can in order to help the latter to get rid of his opponent and to start into the free-throw lane. Then he receives the ball from team-mate 8 ad finishes the attack with a shot at the basket.

Another variant in which, during the second phase, three players co-operate in accordance with the principle of crossing over. Player 6 gains possession of the ball, dribbles to the side the passes the ball to his team-mate 4. Players 7 and 8 have already broken away from their opponents, moved forward and taken up a favourable position for receiving the pass. After receiving the ball, player 8 dribbles to the free-throw line. In the meantime, team-mates 4 and 5 sprint at top speed from the rear court to their team-mate 8, and cross over. Player 8 can now hand the ball to one of them to complete the attack.

The tendency described earlier, i.e. to start the fast break by a fast space-covering dribble to the front court and the shooting area, applies also to this variant of the fast break. Here the two first phases virtually merge (whereby the duration of the attack is reduced even further and only in the final phase, does the dribbler involve his team-mates in concluding the attack.

Set play

In the course of play it is not always possible to start a fast break and bring it to a successful close. Frequently the opponents succeed in organizing their defence and closely guarding all attackers. In such cases the team in possession of the ball must attack with a systematic set play in which all five players participate. Through co-ordinated manoeuvres and team-work, the collective defence of the opposing team is disorganized and a promising situation is prepared for the concluding shot. According to the rules, each team has 30 seconds to do this. This time is sufficient for playing diverse and surprising combinations and, if they are successful, to create conditions for a tactically justified shot from medium or long distances or to effect a breakthrough with a concluding close shot.

In set play, we distinguish between play with and play without pivot players.

The system "with pivots"

This system has been thoroughly perfected in modern basketball and it is part of the tactical arsenal of all top teams. The pivot plays the main role in this system. He takes up the normal position with his back to the opposite basket so that he is in constant visual contact with his team-mates and can receive the ball from a team-mate at any time. In fact, the pivot is the team's main attacker and all efforts and actions of the players are aimed at helping him to get into a favourable (i.e. promising) shooting position near the basket.

Virtually any player in the team can take over the function of the pivot. In general, however, he must meet the pre-requisites.

In this offensive system we usually distinguish between two basic line-ups: 3:2 or 2:3. In relation to the opponents' basket, the first line-up means that 3 players take up front positions and 2 the rear positions. In the second case, there are 2 in front and 3 in the

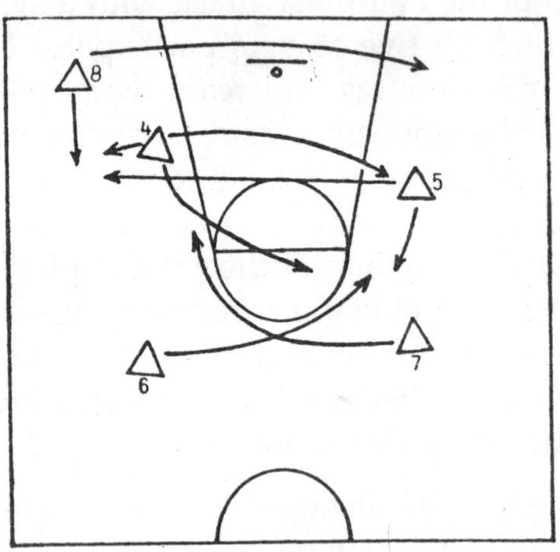

3:2 basic line-up with one pivot

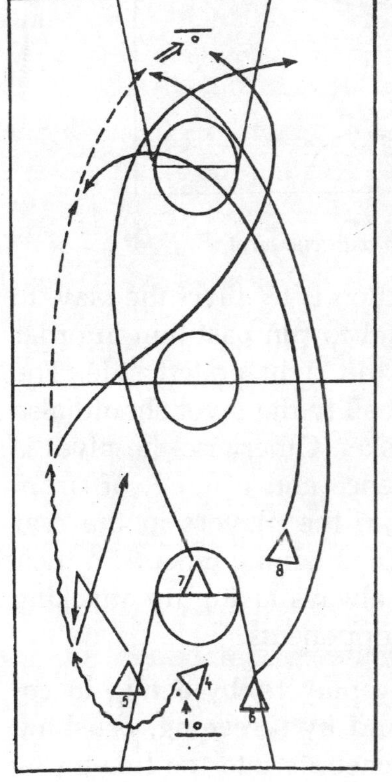

The staggered fast break

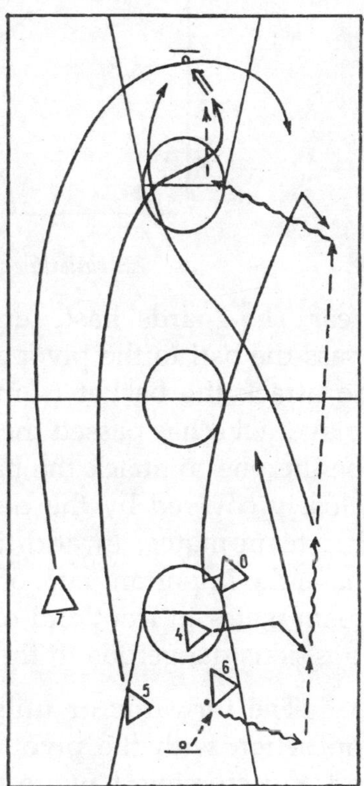

The staggered fast break

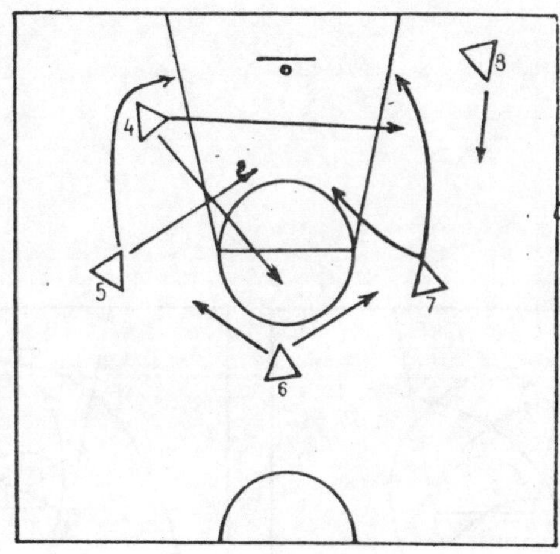

2:3 basic line-up with one pivot

rear. The guards' basic function is to direct the play, to pass the ball to the pivot and to run past him in order to attack the basket from the right or left side. The player who has passed the ball to the pivot should also be the one to attack the basket. Otherwise the pivot is closely covered by the defence and gets cut off from his team-mates. In addition, the players in the rear have the important task of maintaining links with their team-mates in front and of always taking up attacking positions dangerous to the opponents.

The forwards or utility players, by acting in co-operation with the pivot and by screening, brushing off and crossing, have to penetrate into the free-throw lane, attack the basket and rebound. Besides, they also link up with the guards, thus creating favourable possibilities for shots from medium distances. When the pivot gets the ball he has various possibilities:

1. He can shoot directly into the basket or outplay his defender in a one-on-one situation.

2. He can pass the ball to a cutting team-mate.
3. He can set a screen for one of the outside players with a dribble so that the outside player gets free and receives the ball from the pivot for a shot.

An extremely effective tactical weapon is the screening of team-mates by the pivot when he is not in possession of the ball. By doing this, he creates favourable starting positions for his team-mates to initiate positive attacks on the opposing team's basket.

Top teams also use rehearsed combinations based on the typical co-operation of 2 and 3 players.

The combination is based on the triangular play

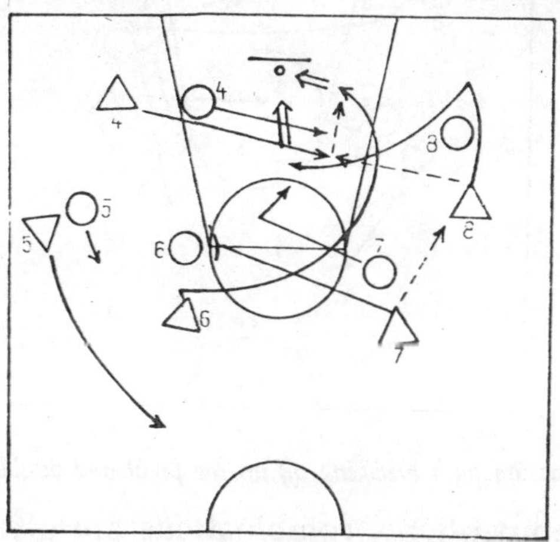

Combination out of triangular play with crossing

with subsequent crossing. The players 7, 6 and 5 form a triangle. The moment player 8 receives the ball from his team-mate, he passes it to the oncoming pivot 4. Then players 6 and 8 cross in front of the pivot past the side line of the free-throw lane. One of them receives the ball and then attacks the basket. Player 5 moves back to cover the rear court. An interesting combination, where the utility player 8 and the pivot 4 team up. By brushing off onto the pivot, an attempt is made to bring player 8 into a shooting position. In case of failure it is possible to set a double screen, by using players 8 and 6, for the utility player 7 who is positioned on the opposite side. Player 7 receives the ball from 5 within the free-throw lane. He can either execute a jump shot from medium distance or pass the ball to 6 who has meanwhile broken away from the screen.

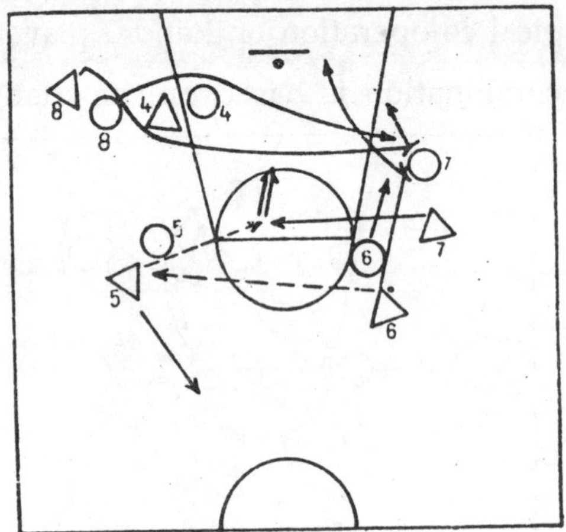

Combination with brushing off on the pivot and double screen

In competitions, combinations are often used in which the pivot stands in line with the free-throw line. Fig. 81 illustrates the combination "merry-go-round". In this combination, a series of brushing off manoeuvres onto the pivot takes place in one direction. Player 7 begins after passing the ball to 5. Then player 8 runs and finishes the attack with a shot at the basket on the move. Should this solution not be possible, i.e. if it has not been possible to hand the ball either to attacker 7 or 8, then the utility player 6 finishes the attack with a jump shot from medium distance.

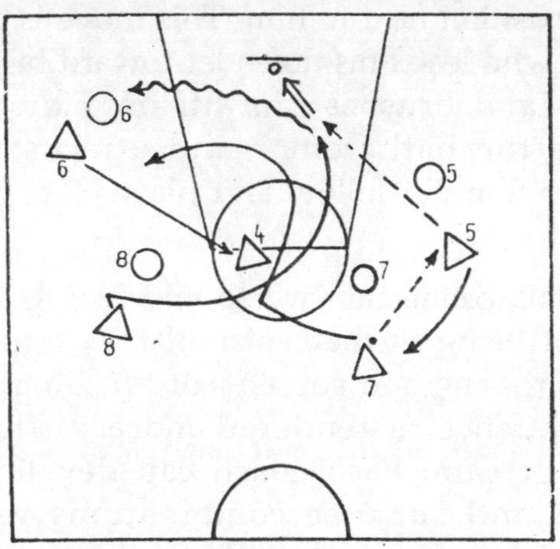

Combination "Merry-go-round"

An extremely effective combination. Here distraction manoeuvres in triangular play are combined with crossing in the free-throw area.

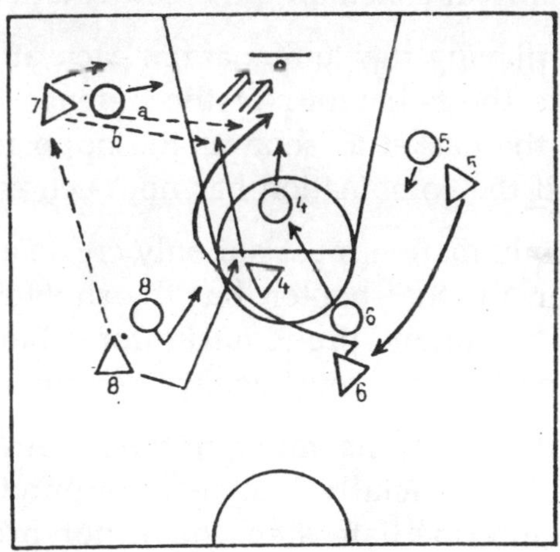

Combination with feints and crossing in the free-throw area

Player 8, after passing the ball to team-mate 7, fakes a change of position. He then runs towards pivot 4 and takes a position next to him. This move is exploited by player 6 who leads his defender toward his team-mates 4 and 8 and brushes him off onto them. He then receives the ball from 7 and attacks the basket. Attackers 8 and 4 follow and player 5 covers the rear court.

In this connection we should like to weaving. By the pivot being in the centre of the "figure of eight" and by crossing and subsequent brushing off onto the pivot, defence is rendered more difficult for the opposing team. Each coach can develop different, original and surprise combinations with the co-operation between two or three players and rehearse them with his team. The following general principles must be observed:

1. The players must be taught to co-operate creatively (especially in concluding the combinations).
2. While playing the combination, each attacker must observe the behaviour of the defence in order to attack the basket as soon as the opposition relaxes (even if the combination has not been completed).
3. Each combination must not only create a favourable position for the shooter, but the shooter must also create favourable pre-requisite for rebounding and covering the rear court against counterattacks.
4. The combinations must not be rendered more difficult artificially because combinations with many intermediate steps have not proved to be successful in competitions.

5. Each combination should begin with a simple, easy to understand signal which cannot, however, be recognized by the opponent.

There are several variants of playing via the pivot. This system can also be played with two or three pivots. These variants are recommended for teams whose players are taller than their opponents. Taller players are at an advantage especially in rebounding and in the attack under the basket. Their disadvantage is, however, that they tend to clog up the area under the basket, impending their team-mates' movements and slowing the pace of the game. With two pivots, setups on both sides of the free-throw lane, on level with the basket or diagonally, can be chosen. With both types of set-up it is recommended that the combinations be carried out by the pivots. These include, above all, such manoeuvres as crossing, screening, etc. An example of how, during weaving, attacker 7 brushes off twice. After brushing off between pivots 4 and 5 he receives the ball and attacks the basket. The second combination illustrates the screening of and by the two pivots.

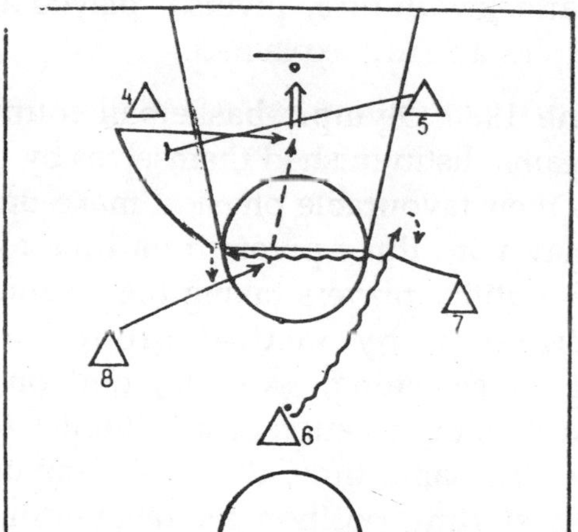

Combinations out of weaving with brushing off on two pivots

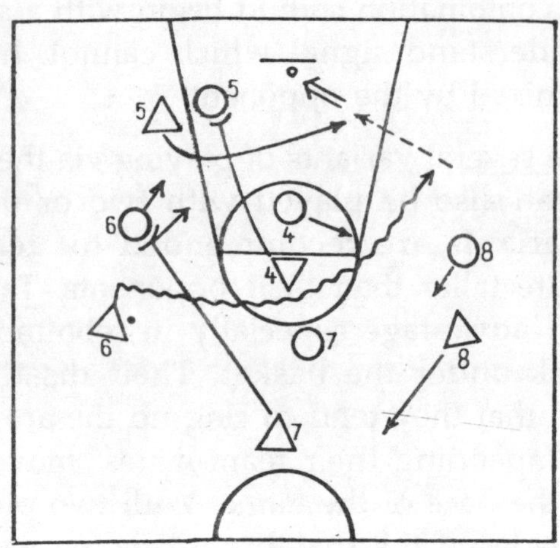

Combinations where the pivots screen one another

Guard 6 who first uses the screen set by team-mate 7 and then brushes off onto the pivot, dribbles to the vacant position on the right hand side. At this moment, pivot 4 sets a screen for pivot 5 who cuts into the free-throw lane, which has now become free, and receives the pass from team-mate 6.

The attack with three pivots is played according to the principles already explained.

At the 1980 Olympic basketball tournament the leading teams distinguished themselves by the fact that thanks to their favourable physical make-up, they were able to play with three pivots from time to time, with one or two utility players taking the positions marked. This facilitated, by tactical group co-operation (brushing off, screening, "swerving out" on the outside positions, etc.), the creation of possibilities to attack the basket. At the same time, this basic line-up created a favourable starting position for rebounding (attacking triangle).

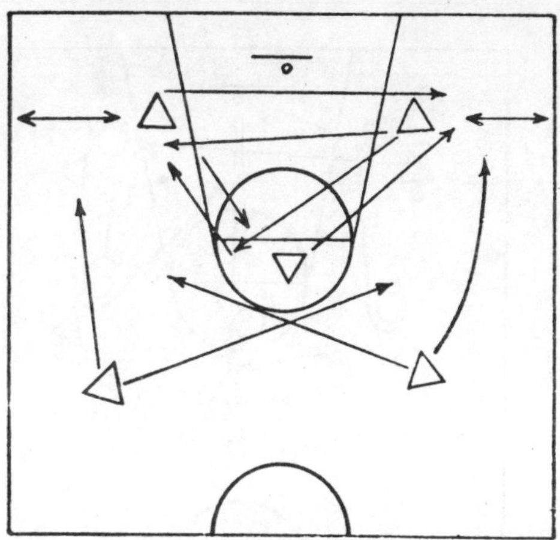

Attack with three pivots

Offensive system "without pivot"

If the team does not have a pivot it can attack either by a series of screens or by weaving (large figure eight). The free-throw area is made free through the 2:3 basic line-up enabling a player to move into the area. The series of screens which are set in succession give each player of the team the possibility to run into the free-throw lane and attack the basket. Player 4 runs, after passing to 5, toward 6 to set a screen. Player 6 now attacks the basket. If player 6 is unable to receive the ball he runs to the right and sets a screen for team-mate 7 who tries to repeat the manoeuvre of player 6. Should the opponent again foil this move, player 7 runs toward guard 8 and sets a screen for him, etc.

In the weave one proceeds in the same way as for the "small figure of eight". The involvement of four to five players for such operations increases the tempo of positional changes, the number of passes and the possibilities for a drive to the basket.

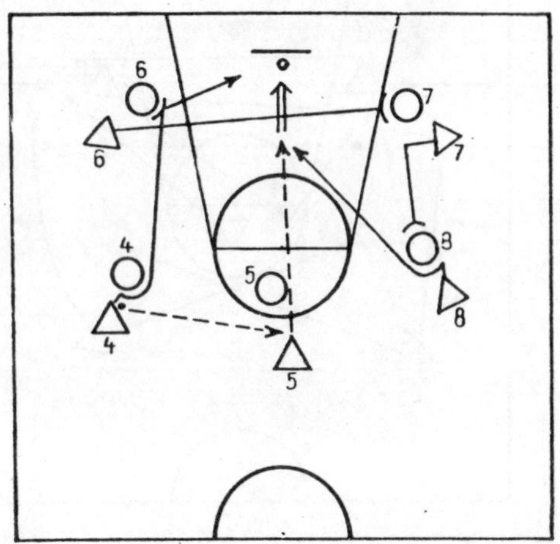

Set play without pivots, with several screens

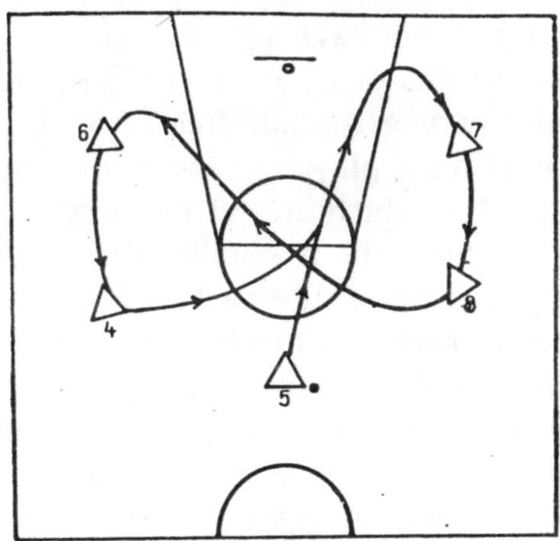

Set play without pivots, with weaving

Throw-in and jump ball combinations

When the ball is to be brought into play, rehearsed combinations prove to be quite successful. They can be applied to surprise the opponent. During the breaks of the game the players can take up favourable positions on the court and then purposefully try to play the prearranged combinations. There are many such throw-in combinations. Several of them are aimed at initiating a fast break. With throw-ins in the midfield one tries to keep the area near the basket free so that it can be used to complete the attack. Distracting manoeuvres are used here.

Combinations during jump ball in the middle of the court and on the free-throw line as well as after an unsuccessful free throw. For example, player 6 uses brushing off at the moment when the referee has tossed the ball up between the players and player 4 has taken possession of the ball.

Player 9, who takes advantage of his height, taps the ball to his team-mate 7 who has cut to the side. The start of the fast break is facilitated by player 6 setting a screen for 9. Players 9, 6 and 5 participate in the fast break.

In case the last free throw is performed unsuccessfully by the opponent, player 8 taps the ball, while jumping, to his team-mate 7 who, together with attackers 5 and 6, starts the counterattack. During he throw-in from the side, screening and brushing off are used. Player 5 passes to 8, who becomes free thanks to the screen set up by 7, and receives the ball (a) after brushing off his opponent onto pivot 4 and forward 6. If the defender succeeds in preventing the pass to attacker 5, players 6 or 4 (b,c) can then receive the ball for a medium-range shot at the basket.

Attack against different defensive systems

Attack against zone defence: The best tactics against zone defence are fast breaks, which make organized defence difficult. But if the opponents still manage to put up organized defence, the attack should be carried out deliberately and with care combinations. All attacking options and variants against zone defence are based on the following principles:

1. Moving the ball precedes the moving of the players, i.e. quick, forceful and accurate passes are the decisive prerequisite for opening up a zone defence. Furthermore, each player should be able to attack the basket. The opposing defence should be kept under constant pressure in order to kept the defenders guessing as to when the direct attack on the basket is going to take place. The attack is completed by accurate long-range shots or drives after fakes with jump shots from a medium distance. If the attacker driving forward is taken on by defenders of the second line the ball is passed to players who have become free. After each shot at the basket rebounds should be made by using.

2. High passes over the zone defence can also be applied successfully. With inexperienced players there is, of course, the danger of the ball being intercepted by the defenders. But with high passes over the zone it is possible to open up a tight defence. High passes to the pivot near the basket can also prove successful against zone defence. We should also mention the front screen as an effective tactical procedure which creates favourable conditions for the execution of an unobstructed long-distance shot.

For example, attacker 6 passes the ball to 5 who, thanks to the screen set by pivot 4, can perform on undisturbed set shot. However, he passes the ball to team-mate 7 who draws the defender by a shooting

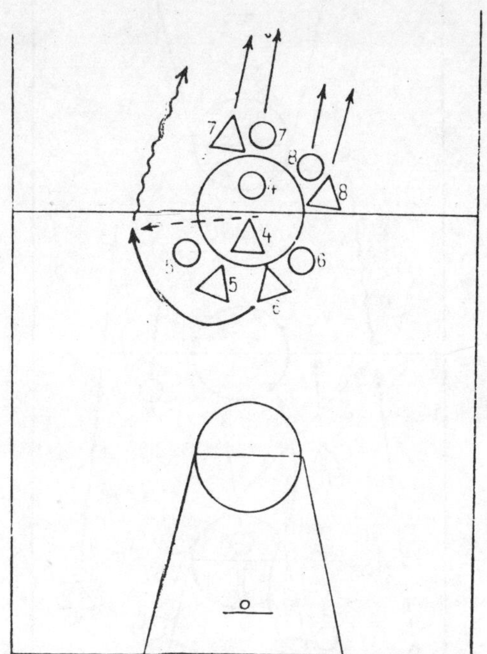

Jump-ball combination in the centre circle

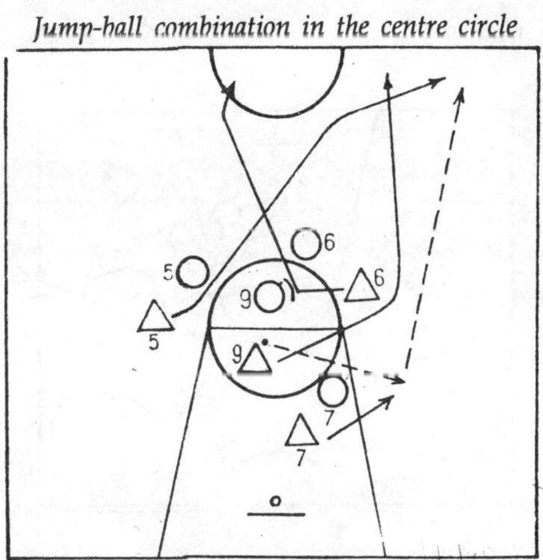

Jump-ball combination at the free-throw line in the rear court

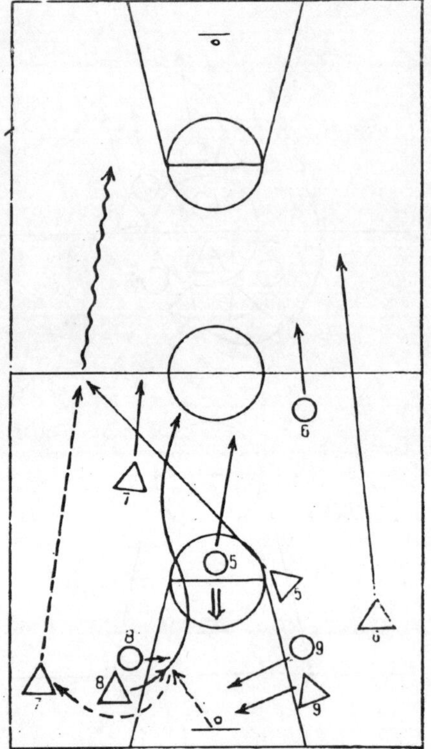

Combination out of the free-throw line-up

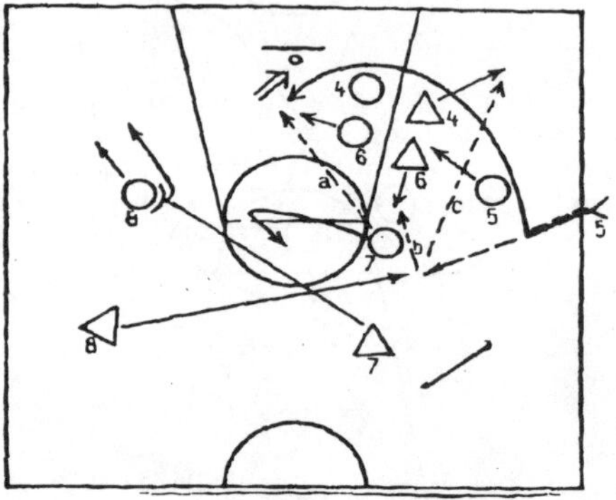

Throw-in combination from the side line

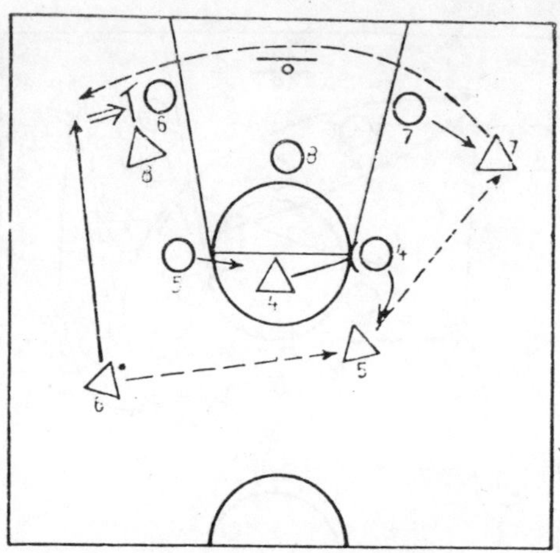

Offensive combination against zone defence, including running behind the zone and setting a front screen

feint and then passes the ball over the zone to team-mate 6. Attacker 6 is screened by pivot 8 and can, therefore, shoot at the basket unhindered. Immediately after the shot attacker 6 has to take over the covering of the rear court. Players 8, 4 and 7 follow the shot. Similarly, attacker 7 can pass the ball to team-mate 5 who is screened free by pivot 4. At that moment, attacker 7 starts running for the free space under the basket and, after receiving the ball from 5, he immediately executes a jump shot. 3. Creating of a situation with numerical advantage in a certain area of the zone defence. This on the right hand side. Attacker 8, who has received a pass from 6, has the following options:

— to attack the basket,

— to pass the ball to team-mates 7 or 4, or

— to pass the ball back to 6 so that this move can be re-started on the other side.

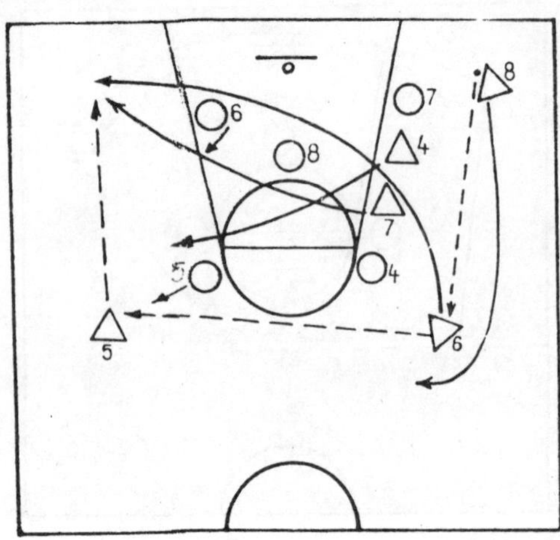

Attack against zone defence with on outnumbering situation

To perform the attack on the left side, 6 passes to 5 and then runs across the zone defence to the left hand corner of the court. The running paths of players 4 and 7 are shown in the figure and require no further explanation. Attacker 8 covers the rear court.

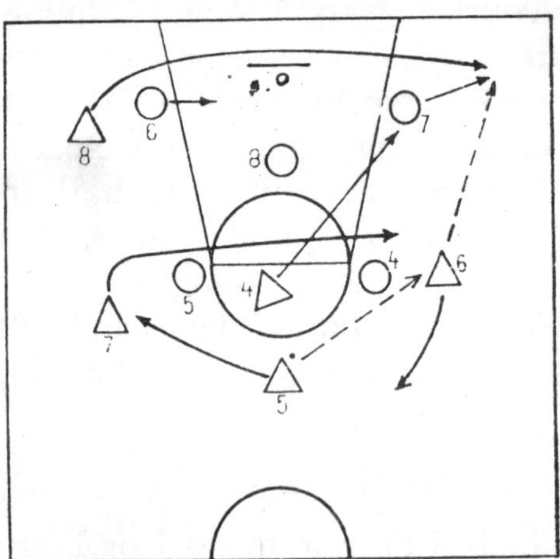

Attack against zone defence by creating on 'overload

4. It becomes necessary to separate the rear and front

rows of the zone defence from each other. For that purpose, the free space in the free-throw lane must be used. Players 4, 5 and 6 pin the front row of the zone defence whereas attackers 7 and 8 pin the rear formation. If defender 8 attacks his opponent after receiving the ball from his team-mate 5, attacker 8 passes the ball to 7 who, in the meantime, has run behind the zone. Attacker 7 completes the attack with a shot at the basket or hands the ball to the pivot 4.

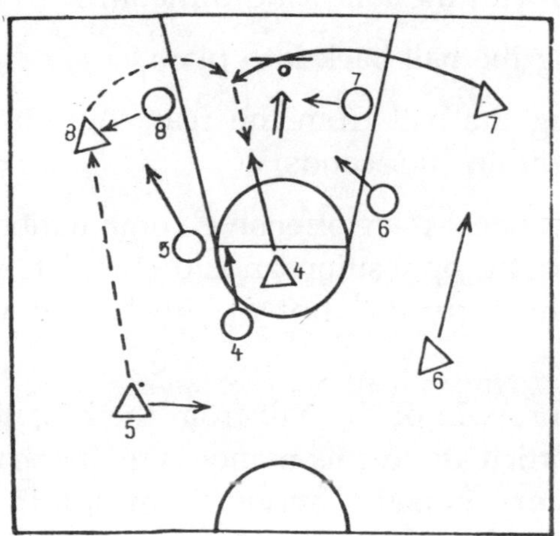

Attacking by using free spaces within the zone defence

The selection and preparation of specific combinations for a systematic set play against zone defence depends, of course, first and foremost, on the composition of the team and its technical and tactical proficiency. It also depends on the basic line-up of the zone defence and its movement towards the ball. Experience shows that every team has some combinations at its disposal in set play against the various types of zone defence (2:3, 3:2, 1:2:1).

Every team which attacks against zone defence must be aware of the fact that the opponents are in a favourable starting position for a counterattack if the ball is lost. Therefore each combination must allow for the covering of the rear court and the rear attackers must always be prepared to defend sudden fast breaks by the opponents.

Attack against man-to-man press

When attacking against man-to-man press every team must cope with the following difficulties:

— to bring the ball back into play;

— to bring the ball from the rear court to the front court within 10 seconds;

— to play one's own offensive combinations despite very strong opposition and to complete the attack with an accurate shot at the basket within 30 seconds.

The throw-in of the ball from the base line. Three players participate in this manoeuvre. If each player is marked very closely, screens similar to those in triangular play tend to be successful. Player 5, after screening free his team-mate 7, immediately joins in the fast break.

In practice, there are quite a number of special combinations designed to bring the ball safely into play during the throw-in and to develop fast breaks out of it. The so-called "wall" set up by players 8, 4 and 5.4 runs back and receives the ball more or less unhindered and passes it directly to 6 or 7 who, supported by players 8 and 5, cut for the fast break.

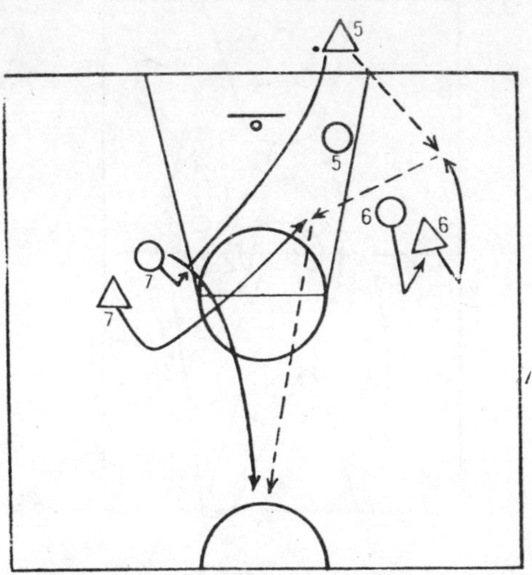

Throw-in combination from the base line against press defence

If the attacking team succeeds in bringing the ball to the front court it has a chance of using the defenders' centralized line-up for the attack. In such cases the attack does not take place via the pivot. The pivot is given the task of keeping the free-throw lane free by taking up a position on the side line. His team-mates can thus use this free space for their movements. If the team has players with excellent fighting qualities (dribbling, drive, etc.), one on one situations should be deliberately created for these players so that they can use their strong points. The other attackers should lure their opponents away from their positions by fakes and keep them occupied so that they do not get an opportunity to support their defender. In the struggle for initiative during the game it has often proved to be quite successful when press is responded to by counter-press. This leads to an extraordinarily high tempo of the game and a strong struggle ensues.

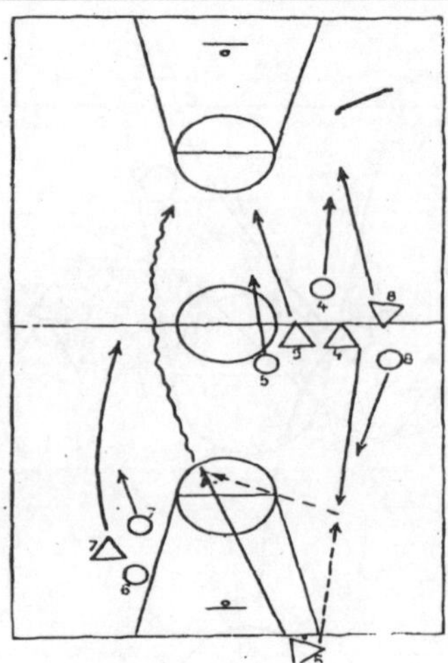

Throw-in combination, "Wall", from the base line against press defence

Attack against zone press

Two variants can be applied when playing against zone press:

— one attacker places himself in the middle of the court between the two formations of zone press, and the attack takes places via this player;

— the main forces of the team are concentrated on one side (wing) of the court and the attack takes place along that side.

If the player in possession of the ball (6) is attacked by the defender 5, attacker 4 moves into the midfield and, together with his team-mates 7 and 8, attacks the opposing basket. In doing this, they must endeavour to obtain numerical superiority over the defence.

Player 5 throws in. He passes the ball to player 7 who has cut to one of the side lines. As soon as he is challenged by defenders 5 and 7 he passes the ball to team-mate 6 who has cut to the same side. Attacker 6 passes the ball on to player 8 who, by moving from one side of the court to the other, has cut to the same side and now dribbles towards the opponent's basket. In this way, the attack against zone press is continued on the left side. Players 8, 4 and 5 then participate in completing the attack.

Attack against a combined defence

When attacking against a combined defence, above all, screens and brushing off should be organized for that player who is tightly marked. Should the defence apply man-to-man defence for two players, then crossing should also be used. These procedures confuse the defence. Fig. 100 illustrates a combination which is applied in the attack against a 2:2 zone defence and man-to-man defence for one player. Player 5, who is marked man-to-man, is screened by his team-mates 6 and 8 so that he can shoot at the basket from a medium distance. If he is taken over the zone defence is destroyed and another attacker is given an opportunity to cut into the free-throw lane and receive he ball from team mate 5 for a shot.

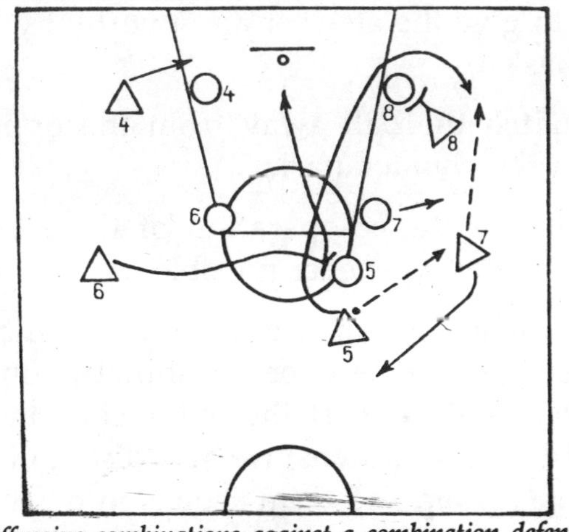

Offensive combinations against a combination defence

3

DEFENSIVE TACTICS

A stable defence does not only stabilize the success achieved in attack, but it also creates the pre-requisites for successful play-making. Each team which has a stable and strong defence can risk shots from medium and long distances and struggle for the missed shots. The actions of the defence depend, above all, on the opponents' offensive actions and tactics, i.e. it is imperative to take note of the reciprocity of attack and defence (alternating responses).

The defence has to solve the following basic tasks:

1. Not to give the attacker an opportunity to shoot at the basket;
2. to snatch the ball away from the opponent and begin the counterattack;
3. to disrupt the co-operation of the attackers and their moves whenever possible.

Each team, which tries to obtain the ball during the defence can take over the initiative in the game and successfully thwart the opponents' tactical plan. As with offensive actions, we also distinguish between individual, **group** and team actions in defence.

Individual tactical actions in defence

The success of a defence is determined by the players' ability to neutralize their opponent, i.e. to take a correct position towards the attacker and to apply successfully such technical and tactical manoeuvres which neutralize the attacker's effective actions. Although, in each case, the opponent must be followed closely and the active tussle for the ball must always be kept in mind, the defence against the player with and without the ball is somewhat different.

Defending against the player without the ball

In the tussle against the attacker without the ball, the defender tries:

1. to give the opponent no opportunity to get to a favourable position which would allow him a successful attack on the basket;
2. to prevent passes to attackers in such a position and
3. to recover the ball which is in the immediate vicinity of the attacker.

The defender must choose a basic position in relation to his basket which permits him to keep an eye on the opponent all the time. The closer the attacker is to the basket, the closer should he be covered. The attacker is in a dangerous position whenever he is between the defender and the basket. There are, however, situations in which the basic rule; that the defender should always be between his opponent and his own basket, must be overlooked. In defending against the opposing pivot close to the basket, it is often necessary to mark the attacker from the front in order to prevent a pass to him. Following figure gives an example of the position the defender should take up in relation to the attacker's position and the basket. Because of the long distance between the attacker and the basket (a) the "fighting distance" towards the attacker is between 1.5 and 2 metres. With increasing proximity to the basket this distance decreases to approximately 1 metre (b). Thus, a pass and a jump shot from a medium distance is rendered difficult. However, if the attacker is close to the basket (c) he poses a direct threat of scoring. Therefore the defender places himself in such a position that the attacker is behind him so that he can prevent a pass to him. The 3-second-rule helps the defender because it forces the attacker to leave the free-throw lane as quickly as possible.

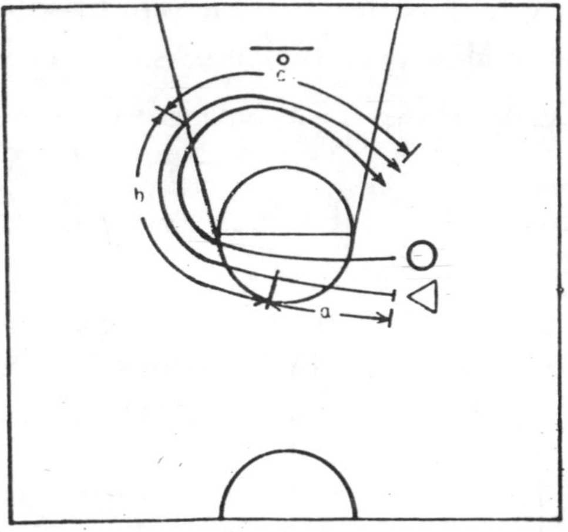

The running paths of the defender in man-to-man defence

Defending against the player with the ball

The defender has to fulfil three basic tasks with regard to the player with the ball. He must not give him an opportunity to:

1. execute a shot at the basket;
2. drive for the basket;
3. pass the ball to team-mates who are in a favourable position, usually the pivots,
4. to gain possession of the ball during rebounding.

It is essential that each defender should be always mentally alert and make every effort to prevent a shot. Should the attacker prefer a certain shooting position he is to be harassed in this position in such a way as to hinder him in preparing for the shot. The defender should try not to be fooled by the attacker's feints. He must always anticipate a shot at the basket following a shooting feint. In the course of the game, the defender should study attentively the attacker's typical peculiarities in preparing for a shot. This permits him to distinguish between real shooting actions from feinted ones and to actively prevent the attacker from concentrating fully on the execution of the shot.

If the player in possession of the ball has not yet completed his dribble the defender has to mark him with extreme vigilance in order to prevent a drive for the basket. During the dribble, the defender must try to stop the attacker or to force him to the side so as to thwart penetration into the free-throw lane. Forcing the dribbler into one corner of the court has proved to be an especially successful measure. This forces the player with the ball to stop the dribble and to remain stationary with the ball. This leads to possibilities to take the ball away from the attacker or to obtain a jump ball.

When the attacker has finished his dribble the defender marks him so closely that he can hit the ball out of this hands or even pull it out. Besides, he must try to have the attacker behind him when near the basket so that the attacker cannot take up a good position for rebounding. An unfavourable position arises for the defender when he is faced with a numerical superiority. If he has to defend two attackers he must run towards his own basket as quickly as possible and try to slow down the attack by feints towards the player with the ball. He then has to provoke the player with the ball to shoot from a medium distance. At the same time, however, he must keep an eye on the passing line to the second attacker. Tall defenders and those with good jumping power have to stand under the basket and give the attacker the chance to execute a shot in order to hit the ball away while it is ascending after leaving the shooter's hand.

In the tussle with his attacker, the defender must always follow the course of the game in order to help, if necessary, one of his team-mates or to call for the active support of one of his team-mates and to be able to time his actions in co-ordination with those of his team-mates.

Rebounding

The main task, when the ball rebounds from the basket, is to take possession of the ball and secure it against the opponents' attack. Usually, the defender is closer to the basket than the attacker, unless he has to mark the opposing pivot from the front. This favourable position should be exploited by screening out the trailing attacker. If, however, the attacker recovers the ball, the defender must take up a favourable position relative to subsequent moves by the attacker. He should try to prevent him from executing a well-aimed shot at the basket. If a team-mate wins the ball the defender has to start the attack immediately.

As the number of unsuccessful shot is performed. He should follow the flight of the ball. But at the same time he should try to take up a good starting position between attacker and basket and prepare for an active tussle for the ball. While he is moving towards the ball he must raise his arms, assess his team-mates' position and calculate the possibility of initiating a fast break.

After the defender has completed a full turn towards the basket he takes a wide straddle position. This position makes it difficult for the attacker to run to the basket without being obstructed. The defender's feet are placed just wide enough apart to ensure his balance and provide a comfortable starting position for the rebound. The knees and the body are slightly bent at the hip, the elbows are raised to shoulder height, and the forearms and wrists are stretched upwards. This bent posture allows a quick start and jump for the ball. The rebounding from the basket or backboard is influenced by various factors, such as the shooting distance, the angle with the backboard in case of bank-shots, the spin, etc. Therefore each shot has to be watched very carefully. For example, balls which are thrown at the basket from the side usually bounce to the opposite side, after touching the backboard. During rebounding at the basket, correct anticipation is more important than excellent jumping power. The defender has to hold the ball in two hands at the culminating point of the jump and to protect it by slightly turning it in. One of the hands protects the ball from above against being knocked out. As soon as the feet of the slightly spread legs touch the ground, the knee joints bend to cushion the jump, and then the player has to look to the side so that he can pass the ball to his team-mate if necessary.

If the opponent applies press defence he must be distracted by a feint. Mean-while the ball must be held in both hands. The first pass is usually made from that side, along the boundary line, where the ball had been recovered. Tall defenders hold the ball above their heads and decide, according to the situation, whether they ought to pass it on immediately or protect it against attacks from the opponent. Short defenders usually protect the ball with their bodies and by spreading out their elbows. In most cases they pass the ball on immediately or dribble out of the dangerous area.

Tactical group defensive actions

Group-tactical actions in defence are aimed at helping a team-mate. They include covering, switching, going 'over the top' of the screen and sliding. When three defenders co-operate, one distinguishes between organized defensive actions against change of positions within the triangle, weaving ("small figure of eight"), crossing, running towards each other, and forming a defensive triangle for rebounding.

Co-operation of two defenders

Covering is a form of mutual assistance. The players must be always prepared to support one another and to take charge of the attacker threatening the basket. This tactical measure is applied, above all, against fast attackers who are able to shoot at the basket very successfully and who master feints and drives for the basket. In the same way, the player who marks the opposing pivot near the basket must assist by trying to prevent the ball being passed to him. If, however, the ball should reach the pivot the supporting team-mate must try to knock the ball out of the pivot's hands or to disturb him when he shoots. Usually, the covering is done by sacrificing the defence against the weakest attacker or against that attacker who, at that particular moment, is not in a threatening position or within shooting distance.

A situation in which attacker 6 outplays his defender 6 and begins to dribble towards the basket.

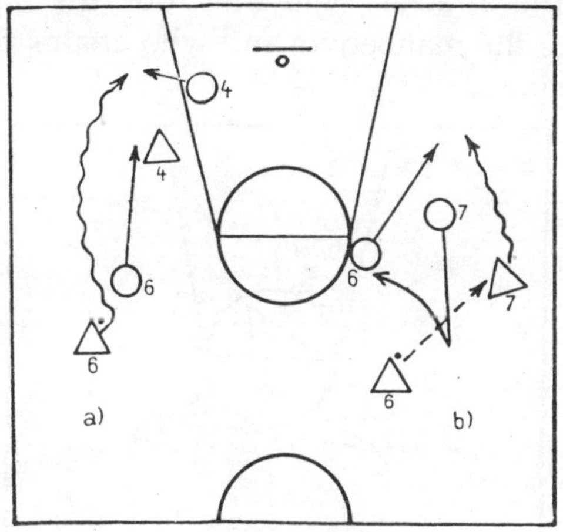

Covering in defence

Defender 4, who marks the pivot 4, assists him team-mate by switching to the dribbling attacker. In that case defender 6 is obliged to immediately leave his opponent and to take over the defence against the pivot 4.

Demonstrates the covering after an unsuccessful

attempt by defender 7 to intercept the ball which is passed to attacker 7. Defender 6 prevents the drive by attacker 7 and defender 7 takes over the defence of attacker 6.

Switching an succeed if the attackers apply screens, splitting the post (crossing) and brushing off while running towards each other. In these instances the defenders switch marking of players for whom they are personally responsible. The decision when to switch is taken by the defender being screened, for this gives him a better chance of assessing the situation. In brushing off, the defender decides which attacker the brush-off is to be used on. In crossing, the defender marking the attacker who first took the initiative in performing the manoeuvre and who attains the highest speed, decides.

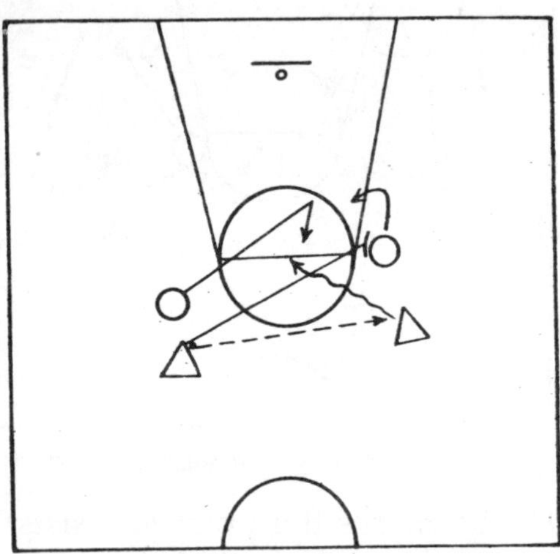

Switching (taking over) during screening

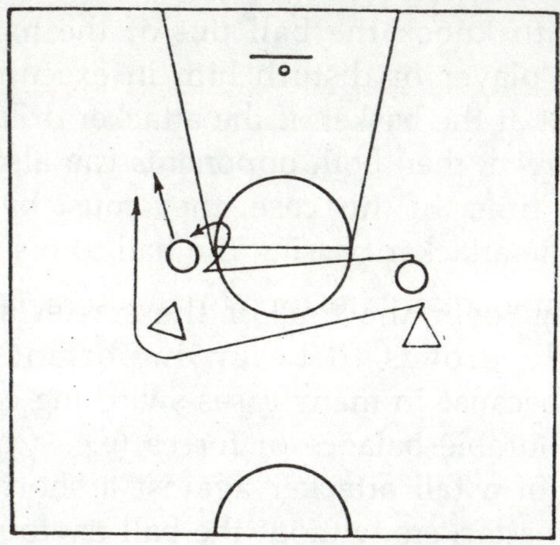

Switching during brushing off

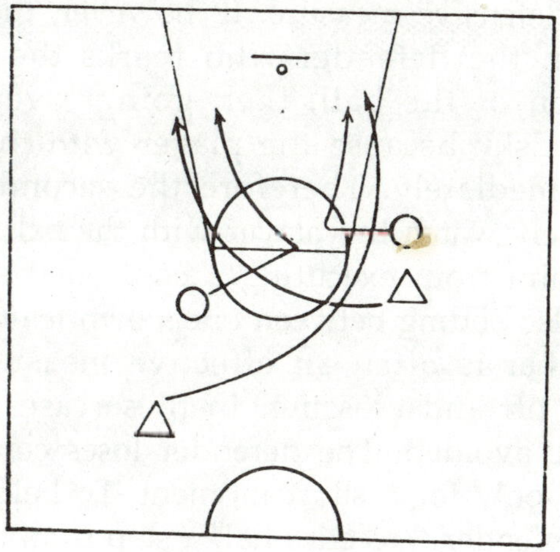

Switching during crossing

Switching against a sliding screen is especially difficult. In this case the defender who is screened must try not to allow the attacker to approach the basket. The second defender must pursue and attack the player in possession of the ball. In doing this, he must try to knock the ball out of the hands of the dribbling player or disturb him in executing a well-timed shot at the basket. If the attacker dribbles with a sliding screen, then both opponents can also defend at the same time. In this case, they must by all means prevent the attacker passing the ball to his team-mate.

Going 'over the top' of the screen and sliding frequently proves to be an important defensive measure because in many cases switching can result in an unfavourable balance of forces (e.g. a one on-one-situation of a tall attacker against a short defender). When the attackers without the ball try to screen their team-mate's defender then slight falling, back and on immediate approach towards the attacker is an effective defensive measure. If, however, the screen is placed on the defender who marks the player in possession of the ball, then going 'over the top' becomes risky because the player with the ball can shoot immediately. Therefore the second defender must closely watch the player with the ball and try to prevent him from executing a controlled shot at the basket. Also sliding between one's own team-mate and the attacker is often an effective measure against brushing off and crossing. In these cases switching should be avoided. The defender loses control of his opponent only for a short moment. To help his team-mate 5, defender 6 recedes half a step from his attacker thus creating a free running path. The defender who is sliding through must slightly twist his hips to diminish his profile and reduce the obstruction. However, a better technical solution is to use sideways sliding steps so that he can nimbly slide through between the team-mate and the attacker.

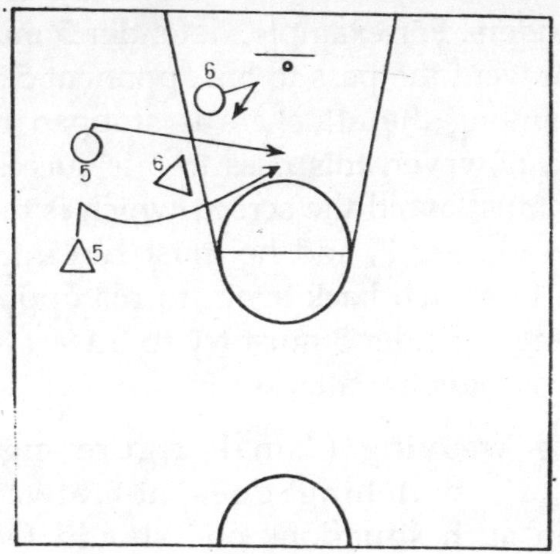

Stepping back to allow team-mate to pass against brushing off

Double teaming is frequently used in modern basketball, mostly during press defence. Here, two defenders simultaneously attack the player in possession of the ball. There are two variants of double teaming. In the first case, the defender forces the player with the ball to the side line making him end the dribble and to take up the ball. The attacker usually finishes up with his back towards the opponent and the court. At that moment the second defender who has approached the attacker unnoticed tries to pull or knock the ball out from the other side. In the other variant, the second defender must knock the ball out from behind or from the side when the dribbler is harassed and distracted by his team-mate.

Co-operation of three defenders

The defence against the change of positions within the triangle, weaving ("small figure eight") and crossing requires organized and well co-ordinated co-operation of the defenders. For example, defender 5 must, first of all, try to prevent the pass to his opponent 5 so that co-operation among the attackers is stopped right from the start. If, however, this pass to 5 is successful, then defender 6 must avoid the screen which is to be set up for him by attacker 7, and he must run into the free-throw lane to switch back again to his opponent 6. In the meantime defender 5 must try to thwart a pass into the free-throw lane by attacker 5.

During weaving ("small figure eight") and brushing off, switching does not always prove effective. In such situations one should temporarily change from man-to-man defence to zone defence.

Defence against triangular play

The possibility to neutralize splitting the post (crossing) is illustrated. Defenders 4 and 5 step back towards the defender who marks the opposing pivot (6), thus making the crossing of attackers 4 and 5 in front of their own pivot much more difficult. The defenders take over their team-mate's attacker. During

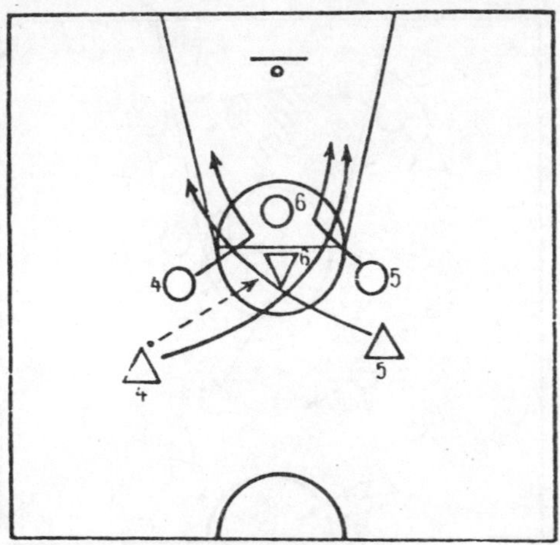

Defence against crossing in front of

rebounding, the correct and well-timed co-operation of the three defenders determines the success of this important element of the game. The defenders 5, 4 and 7 form a defensive triangle in the free-throw lane after attacker 4 has taken a shot at the basket. They place themselves in such a way that their opponents are behind them, depriving them of an opportunity to assume a favourable starting position in the tussle for the rebounding ball. Defender 6 also covers the area around the free-throw line in case the ball bounces farther away from the basket.

Co-operation in case of numerical superiority of defenders

Nowadays attackers make increasing use of the possibility of outplaying a disorganized defence by means of fast breaks. They also tend to increasingly attack the basket when the forces are balanced or even when they are outnumbered. Therefore allowance should be made for a defence in such situations.

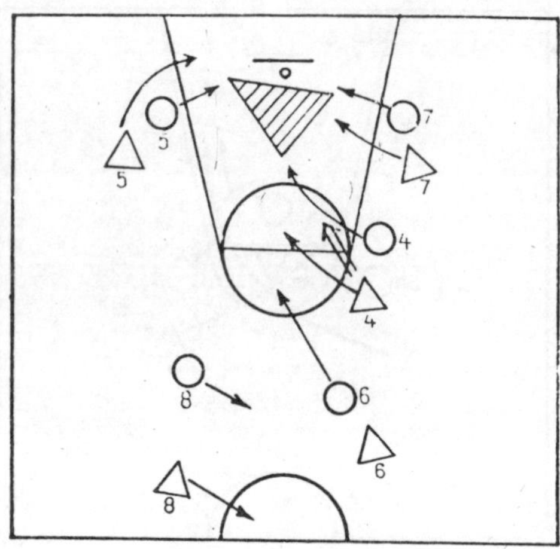

Formation of the rebounding triangle in defence

It often happens that the player with the ball is far in front of his team-mates (e.g. after a successful long pass) and consequently challenges the two defenders. If this situation occurs one defender must try to stop the attacker while the other tries to gain the ball from the so-called "blind" side. The best they can do is gain possession of the ball or bring about a held ball. But even provoked uncontrolled shots at the basket or an inaccurate pass do well. However, the defence must always make sure that no attacker can cut into a position near the basket. With three defenders against two attackers, the nearest defender stops the dribbler and the second defender actively attacks the player with the ball, while the third covers the passing line to the second attacker.

Defence against throw-ins

In practice, there are mainly, two methods of

successfully defending against the throw-in. In the first instance, all defenders are between their opponents and the ball. The defender who marks the attacker who throws in tries to unbalanced him and to provoke him to make an inaccurate pass by very active arm and leg action.

In the second variant, which is very common, the player who throws the ball in remains unmarked. The defender takes up a position between the player who throws the ball in and the basket, while all the other defenders cover the passing lines without losing sight of their personal opponents. The free defender now tries to intercept the pass to the attacker who cuts to the free-throw lane. When the player who throws the ball enters the court he must be forced away from the basket in order to eliminate a give and go situation (wall pass) between the attackers.

Co-operation between outnumbered defenders

After losing the ball in attack, situations frequently arise in which the attackers outnumber the defenders. The player who, due to a mistake, has lost the ball to the opponent, acts wrongly if he tries to regain the ball immediately. In such situations a quick return into one's own half of the court is the right thing to do. If, however, he rushes at the attacker he is usually outplayed in the duel and the attacker can drive for the basket unhindered, with little chance of preventing a short distance shot by the attacker. Most frequently the following outnumbering situations of the attackers arise: 2 on 1, 3 on 1, 3 on 2, 4 on 2, 4 on 3 and 5 on 4. In a 3-on-2 situation the defenders have two possibilities. To start with the two defenders place themselves diagonally behind one another. One defender takes his position level with the semicircle of the free-throw lane and the other about 2 to 2.5 metres in front of the basket. The front player stops the dribbler and forces him to pass the ball (the more passes have to be made, the higher the possibility of a mistake). The second defender moves in the direction of the pass, but not before the ball has left the passer's hands. If he reacts to a passing feint then the third attacker is completely unmarked under the basket. After the pass, the first defender turns into the direction of the pass and runs back to the basket. At the same time, he keeps an eye on the position of the third attacker. In the meantime, the rear defender harasses the player with the ball with the aim of delaying the attack and preventing another pass. If the dribbler continues his run and does not pass the ball, the defender has to force him to the side line thus restricting the possibility of a pass. If this has been achieved the front defender withdraws in the direction of the basket. Meanwhile a third defender should come up level with the free-throw line.

With the second variant, the defenders stand parallel to and level with the free-throw circle, 3 to 4 metres apart from one another. This move is used if the opponent does not have excellent dribbling qualities and, consequently, the team, as a whole, makes only limited use of the fast break as an offensive weapon. The defenders simultaneously watch the dribbler and the two attacking team-mates who run along on the outside. However, the distance kept between the defenders should not allow the dribbler to advance to the basket and shoot unhindered. The defender who is positioned on the dribbler's side must try to force him to stop dribbling.

If he manages to do this, both defenders then cover the passing line and try to prevent a pass. If they do not succeed, the defender in question should place himself between the opponent and the basket in order to prevent a shot at the basket. In the meantime, the team-mate turns to the side where the ball is and takes up a favourable position for rebounding in case the ball misses it target. He also tries to prevent a possible pass.

Meanwhile a third defender who can cover the player in the middle should have returned to give support.

In a 4-on-2 situation, a parallel formation, level with the free-throw line, is preferable. Both defenders aim their actions at slowing don the attack so that their team-mates can intervene and to prevent a shot from the immediate vicinity of the basket. To do this, they should by no means try to actively prevent the player with the ball from making a long distance or medium distance shot. In an extreme case, a close shot can be prevented by infringing the rules. In a 4-on-3 situation, one should proceed according to the above principles using zone defence. The defenders place themselves in a triangle. The middle player takes up his position level with the semicircle of the free-throw lane, and the two team-mates position themselves a long the side lines of the 3-second area. They try, by means of active arm and leg action, to cover the relatively large space within the shooting area. The front player must induce the attacker to pass to the side with the least number of attackers, forcing the latter to follow the ball. The defender on the far side turns to the ball and moves immediately into the free-throw lane in order to help his two team-mates foil drives and to intercept passes under the basket. The defender who is on the same side as the play switches onto the player in possession of the ball to prevent a shot at the basket. In order to prevent shots from favourable positions, switching also takes place within the zone defence. If the defence is complemented by a fourth player then one can switch to man-to-man defence or a 2-on-2 zone defence line-up.

In 5 on 4 situations, zone defence should also be applied. When the middle player has the ball, the defence should take the shape of a rhombus. But when the ball is passed to the side lines the defence takes the shape of a square. The general defensive principles described above also apply here.

If full strength is available, the team can successfully fulfil the basic tasks of defence by well organized and well co-ordinated collective actions. According to the basic task, the collective defensive actions are subdivided into two different forms-concentrated defence and spread out defence, i.e. open-court and wide defence. In concentrated or sagging defence, the opponent must not be given a favourable opportunity to shoot at the basket from a close or medium distance. Therefore the struggle with the opposing attackers takes place mainly within the free-throw area where all, or nearly all, defenders position themselves.

This type of defence is played in two systems: man-to-man defence and zone defence.

In the spread out or open-court defence, the tussle with the opponent takes place throughout the court.

The defenders try to gain the ball or to disturb the opponent' combined play so that they are forced to change their offensive conception, i.e. they cannot as planned.

This type of defence is played in two systems: by man-to-man press and zone press.

Besides, it is possible to apply a combination defence which combines various elements of man-to-man, zone and press defence.

Man-to-man defence

When this system is used each player of the team has to mark an opposition attacker for whom he is fully responsible. All players place themselves in the free-throw lane area. That is why this defensive system is also called sagging defence. It is mainly used in the following situations:

1. the opposing team does not have proficient long range shooters;
2. the attackers have an excellent pivot, and the marking of this pivot, in a one-on-one situation, is either not possible or difficult;
3. the team is leading by a few points and is trying to keep this lead until the end of the game.

The principle of man-to-man defence is on excellent means of developing a player's feeling of responsibility for his own individual defensive performance. It permits the deployment of defenders according to the peculiarities of the attackers. At the beginning of the competition each defender studies his attacker's peculiarities and tries to utilize his weak points for a successful defence. The weakness of this defensive system, however, is that the attackers can apply the well-known manoeuvres of playing one of their team-mates free in such a way that they have enough time to prepare their attack and that they can apply their set combinations. After losing the ball in the attack, all players move back to defend their own basket. Each player looks for and takes on the attacker assigned to him. Also, all defenders position themselves in such a manner that they can support each other, if necessary. Sagging defence is directed mainly against the opposing pivots, against individual breakthroughs and against close and medium range shots.

The defenders focus their attention on the player in possession of the ball and on the pivot. All other attackers who are outside the free-throw lane are either not guarded closely or are not marked at all. Defender 5 demonstrates the active hindrance of player 5 who is in possession of the ball. Defender 4 takes up a position which prevents a drive to the basket by 5 or a pass to pivot 8. Defender 7 is prepared to help his team-mate 8 if pivot 8 prepared to help the free-throw lane. Defender 6 marks his attacker closely and attentively in order to prevent a shot from long or medium distance or breakthrough to the basket.

Zone defence

This system is also characterized by a concentration of the defenders in the area of the free-throw lane. It is used mainly against relatively slow and tall players who try to achieve their ends via their pivots and who do not have excellent shooters from long and medium distances. Zone defence is especially effective against teams which are not able to execute fast and accurate passes. In zone defence, each player is responsible for a certain are (zone) in which he has to defend against any attacker moving in that area during the game. The advantages of this system are that it does not require constant changing of positions by the defenders along with their own attackers, it facilitates organized rebounding and the planned transition to fast breaks and it makes it more difficult for attackers to apply combinations, screens, splitting the post and brushing off.

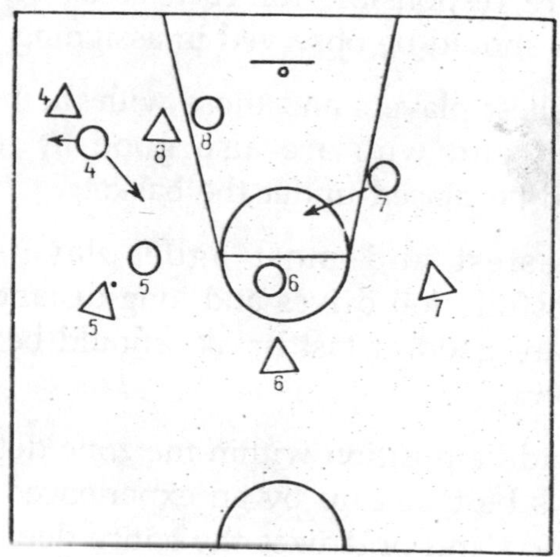

Basic formation of the defenders in sagging defence

The disadvantages lie in the relatively passive nature of the defence because it does not allow an active tussle for the ball which is outside the defender's own zone. It also enables the attacker to apply set shots and makes it difficult to guard several attackers who group together in one zone.

The basic formation of the zone defence depends on the composition of the defending team, the opponents and their offensive system. Currently, two variants of zone defence are used: the 2:3 formation, three players place themselves under the basket and two on level with the free-throw circle. In the 2:1:2 formation, two defenders, the so-called "chasers" or "hustlers", take up their basic positions level with the free-throw circle, two under the basket and one within the free-throw lane. This variant of zone defence is applied especially when the opposing team attacks with two pivots. A basic formation of 2:1:2 and which players are responsible for each zone. The following principles should be observed in assigning the players:

1. The tallest players and those with the best jumping power, and who are also good at rebounding, should be placed under the basket;
2. the fastest and most agile players who can successfully foil drives and long-distance shots and who are good at fast breaks should be used in the front line;
3. the middle position within the zone defence should always be taken up by an experienced player who conducts and organizes the entire deployment.

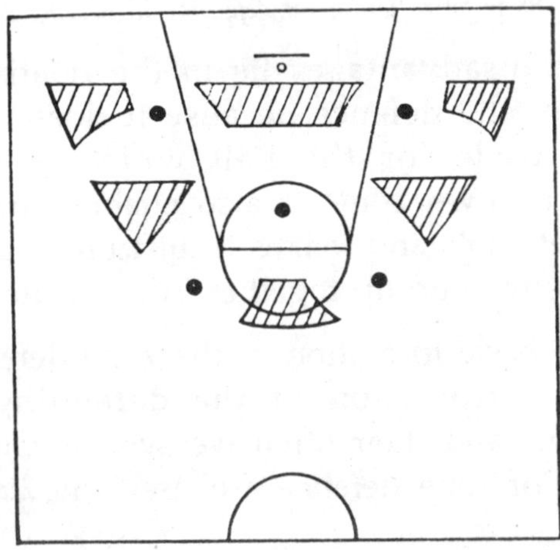

2:1:2 basic formation of zone defence

Steady and marked improvements in the accuracy of medium-and long-distance shots and the development of new, successful combinations against these zone defence continues, which led to the attackers' numerical superiority in the various zones, have resulted in the increased use of the 3:2 and 1:3:1 basic formations. The division of the court within the shooting area into zones must, of course, not restrict let alone forbid the defenders' mobility on the court. Each player is obliged to help and assist his team-mate if an acute threat to the basket develops in his zone. The defence must be able to react flexibly and in various ways, according to the positions of ball and attackers. The basic running directions of each defender in the 3:2 basic formation.

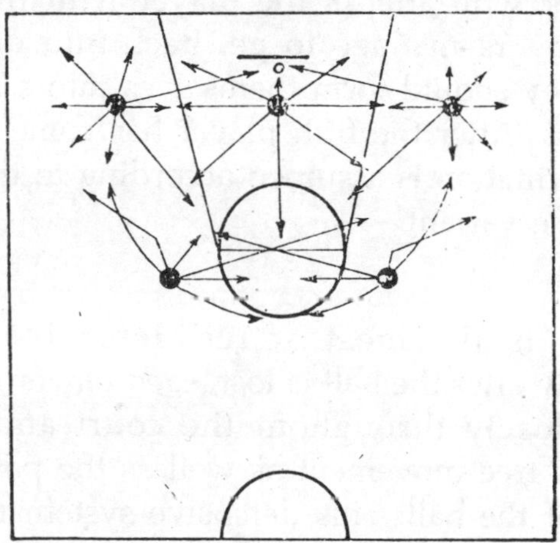

Basic running directions in the 3:2 zone defence

The success of any zone defence operation depends, first and foremost, on the well co-ordinated, circumspect and collective action of all players of the team. Unwise individual action (e.g. risky intercepting of passes) endanger and disorganize the team's collective defensive strength.

After losing the ball in attack, each player must take up his position as quickly as possible in the basic formation. However, this is not always possible, i.e. when the opposing team counterattacks, the players who are retreating back into defence must take up the following positions:

1. one player stands at the middle of the free-throw line;
2. two defenders place themselves on the sides of the free-throw lane, i.e. the three players are in a triangular formation whose vertex is formed by the defender who attacks the player with the ball. If four players manage to get back into defence in time, they should form themselves into a square or rhombus. After the fifth player has come back, the basic formation is assumed according to the chosen defensive variant.

Press defence

The press is the most active defensive system. Immediately after the ball is lost, each player marks his attacker closely throughout the court and tries to prevent his free movement as well as the passing and receiving of the ball. This defensive system makes for an active play, which increases the pace of the game and prevents the opponents developing their game. The press provides the team with more opportunities for counterattacks. In addition, it is more difficult for the attackers to play their set combinations. There is no time to prepare the attack, for the players to take up their attacking positions and the attackers cannot make use of their physical advantages. The press also tends to be a successful weapon if the opponent uses delaying tactics in order to retain the lead. This active type of defence is especially effective if the players of the opposing team are not sufficiently prepared athletically and technically and if the opposing team are not sufficiently prepared athletically and technically and if the opposing team does not have a sufficient number of equivalent substitute players.

It is imperative for all players to adhere to the following rules:

1. Having forced his opponent to stop dribbling, the defender restricts the freedom of action and orientation of the player with the ball by active harassment. All team-mates must cover the passing line so that the ball can be intercepted.
2. When there is a danger of a direct threat to the basket, because the attacker has outrun his opposing defender and received a pass from his team-mate, the defender should fight all out for a position between the opponent and the basket.
3. Each defender should try to force the dribbler to the side (if possible towards the side of the weaker hand). In any case, he must not give him an opportunity to drive to the basket across the middle of the court. Besides, the dribbler must be forced to terminate his dribble and to take up the ball.
4. During and especially after ending the dribble, double teaming should be used. For that purpose the second defender temporarily leaves his personal opponent free or has him covered by a third team-mate. Both defenders try to pull or knock the ball

out of the attacker's hand or cause him to make a risky pass.

5. Although during press defence all players are usually dispersed over the entire court, they should always be ready to guard and take over the most dangerous shooter in the opposing team at a moment's notice.

The space and character of the operation change as the dribbler approaches the basket. If one subdivides the court arbitrarily into four sections, then

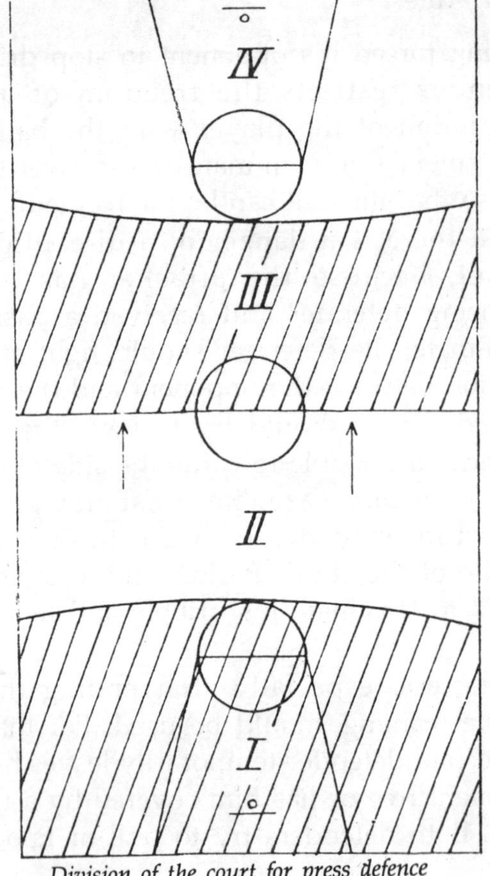

Division of the court for press defence

in section 1 one should play with maximum warrantable risk, two defenders using all possibilities of defence against the dribbler and trying to take the ball away from him. In section II the team fights for the ball rather actively by harassing the dribbler and forcing him to take up the ball. If adequate protection is given all defenders prepare themselves for intercepting the pass. In section III the defenders must mark the attackers closely by switching and covering without losing control of their attackers. The general aim must be to always disturb the opposing team in developing a pre-planned combined play. If the player in possession of the ball advances to the area near the basket the team has to apply the basic techniques of man-to-man defence in the free-throw lane area.

Three typical uses of the press defence are:

1. The defenders leave the player 4, who throws the ball in, free. Attacker 8, the opposing team's best dribbler, is covered by the two defenders 8 and 4. If the pass to attacker 5 succeeds, defender 5 forces him, while he is dribbling, to the side. In the meantime, defender 4 switches to player 4 who originally threw the ball in and has now started for the midcourt. Defender 8 keeps attacker 8 under surveillance. Defender 6 utilizes the difficult position of dribbler 5 by breaking away from his opponent 6 and forces attacker 5 to take up the ball. Together with his team-mate 5, he now harasses the attacker. Defender 7 covers the passing line to the attacking pivot 6, and his team-mate 8, after having spurted back, takes on attacker 7. Attacker 8 remains temporarily unmarked as he is the least dangerous at that moment.

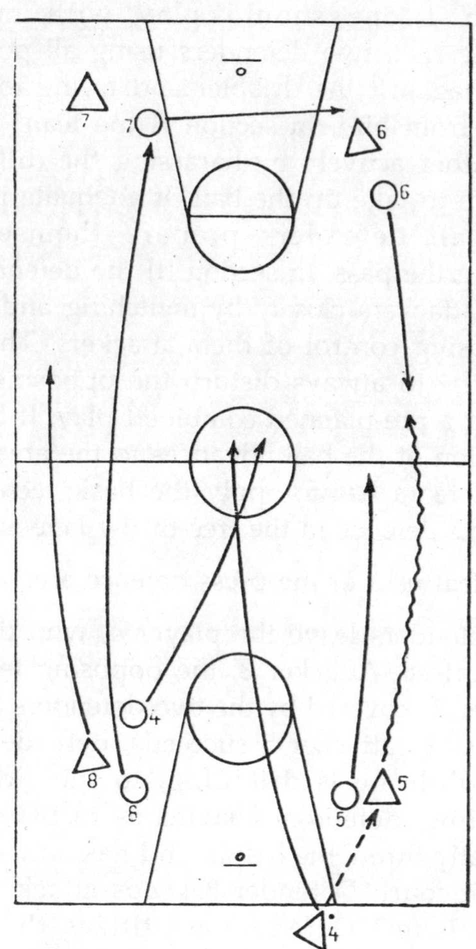

Application of the press defence (first variant)

2. A series of switches of attacker 4 who is an excellent dribbler and passer. In section II, he is successively harassed by two defenders, but this is a bit risky. Initially, he is taken on by defender 5. Defender 4 switches to attacker 5 instead. In section IV, defender 6 blocks the way of the dribbler 4.

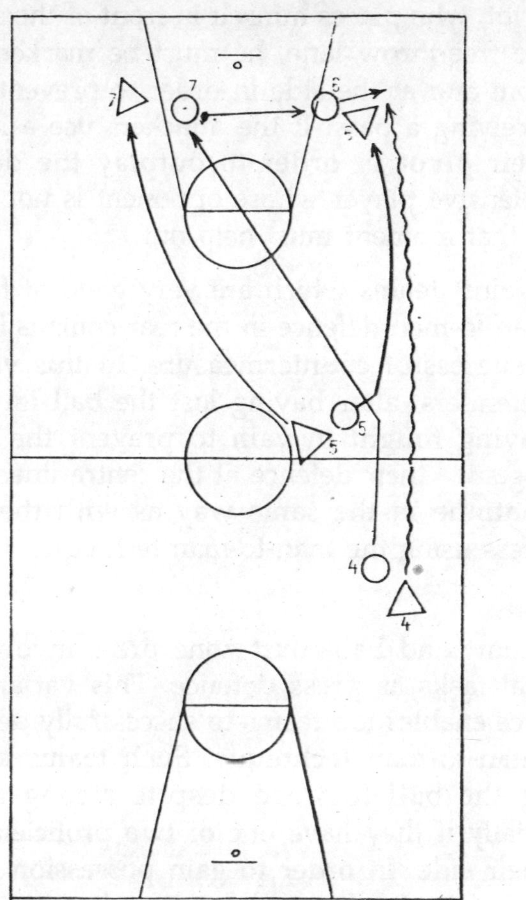

Application of the press defence (second variant)

This move entails a triple switch. Player 7 places himself between the basket and the dangerous pivot 6. He is supported by defender 5 who marks pivot 6 from the front. Defender 4 switches to attacker 7. Attacker 5 remains temporarily without a defender. If the attackers try to involve their pivot, who places himself in front of the side line of the free-throw lane, he must be marked from the front and at the side in order to prevent him from receiving a pass. If the attackers use a lob pass to their pivot in order to outplay the defender, a defensive player whose opponent is not dangerous at that moment must help out.

3. Against teams which are very good at fast breaks, man-to-man defence in the rear court is likely to be a successful countermeasure. In this variant, the defenders, after having lost the ball in attack and having fought in vain to prevent the first pass, organize their defence at the centre line. Then they continue in the same way as with the full-court press using the man-to-man technique.

Zone press

Full-court and half-court zone press involves similar tactical tasks as press defence. This variant of press defence enables top teams to successfully defend using the man-to-man technique. Such teams are able to bring the ball forward despite strong resistance, especially if they have one or two proficient dribblers on their side. In order to gain possession of the ball several defenders must attack the player with the ball. If, however, two or even three defenders attack the player with the ball the remaining attackers outnumber the defence. This forces the defence to apply zone principles.

The following important and basic demands are to be met in building up this defensive system:

1. The player with the ball should be forced into an

unfavourable position for the pass by the aggressive play of two defenders. A held ball situation should be created, if possible, or lob passes should be provoked which the defenders can intercept. This requires maintaining double teaming of the player in possession of the ball.

2. Thanks to the standard disposition of players characteristic of this variant and the interchange between the guards and the forwards, this system is not quite as tiring as press defence.

3. In case of a possible splitting of the zone press, the reorganization must be as easy as possible by making appropriate arrangements for a systematic supplementation of players.

4. It should be made possible to "share" the defending fouls appropriately among the team.

In order to meet these demands, different variants of full-court and half-court defence are applied.

With the 2:1:1:1 line-up, also called Y-formation, two defenders attack the player with the ball in the front court and the others cover the possible passing paths. If three defenders (3:1:1 formation) form the first line in zone press, the player in the middle must anticipate action on either side. It is his task to stop the dribbler or to double team him with a team-mate. With the 3:2 zone press, two players form the rear defensive line. With a 3:1:1 line-up, they stand behind each other in staggered formation.

Should the attackers succeed in penetrating into sections III and IV of the court, the principles of 3:2 zone press must be applied only temporarily. If, however, attackers move into the free-throw lane or into another favourable shooting position, it is imperative that they be marked man-to-man. A 3:1:1 formation if the tussle with the attackers takes place in section 1 of the court.

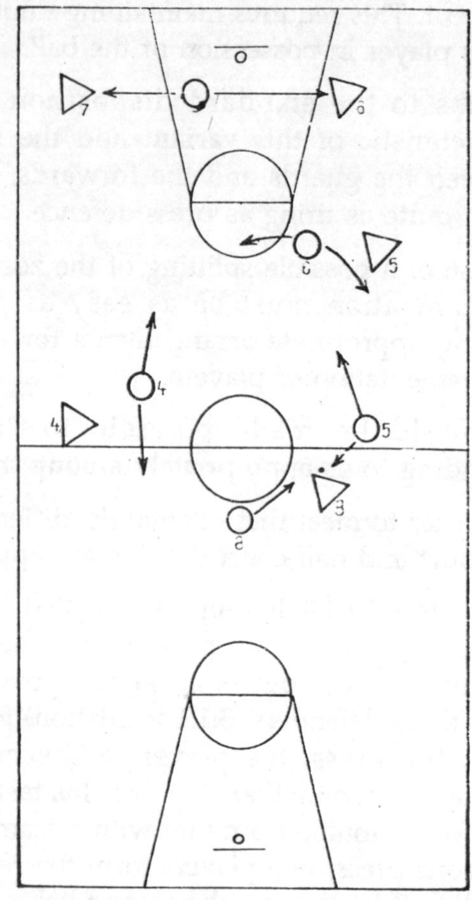

The continuation of zone press from a 3:1:1 starting position

The weak points of zone press include:

1. the difficulties which arise when several attackers concentrate on one wing, and

2. the changing of positions of defenders which is necessary after an unsuccessful pursuit and failure to prevent the initial pass when the tall forwards and pivots run into the middle and rear court for defence; and when the quick, mobile guards have to race forwards to occupy their defensive area. This manoeuvre becomes unnecessary for teams whose players are of more or less equal height.

Thus, with zone press, in general,

— no personal responsibility (marking assignment) is fixed;

— a particular formation is organized immediately over the entire court or half court (e.g. 3:2, 3:1:1 basic formation, etc.);

— double teaming is always organized for the player in possession of the ball, thus enabling the systematic continuation of double marking in the situations which follow;

— the remaining defenders organize, against numerical superiority of the attackers, a zone defence which covers the passing lines near the ball and the areas which are farther away against long passes.

Also important are

— the use of dummy man-to-man press in order to obtain advantages for zone press afterwards;

— the development of intense activity when changing from defence to attack, especially when the opponent scores a basket.

Thus, successful zone press cannot be completely based

on principles of safety, Therefore the players are to be trained in such a way that they are prepared to take risks and play all out in order to get possession of the ball and to keep it in control.

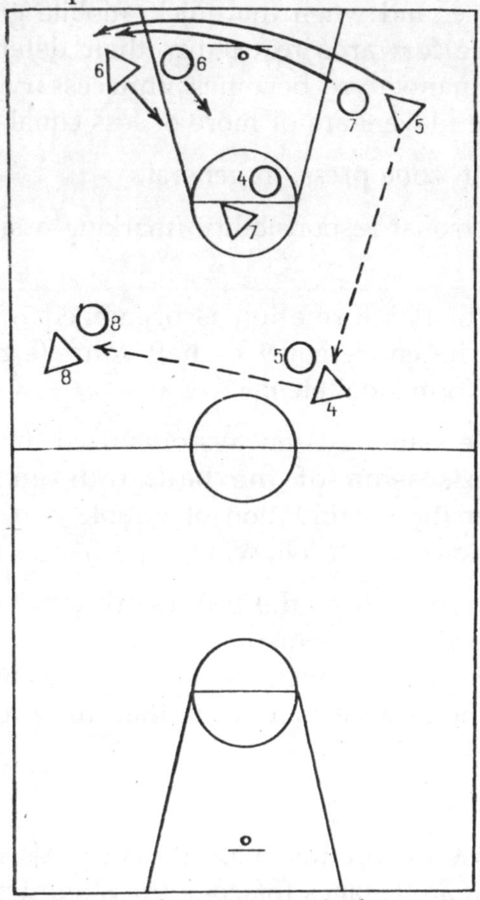

Final phase of 3:1:1 zone press in the rear court

Combination defence

If the opponent possesses players with above-average shooting and play-making qualities, it is recommended to apply combination defence by employing zone and man-to-man principles. A tight man-to-man principles. A tight man-to-man defence (personal press) is played against one or two strong attackers whereas the others engage in active zone defence (2:2 or 2:1 zone defence). However, within the free-throw lane, the defence can be based on the principles of sagging defence.

The ."basket hunter" 4 is closely marked by defender 4. The other team-mates, 8, 5, 6 and 7, employ

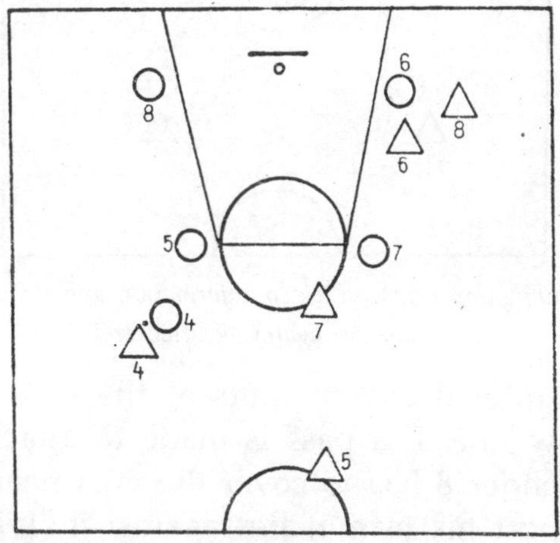

Combinations defence (2:2 zone formation and man-to-man defence)

a 2:2 zone defence. If the defenders have a tall player who can jump well and is experienced in one on one play and rebounding, the zone formation of the four defenders can take the shape of a rhombus. If the pivot is the most successful of the attacking players, he is marked closely from the front by defender 4 to deprive him of an opportunity to receive a pass, and the other defenders behind him set up a tight and mobile zone defence.

If the attacking team has two "basket hunters", they are marked closely by the defenders 4 and 5. The three remaining players, 8, 6 and 7, then organize a zone defence in the form of a triangle.

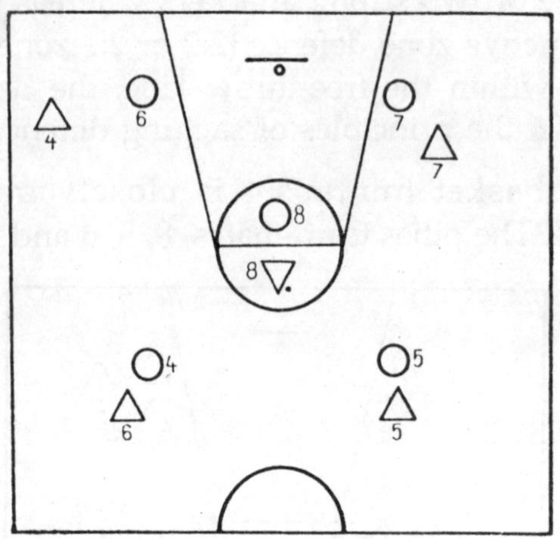

Combination defence (2:1 zone formation and man-to-man defence against 2 attackers)

Defender 8 covers shots at the basket from the free-throw line. If a pass is made to attackers 4 or 7, then defender 8 has to cover the area near the basket and support his team-mates against individual drives for the goal and he is responsible for rebounds of missed shots.

Changing over from defence to attack and vice versa

This "play reversal" is mastered by all top teams with a high degree of perfection. It can be used effectively if the collective preparation of attack and defence is excellent. Preparations for the fast counterattack are made by the defending team by aggressive defensive actions and well-timed rebounding. The same applies to the preparation of the defence. Preparation for the defence takes place, through effective offensive rebounding, prevention of the initial pass and organized covering of the rear court, during the concluding phase of the attack.

Changing over from defence to attack

Based on the fact that the fast break, as the most effective offensive action, plays a dominant role in modern basketball, the preparation and execution of the fast counter attack must be regarded as a routine procedure in a team's organization of its mode of play.

The preparation is aimed at gaining balls from the opponent by proficient individual collective defensive manoeuvres by:

— taking the ball away from the dribbler;

— intercepting passes;

— active defence against all shots;

— successful rebounding of shots missed by the opponent.

After gaining possession of the ball, the fast break is initiated with the outlet pass or a fast dribble. Possession of the ball means, however, that all players must move towards the opposing basket. The actions on the court are co-ordinated by using the free spaces and by keeping an eye on the ball play.

Changing over from attack to defence

The defence is usually prepared in the concluding phase of the attack. By giving the example of offensive rebounding, we can illustrate the tactical tasks. Attacker 3 shoots at the basket and follows the ball. Players 4 and 5 also go for the rebound near the basket. Player 1 tries to find a favourable position for rebounding on the free-throw line while player 2 covers the rear court. The tactical tasks can, however, vary, depending not only on the quality of one's own team but also of that of the opposing team.

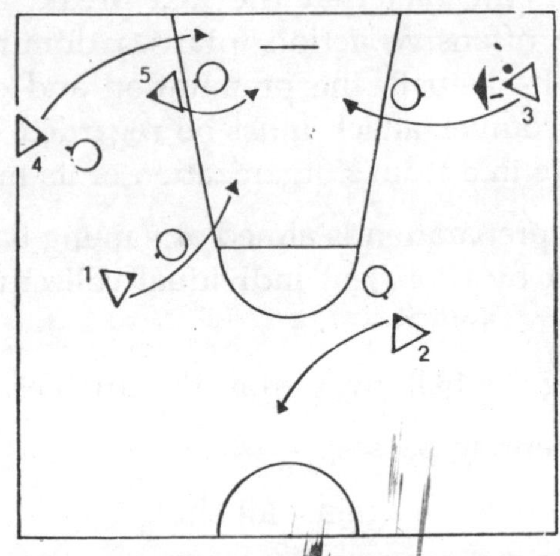

Basic tactical requirements in offensive rebounding

For example, two attackers who are near the basket and the one on the free-throw line can go for the rebound and the remaining two players cover the rear court.

Every effort should be made, after the ball has been lost, to prevent the initial pass in order to thwart a fast break by the opposing team. Usually the first pass is made on that side of the court where the ball has been lost. Therefore the defender who plays on that side must try, at all costs, to prevent the attacker from cutting and receiving a pass. In any case, he has to prevent the initiation of a fast break and delay the development of the counterattack. To do this, he must force the player in possession of the ball to dribble or pass the ball into midcourt. He must prevent a pass or dribble along the side line by all means at his disposal.

Finally, it must be reiterated that good offensive rebounding the prevention or disturbance of the outlet pass and stable covering of the rear court are the basic pre-requisites for the organized preparation of defence because, after losing the ball, the full-court defence, i.e. press or zone press, can be immediately reorganized out of these offensive activities.

4

TECHNIQUE IN ATTACK AND DEFENCE

The correct teaching of techniques is of great importance and constantly trying to attain technical perfection of the elements of attack and defence should be part of it. An athlete's concept of tactics begins to take shape when he learns the techniques in simple forms of exercises and in difficult attacker-defender situations. These two elements of basketball are interdependent and inseparable. In this manual, however technique and tactics are dealt with in two separable. In this manual however, techniques and tactics are dealt with in two classifying the subject-matter. In the paragraphs which follow and in dealing with the fundamentals and methods of training of technique and tactics, the close relationship between both components is dealt with in detail. Practical experience in the course of the development of the game has shown that each player's individual peculiarities are reflected in the technical elements. Therefore, in presenting the elements we start with a general basis which has so far been characteristic of basketball technique in its evolution till now. From this follows that the player should not be forced to learn the elements mechanically but that the technical development has to be directed within a universally valid framework. Practical experience also teachers us that players should constantly strive to improve their techniques. The player's development comes to a standstill as soon as the work on improving technique is subdivided in to two major sections. The respective attacking and defending movements; the technique with the ball comprises the elements of receiving the ball, pivoting passing dribbling shooting and feinting.

Technique without the ball

Basketball is characterized by sudden bursts of speed by unexpected stops, jumps turns changes in direction and pace without and with the ball in response to the direct action of the opponent. This requires proficient command of the technique without the ball in a very cramped space.

A close connection has to be established and the players athletic development, such as speed, strength, explosive power and endurance. The players insufficient technical development can restrict the special physical preparation tremendously. Therefore players and coaches have to pay attention to systematically developing technique and physical preparation and to constantly increasing the technical arsenal.

The basic stance

All movement of the players starts from the basic stance which facilities fast movements in all directions at any time. All movements of the players are related to the basic stance and the maintaining of one's good body balance which are expressed in the so-called "footwork".

The basic stance and the movement connected

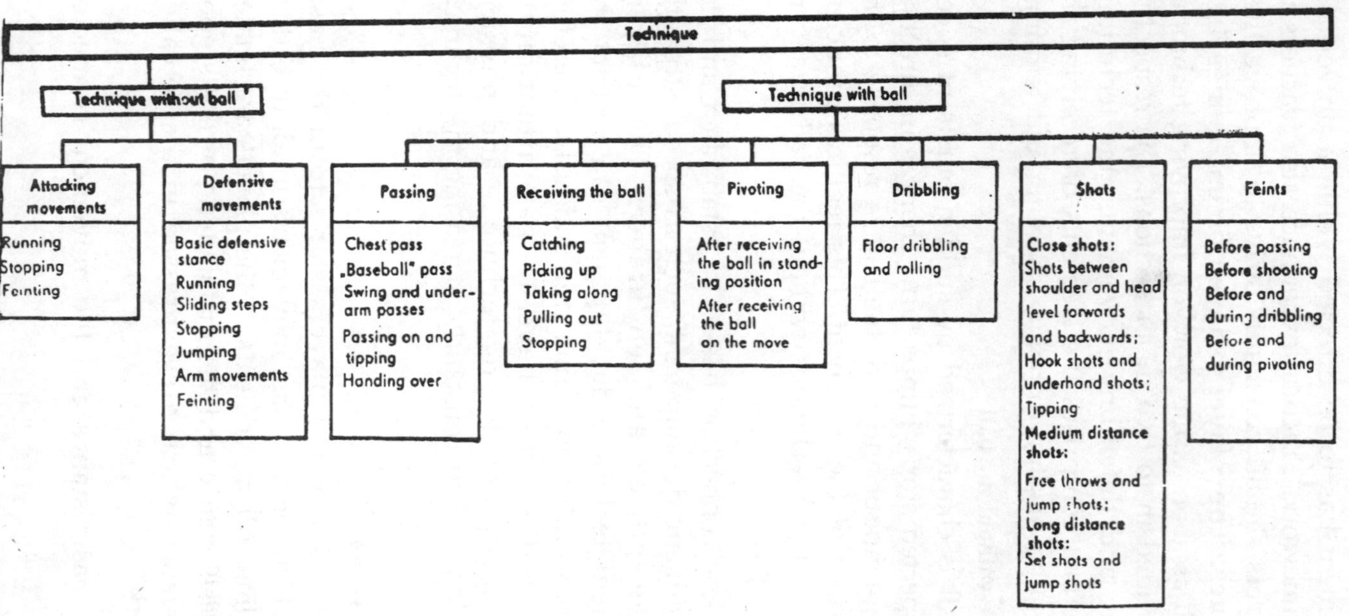
Technique
Technique without ball
Technique with ball
Attacking movements
Running
Stopping
Feinting
Defensive movements
Basic defensive stance
Running
Sliding steps
Stopping
Jumping
Arm movements
Feinting
Passing
Chest pass
„Baseball" pass
Swing and under-arm passes
Passing on and tipping
Handing over
Receiving the ball
Catching
Picking up
Taking along
Pulling out
Stopping
Pivoting
After receiving the ball in stand-ing position
After receiving the ball on the move
Dribbling
Floor dribbling and rolling
Shots
Close shots:
Shots between shoulder and head level forwards and backwards;
Hook shots and underhand shots;
Tipping
Medium distance shots:
Free throws and jump shots;
Long distance shots:
Set shots and jump shots
Feints
Before passing
Before shooting
Before and during dribbling
Before and during pivoting

Attacking movements without ball

- Attacking movements without opponent
- Attacking movements with opponent

- Taking up positions in the game
- Cutting
- Technique of setting screens and brushing off opponent

Runs — in various directions
— at various speeds
— in association withturns and changes in pace and directions

Spurts — in various directions

Stopping — in various speeds
— in association with turns

in association with feints

The basic stance

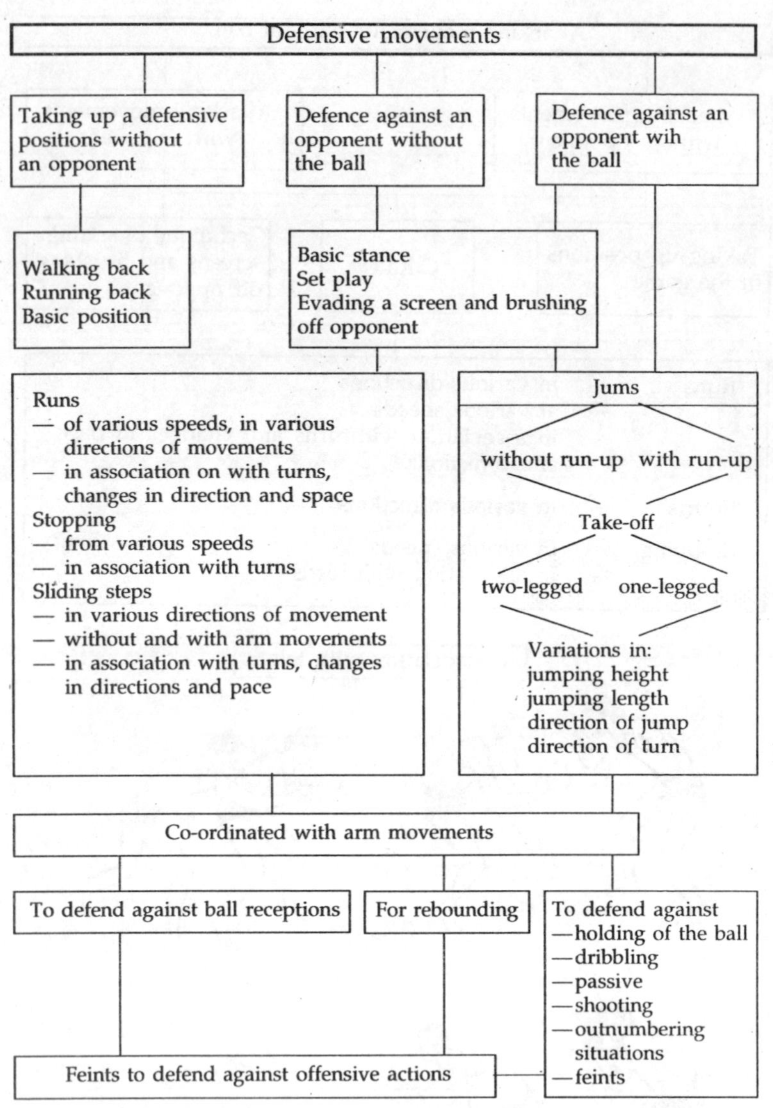
Defensive movements
Taking up a defensive positions without an opponent
Defence against an opponent without the ball
Defence against an opponent wih the ball
Walking back
Running back
Basic position
Basic stance
Set play
Evading a screen and brushing off opponent
Runs
— of various speeds, in various directions of movements
— in association on with turns, changes in direction and space
Stopping
— from various speeds
— in association with turns
Sliding steps
— in various directions of movement
— without and with arm movements
— in association with turns, changes in directions and pace
Jums
without run-up
with run-up
Take-off
two-legged
one-legged
Variations in:
jumping height
jumping length
direction of jump
direction of turn
Co-ordinated with arm movements
To defend against ball receptions
For rebounding
To defend against
—holding of the ball
—dribbling
—passive
—shooting
—outnumbering situations
—feints
Feints to defend against offensive actions

with it through the respective foot and arm actions are characteristic of the defensive and offensive play. They are the players fighting positions.

Body position bent knees and the shifting of the weight are identical for attackers and defenders. The player stands in a stable position with slight or pronounced flexing of the knees. The body is slightly bent forwards, but upright, and the feet are slightly apart or parallel, with the points of the feet pointing forwards and inwards.

Thereby the centre of gravity is somewhat lower and shifted more towards the balls of the feet. The position of the head is upright so that the peripheral vision for maintaining a grasp of the game is increased. The defender's arms are bent sideways and forwards up to medium reach so that the hands are at about shoulder height.

The opponents arms for defending a short can be changed in such a way that the left or right arm is held forwards and upwards to stop a short and the other arm is held loosely sideways and downwards to catch the ball.

The attacker's arms are bent and kept somewhat closer together at waist height ready to receive the ball.

The distance between defender and attacker is determined by the individual tactical aspects and depends on the developing situation. During the first hours of training the players are familiarized with the basic stance. Throughout training the other technical elements and continually developed.

Following mistakes occur most frequently:

— the feet are not parallel but distinctly spread out or very close together:

— the centre of gravity is contained on one foot, mostly forwards making for an unstable body posture;

— the trunk is bent too much forwards and the knees thereby become automatically excessively stretched.

In most cases the faults occur together with other technical elements which have to be corrected individually.

The run

The run in basketball is the basic from and the main means of the player's movement. It is characterized by great variety and differs from the rhythmical run in athletics by quick changes of the various forms in short intervals (forwards, backwards, sideways) by a change of direction and pace from the various starting positions in attack and defence. The peculiarity of the straight run is that the feet must touch the floor by putting down the heel first and then rolling onto be ball of the foot or by placing the whole sole softly on the floor. This enables a natural elastic movement of the legs (bending of the legs) which is characteristic of all running movements for a basketball player. In pushing the floor off the ground a strong bending of the leg takes place by lifting the thigh into the running direction. The arms are subsequently relaxed and move freely with the rhythm of the run.

The sudden starts from the basic stance or from the relaxed run are of great importance. The attacker uses the quick starts, changes of direction and pace which the defender does not expect mainly to get away from the defender.

The first three to five steps of these running starts are short and quick and are performed on the ball of the body is bent forwards and the arms are strongly flexed. Thereafter the speed is increased by making longer and faster steps. The player must be ready to receive the ball in this state of concentrated running. Changes of direction in connection with changes of pace during the run are typical of basketball. They occur frequently and are executed suddenly. In order to change the direction of run the body weight is shifted to the inside by pressing the outer leg to the inside and throwing the inner leg and pointing the foot in the new direction. The defender's initial position is at the attacker's side or with his back to his own basket, depending on the attacking situation. If the distance to the basket is longer he engages the attacker by making short steps forward and subsequently returning to the basic stance. Running movements covering a large distance to the basket and near the basket are carried out with shuffling steps keeping an appropriate distance from the attacker. Short, fast shuffling steps backwards and sideways should be avoided in these situations as they are ineffective for gaining ground and they often make the defender lose his balance. In using shuffling steps it must be borne in mind that the knees should be sufficiently bent as in the basic stance and that the legs should glide (not jump).

Stopping

Attackers and defenders apply the stopping technique from various forms of running in order to suddenly stop the run; for a change in the direction of the run; or for other subsequent movements of play, such as jumping receiving throwing the ball. The attacker does this to outwit the defender, and the defender uses it to prevent the attacker from taking a short at the basket. Stopping can be performed by two techniques: by a jump landing or with two steps.

The player carries out the stop by making a flat, often gliding jump in the direction of run. He touches the floor with both feet parallel and slightly apart. The upper part of the body is bent backward and the legs are pronouncedly flexed to lower the centre of gravity. The forward jump is achieved by the opposing braking effect of the legs and strong springing action. The two-steps stop is performed in the normal sequence of steps (take-off, left, first step right and second step left, or vice versa). This is also known as the two count rhythm. The player's; last but one step is short and the centre of gravity is above this leg. On the last step the heel is pressed against the floor, thereby counteracting the forward movement of the body and leaving the body in the starting position for the next movement or action of play.

The effectiveness of both kinds of stopping techniques lies in the elasticity and the strong flexing actions of the legs in the quick reaction to restore body balance whereby the centre of gravity is shifted to the standing leg. The posture assumed after stopping is effective for continuing the run into various directions, for another jump, receiving the ball feinting etc.

The turns

The attacker uses turns to secure the ball as a feint for the drive to the basket in a one-on-one situation, for getting free with or without the ball, for other situations. Almost always it is performed after stopping near the opponent in order to get away from him and/or to effect a successful movement towards the basket.

The reactions of the defenders either consist of small turns and shuffling steps which cover a lot of space or turns at the start in order to quickly re-establish a stable defensive position at an appropriate distance from the attacker. We distinguish between two types of turns forward and backward turns. The direction of a turn is determined by the moving away of one leg (swinging leg) moving away of one leg (swinging leg) and the simultaneous movement of the body.

Forward turns are turns where the feet and the face point in the direction the turn. Backward turns are those where the heels and backs face the direction of the turn. A turn on the move near the opponent is carried out on the ball of the foot of the supporting leg into the intended direction with only a brief stop. Thus, the attacker leaves his opponent behind him and

The turn

the has a free path towards the basket or in the direction of the pass if no other players intercede. Also after receiving the ball and stopping at the beginning of the dribble, such a turn can be very effective in order to get away from the defender. It is, however necessary to stop with both feet at the same time if the turn is to be made on the front leg (danger of travelling!).

The jumps

Jumping in basketball is multifarious and rich in variants. As the game developed the jumping elements have multiplied. The number of jumps a good player makes has increased to between 100 and 130 per game. The jumps are performed as independent elements but they are mostly applied in connection with other technical elements. The most frequent jumps are upward jumps in which the body is stretched the forward jumps, which cover a long distance, and the jump sequences in attack and defence.

For advanced players, explosive poser and jumping endurance and, above all, jumping agility are attributes of high performances. In mastering the manifold combined technical elements the players must not only master the take-off and the safe landing, but they must also control the body position, the turn and arm movement after take-off for a successful continuation of the movements of play that follow.

There are two types of jumps: one-legged jumps and two-legged jumps.

The *two-legged take-off* is mostly applied from the basic stance, with and without the ball. The assuming a half square and by flexing his arms and moving them

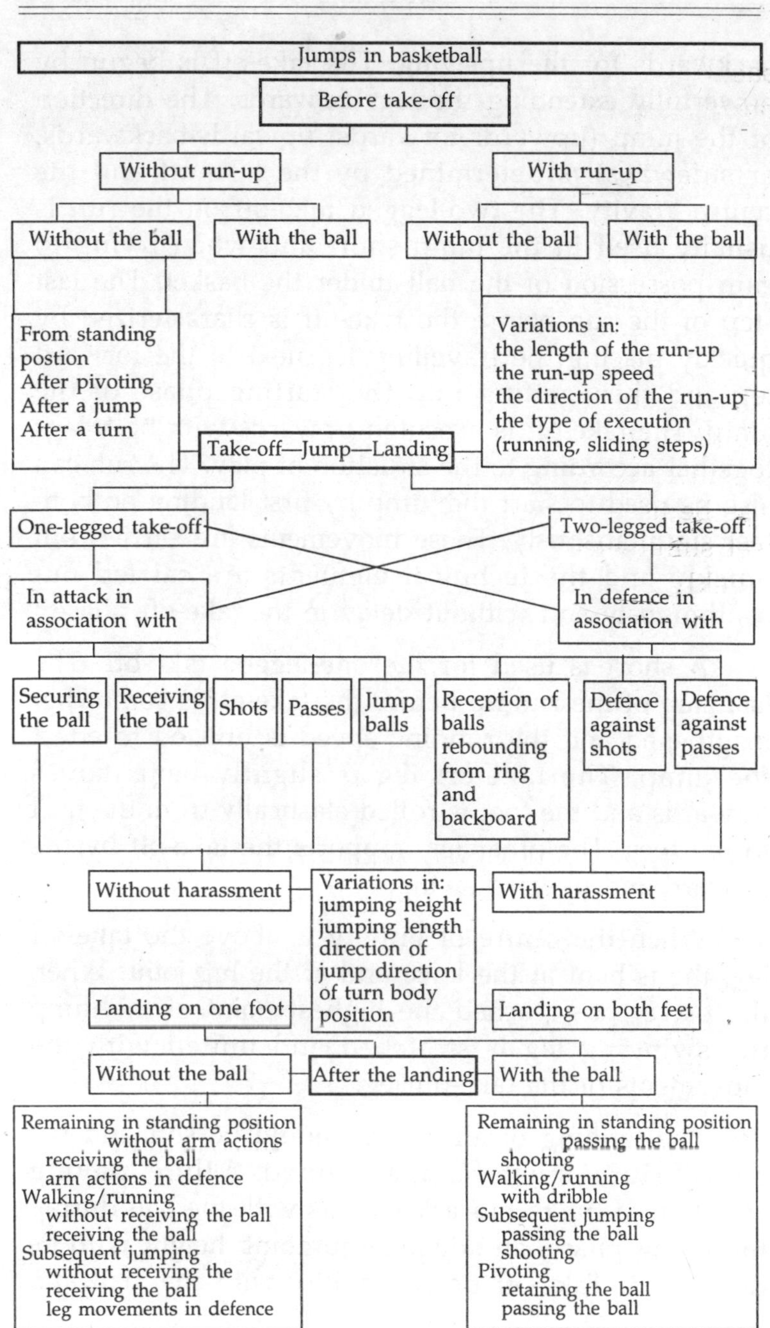
Jumps in basketball
Before take-off
Without run-up
With run-up
Without the ball
With the ball
Without the ball
With the ball
From standing postion
After pivoting
After a jump
After a turn
Variations in:
the length of the run-up
the run-up speed
the direction of the run-up
the type of execution
(running, sliding steps)
Take-off—Jump—Landing
One-legged take-off
Two-legged take-off
In attack in association with
In defence in association with
Securing the ball
Receiving the ball
Shots
Passes
Jump balls
Reception of balls rebounding from ring and backboard
Defence against shots
Defence against passes
Without harassment
Variations in:
jumping height
jumping length
direction of
jump direction
of turn body
position
With harassment
Landing on one foot
Landing on both feet
Without the ball
After the landing
With the ball
Remaining in standing position
without arm actions
receiving the ball
arm actions in defence
Walking/running
without receiving the ball
receiving the ball
Subsequent jumping
without receiving the
receiving the ball
leg movements in defence
Remaining in standing position
passing the ball
shooting
Walking/running
with dribble
Subsequent jumping
passing the ball
shooting
Pivoting
retaining the ball
passing the ball

backwards for the upswing. The take-off is begun by powerfully extending the legs upwards. The direction of the jump (upwards-forwards, upwards-backwards, or sideways) is determined by the take-off and the centre gravity. The two-legged take-off on the run is usually used in the jump short and when trying to gain possession of the ball under the basket. The last step of the run before the take-off is characterized by quickly placing the travelling leg next to the forward leg and then getting into the starting phase of the jump. The take-off is executed upwards with both legs together according to the situation of play. The run can also be used to start the jump by first landing on both feet simultaneously. These movements are carried out quickly and the technical elements are carried out continuously and without delay in the take-off phase.

A short is used for the one-legged take-off. The last step of the run-up before the take-off is somewhat lengthened and the running speed is utilized to effect the jump. The take-off leg is slightly bent moves forwards and the foot is rolled elastically from the heel to the toes. The other leg supports the take-off by the forward and upward swing.

When the centre of gravity is above the take-off leg, the is bent at the knee and at the hip-joint. When the player has reached the highest point of the jump the swinging leg is stretched and united with the movements of the take-off leg.

The landing of all jumps should be soft and the equilibrium must be maintained. While paying attention to the technical elements with the ball during the flying phase, an adequate jumping height is to be developed. Take-off power, agility with the, ball and speed, coupled with tactical understanding determine the success in these situations. Concerning the individual tactical application of the jumps, the player must learn to jump at the correct moment, to organize the gaining of space in changing directions in attack and defence, and to take these movements effectively in the preparation for the jump.

Technique with the ball

Receiving and passing the ball, dribbling and shooting and the use of feints in basic elements of basketball. The grade of a team can be recognized by its mastery of the technical elements. Safety efficiency, accuracy and speed are the pre-requisites for wise tactical play. The corresponding defensive component of the game is equally important. To defend in the modern sense means to defend actively; i.e., to intercept, deflect knock out and pull out the ball or grasp it at the same time when the opponent catches it.

Receiving

We distinguish between receiving with both hands and with one hand while standing running and jumping. Depending on the accuracy of the pass, the opponents action and one's own reaction speed, there are some variations which must be taken into consideration when learning and practising. Correct receiving in all variations is one of the most important pre-requisites for good ball handling as a whole. Safety and confidence in catching any pass are the basis for the players subsequent successful actions.

Receiving the both hands

Usually one moves towards the oncoming ball with one's body and arms from the basic stance.

When the finger tips touch the ball, the arms and the upper part of the body flex and the impact of the ball is cushioned.

The fingers are spread and they hold the ball in such a way that the thumbs and forefingers of both hands are positioned opposite each other and are clearly behind the ball. Right from the beginning it must be kept in mind that the ball lies on the fingers and the roots of the fingers and does not touch the whole palm of the hand. In receiving balls which

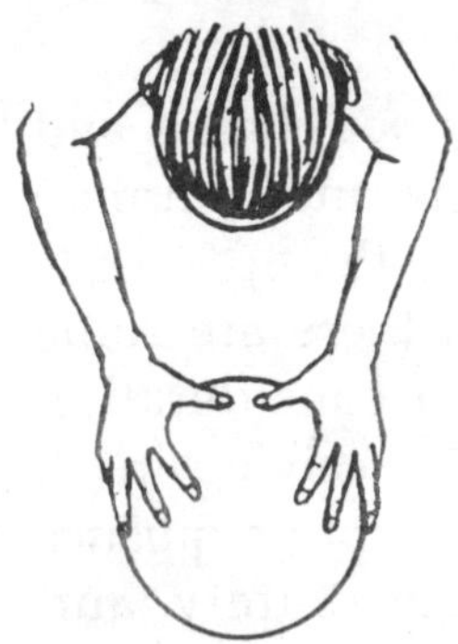

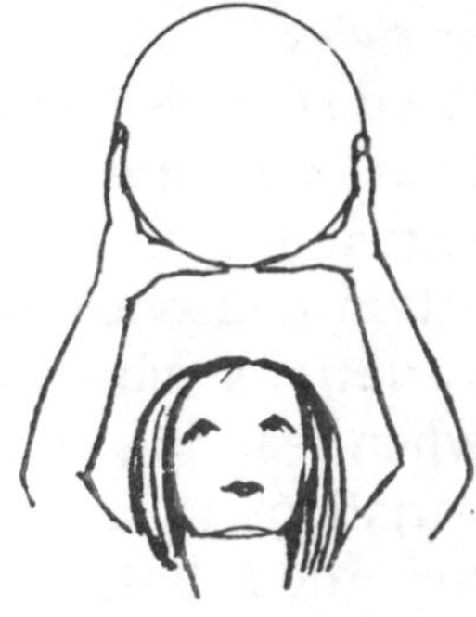

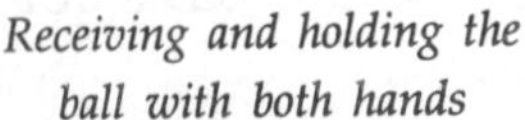

Receiving and holding the ball with both hands

arrive from the side or over the head, the cushioning of the ball is executed by a short springy movement of the stretched arms and the upper part of the body, and consequently the movement is shorter and harder. Therefore elasticity of the fingers becomes essential. Only when the ball is securely gripped it is pulled to the body.

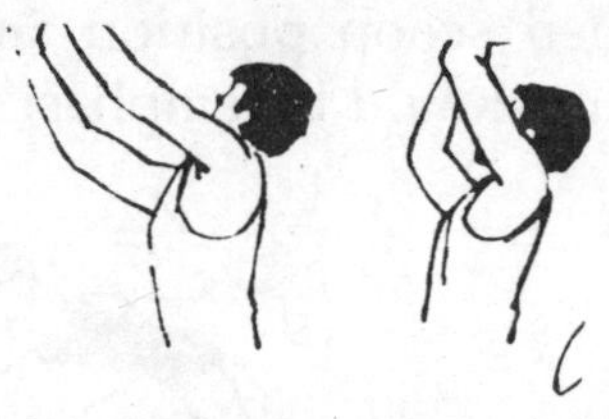

Receiving high balls

Low balls are caught from below the arms pointing diagonally downwards to meet the ball. The fingers are spread out and point downwards and the little and ring fingers are behind the ball. The springy movement is done by slightly pulling the arms and the forearms backwards.

Receiving the low balls

Rcceiving with onc hand

Receiving with one hand is used mainly for passes which can just be reached at the side, at reaching height or by jumping. The starting position is the same as in catching with both hands. However, when catching the ball with one hand the whole hand is behind the ball. At the moment of touching the ball it is important that the fingers not be stiffened and that especially the wrist and shoulder joint should give a little. In receiving low balls and rolling balls with one hand the so-called scoop position and movement of hand and forearm should be emphasized.

Receiving low balls with one hand

All catching movements should be well co-ordinated such the appropriate body movements such as walking running jumping, turning lunging falling kneeling, etc.., After catching the ball with one hand in most cases the ball is then transferred to the other hand and for, securing it down up to the body. This is important because of the one-handed catch, the ball can be last, as often happens, for example in rebounding at the basket. It is also important to master the immediate passing on of the ball after receiving it with one hand. The receiving and passing of the ball is executed in one continuous movement mainly of the forearm, hand and fingers.

Receiving the ball on the move

In receiving the ball on the run or jump, the rules must be observed which only allow two floor contacts while holding the ball. This means that only two steps are allowed with the ball and touching the floor at the moment of receiving the ball already counts as one step. Therefore, in order to make full use of the rule on travelling and land after making contact with the ball (first contact). Thus, he can make a second step or jump and land again (second contact) and thereafter take off again and pass, the ball while jumping or he can shoot at the basket. For a right-hander the rhythm is left-right-left and for a left handed, it is right-left-right. As far as the stepping is concerned, it is three-count rhythm to the beat; tam-ta-tam). This rhythm is also maintained when stopping by checking the forward motion with the take-off foot after the second contact and then coming to a standstill. This can be followed by a pivot and the pivot leg can be disengaged from the ground for a take-off to pass or throw at the basket. It is within the rules and sometimes necessary to apply the so-called "limping step" in the two-count rhythm. The sequence of steps will then be like in triple jump, right-right-left or left-left-right. The modern interpretation of the rules of recent years permits also landing on both feet after receiving the ball and to allow one more step and a take-off thereafter. Hence the sequence becomes: left or right-ball reception-two-legged-left or right-take-off-pass or throw at the basket. In doing so the two-legged landing must be simultaneous and parallel and at right angles to the direction of movement.

Pass interception

As important as the receiving of the balls its interception. Often the opposing team cannot be prevented from scoring if they complete a pass. What matters however, is an active defensive action which is directed at gaining possession of the ball.

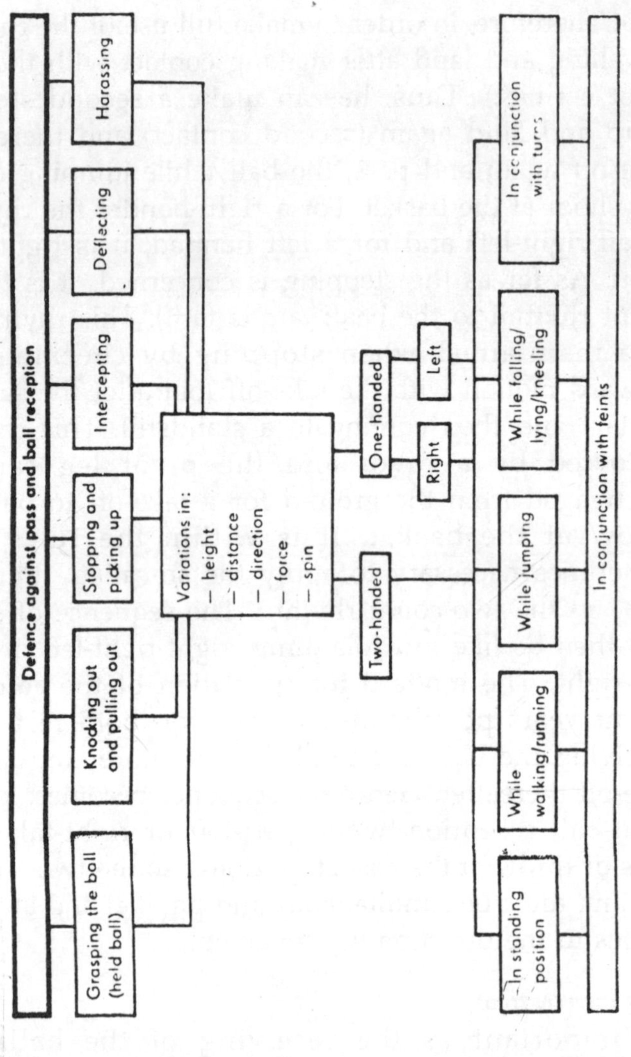
Defence against pass and ball reception
Grasping the ball (held ball)
Knocking out and pulling out
Stopping and picking up
Intercepting
Deflecting
Harassing
Variations in:
— height
— distance
— direction
— force
— spin
Two-handed
One-handed
Right
Left
In standing position
While walking/running
While jumping
While falling/lying/kneeling
In conjunction with turns
In conjunction with feints

The defence in this situation is realized by obstructing, deflecting and intercepting. To do this the defender has permanently to react to his opponent's movements from a good basic stance and to assume an appropriate position in relation to his opponent. Arm actions well co-ordinated with body movements can be executed in such a way as to constantly harsh the opponent and to increase the possibility of deflecting or intercepting the incoming ball. The technical execution of the various defensive movements is identical with the elements of the technique without the ball.

Holding the ball and pivoting

Holding the ball

After receiving the ball it must be held securely so that the opponent cannot knock it must of the hand or grab it. The ball should always be held with both hands from the top or from the bottom in readiness for actions to follow. In exceptional circumstances, players with large hands and corresponding finger strength can hold the ball with one hand, the ball being often pressed against the forearm for a safer grip. The ball is always shielded from the opponent with the body and by appropriate movement.

Pivoting

Pivoting is used to escape persistent attacks from the opponent to secure the ball and to create a good starting position for subsequent movements. Pivoting is done in conjunction with other technical elements. Pivoting takes place from a safe basic stance. The upper part of the body is bent and the ball is usually held at chest or waist level. When beginning the pivot the weight is shifted to the pivot leg and the free leg is pushed off the ground so that it is placed forwards backwards or sideways in the from of a lunge. The turn is made on the ball of the anchor foot. After the turn the body weight comes to rest on both feet again.

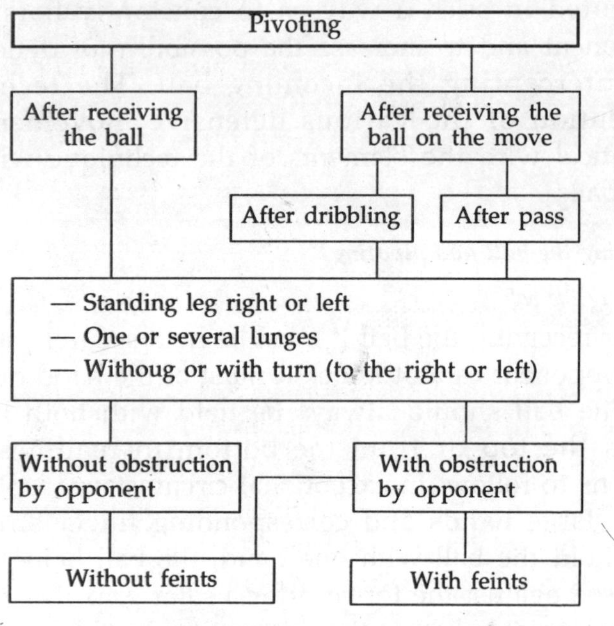

Pivoting

Special attention must be paid to the correct choice of the pivot leg. Basically, it has to be that leg which, after receiving the ball in the two-contact rhythm touched the ground first (in most cases the rear leg). If the player receives the ball in a standing position of it after the jump he touches the ground with both feet simultaneously the choice of the supporting leg can vary. While pivoting the anchor leg must not be changed (Travelling!).

Defence against ball holding pivoting

Just as during ball reception. The defender is also very active during ball holding and pivoting. Especially when the player in possession of the ball has already dribbled he is confronted with a very close defensive position and numerous active movements are made by the defender. In this situation the defender has possibilities to apply feints with his arms and legs in order to force the player with the ball into the wrong direction and also to distract him so that he the defender can knock the ball out etc.

Two-handed passes

The continuous development of the technique and tactics of basketball has resulted in numerous types of passing. The constant improvement of the technique can only be achieved when the players are efficient at all basic types of passes with one or two hands. The players can then learn without major difficulties special variations of the passes in relation to their respective positions and roles in the game. Almost all the types of passes can be broken down into three categories based on tactical consideration; the direct straight pass, the curved pass (lop passes) the bounce pass (touching the floor).

The two-handed pass is of fundamental and precision of this basketball. The dynamics and precision of this fast small-court game is increasingly determined by the fusion of the receiving movement and the execution of the pass. And since most balls are received with both hands it is most convenient to pass the ball on with both hands.

The two handed chest pass

The two-handed pass is the basic type of pass in basketball. During its execution the player assumes the basic position-the legs somewhat bent, one leg slightly in front, the body leaning slightly forward in the direction of the pass and holds the ball at chest level. During the pass the body movements should be harmonious. The ball is pushed with both arms with a parallel forward thrust the last impulse being given with a loose wrist and finger movement, the palms being turned slightly outwards. When passing the ball the rear leg is stretched and the upper part of the body follows the direction of the pass. Often, to support the whole movement a more or less pronounced lunge is performed with the front leg.

The two-handed chest pass

Two-handed chest passes over short distances are performed with a very short arm action and often only with wrist and finger movements. When passing on the run to while jumping the receiving and wind-up phases must merge in order to achieve a flowing transition to pass on the ball.

The chest pass is practically applied in all situations of the game provided there is enough space to move in. Chest passes are useful, above, for making fast breaks for crossing the midfield and for playmaking. It is often applied as a bounce pass or a lob pass when passing the ball to the centre. Depending on the position of the opponent and the whole playing situation it is often appropriate and effective to use passing feints. In the chest pass feints movements in another direction than the intended one are usually made and the ball is then drawn back towards the body. If the opponent reacts to the feint the player in possession of the ball can pass it without interference. These feints can also be effectively combined with pivoting and other types of pass feints with one or both hands. (e.g. high or low) before passing the ball with a chest pass at medium height.

Experience has shown that the following errors are partially frequent and special attention should be paid to them when correcting mistakes: the legs are kept too stiff especially at the knee joints; the elbows are spread out too wide while holding the ball and leaves the hands too early (before wrist and finger action becomes effective); the right and does not follow the passing movement.

The two-handed overhead pass

The feet are kept slightly apart and the ball is held in

both hands as high as possible above the head. The arms are slightly bent at the elbows. The ball is released with a short and forearms mainly, from the wrists with vigorous action of the fingers. Players who do not yet have sufficient strength for the wrist and finger movement compensate by exaggerating the bending of the arms and by pronounced stretching of the legs and by trunk movements.

The two-handed overhead pass

The overhead pass is excellent for tall players when passing over short and medium distances. The advantage is that the ball can be passed in any direction with out having to twist the body too much feinting in conjunction with the overhead pass is done mainly by deceiving the opponent about the intended direction of movement and by using the overhead pass by bending sideways (variation of the overhead pass from the shoulder). Other types of deceptive passes and raising the ball as if about to make an overhead pass are also suitable as feints. In this type of passing the most frequent faults are: the ball is held too for behind the head (danger of losing the ball); the ball is passed solely by swing-finger to give if the necessary accuracy.

The two-handed underarm pass

The two-hand underarm pass is applied as low underarm pass or as what is called a hip pass. The player takes a stable stance with the body in crouched position and with feet well apart. The ball is held on one side of the body the elbow of the outer arm pointing slightly upwards the other elbow being close to the body. During the execution of the pass the weight is shifted onto the front foot and with a short movement the ball is swung forwards in front of the body. The ball is released with a smart snap of the wrists and fingers. In the final phase the arms are fully extended.

The two-handed underarm pass

The two-handed underarm pass is generally suitable for low passes over short and medium distances as well as for handing the ball to team mates who cut closely by. This type of pass can also be used for longer distances. But inaccuracies occur very often unless this pass is fully mastered. The most frequent faults are: the whole passing movement is performed with extended arms and with a long wind-up of the arms; the turning of the body is exaggerated which leads to instability.

Defence against two-handed passes

By being active and constantly on the move the defender should always try to effectively disturb the pass or even deflect the ball. Especially when the player with the ball has already dribbled very close making with arm, trunk and leg actions. In most cases it is, however not possible to prevent a pass by an attacker with a stable body position. But a defender has achieved a lot if he managers to prevent an individual attack or an out side shot at the basket and forces the opponent to pass the ball. Or if he managers to force the attacker to pass inaccurately or deflects the ball.

One-handed passes

The one-handed pass with its numerous types and variants contributes very much to the dynamic and efficient mastery of one- handed passes is the basis of an individual range of tactical diversity and provides the player with the ball with a wider scope of action then two-handed passes. Thus, for the advanced player the sensible combined application of both types of passes and the mastery of the one-handed pass with both the right and left hands will be effective.

The one-handed chest pass

For this pass the starting position is the same as in the two-handed chest pass. The ball is held with the hand placed fully behind the ball (? turn of the ball) and the arm being quickly and forcefully extended. In the final phase there is pronounced wrist and finger action.

The one-handed chest pass

The one-handed chest pass is used for passes over short and medium distance. The pass is performed in a somewhat oblique direction. This type of pass is frequently applied after feinting another one handed pass. This is done by taking the ball briefly back in the other hand and then executing the one-handed chest pass. Other wise the same principles as for the two-handed chest pass apply.

The one-handed baseball pass

The one-hand baseball pass is very similar to the baseball pass used in handball. During the preparatory wind-up the bail is held above the shoulder with one hand at head level of higher. The arm is bent accordingly. The wind-up movement should not extend for behind the head. The passing movement is performed by a short forceful forward armswing in which the arm is stretched and in the final phase, wrist and fingers are extended and snapped. From the stride position (right-hand-left foot in front) the passing movement is executed with the rear foot being placed forward thus supporting the movement of the whole body.

The one-handed baseball pass

The very common one-handed baseball pass is mostly used for medium and long range distances. This pass is therefore very important for the fast break (long passes) and it is frequently performed while jumping. The baseball pass although less forceful can also be used as a lob pass over opponents (e.g. for passing the ball to the centre). When correcting mistakes the following should be observed: during the wind up the ball is often taken too far behind the head (defence from behind); the hand with the ball is twisted which leads to an undesirable spin of the ball and inaccuracies in passing: when performing the pass while jumping the take-off is performed with the wrong foot to so that a wrong action of the swinging leg leads to countermovement of the body, and the whole movement fails.

The one-handed underarm pass

The one handed underarm pass is performed as a low swing pass at knee level. The stride position is assumed in which the legs and the body are bent and the ball is held with both hands at the side of the body. The preparatory wind-up is performed with one hand moving back and upwards and then the arm is flicked forward with the so-called "shovel movement". In the final phase, the hand opens out and the fingers give the final push. The body weight rests on the front leg and the rear leg accompanies the entire forward movement of the body more or less forcefully, depending on the distance of the pass.

The one-handed underarm pass

This type pass is especially suitable for covering short and medium distances. It is particularly effective after feinting a high pass or when tussling for the ball during jumping. By taking the ball suddenly down, the lower passing paths become free. Often the ball can be safely passes in any direction under the arms of defenders whose arms are usually still up in the air at this point. The most frequent mistakes are an excessively long swinging movement backward and upwards (defence from behind the passing time is too long) and delayed opening of the hand in the final phase ("shovelling"), the ball resulting in upward curved unaccurate passes.

The one-handed swing pass

The one-handed lateral swing pass is performed from the basic stance, mostly in connection with a lunge to the side. The ball is held in both hands. Then the passing arm is moved to the side and almost fully extended. The hand with extended fingers is directly behind the ball. The pass is executed with a brief forceful movement of the forearm and chiefly by means of wrist and finger action. The body weight is shifted to the lateral leg of the passing arm side. In case of a very wide lunge, the other leg is slightly dragged along.

The one-handed swing pass

The one-handed swing pass is used mainly for passes over shorter distances and is particularly suitable for playing round the opponent. Frequently this pass is also performed as a bounce pass under the opponent's arms and it is therefore suited passes to the centre. If executed the one-hand swing pass is very difficult to intercept. The most common mistakes are: very often the laterally stretched arm resulting in an excessively long wind up (danger of being blocked); the long wind-up also causes a marked turning of the body and inadequate ball control; when holding the ball laterally with one hand, the hand is not behind the ball but diagonally underneath it this results in a "shovel movement" and in the hand slipping off (undesirable ball spin and passing inaccuracies).

The hook pass

The one-handed overhead swing pass is called the "hook pass". With the legs slightly apart, the body is turned 90° away from the direction of the pass. The ball is held in both hands and it is then taken over the head with one hand the throwing arm describing a curve until it is fully extended. The ball is released above the head with a wrist action and the forceful push of the fingers results in a flat trajectory of the ball. The shoulder opposite the throwing arm points in the direction of the pass. In the final phase of the hook pass, the body weight is shifted to the swinging leg (right leg with the right-hander, and vice versa). The pass is usually connected with a powerful one-handed take-off. The hook distance. This high pass is especially useful for passing over opponents on either side and for passes to the centre. It is therefore effective for use by tall players. It can also be applied as a long pass, e.g. after rebounding at the basket to initiate a fast break.

The hook pass

The most frequent mistakes are: the throwing arm remains bent at the elbow; the hand is laterally behind the ball; the trajectory movement of the throwing arm is executed from too far behind or in front of the head; the ball is released too early resulting in a steep trajectory.

Behind-the-back pass

The behind-the-back pass is performed with two variations as a backward pass or as a sideway pass behind the back. When passing backwards the ball is held with both hands at the side of the body. With a short backward forearm swing the ball is passed with an intensive wrist and finger snap so that after the ball has been released the fingers point downwards. When passing sideways behind the back, the ball is taken round the body, at waist level, by means of a circular movement and passed from behind the back. The wrist and finger snap is of great importance in this type of pass.

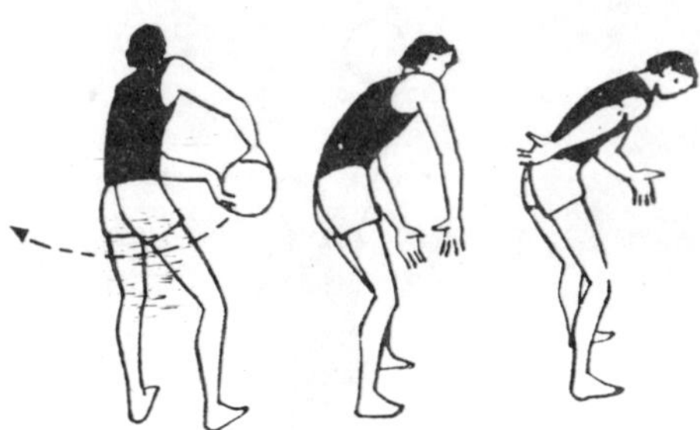

The backhand pass

The behind the back pass is applied mainly for passes over short distances and it usually surprises the opponent particularly since it is often applied in connection with feints and without any specific line of sight. Most mistakes and, thus, inaccurate passing arise out of body wrong positions of the hands on the ball in the final phase (under the ball). This causes "upward shovelling".

Passing on and tipping

The direct passing on and tipping of the ball is performed with one or two hands. It is mostly executed on the move or while jumping. It is similar to the pass in volleyball. The difference is that ball is led longer. The forms of tipping are as numerous as the types of passes and their variations. Due to the increasing dynamics of basketball the "volley game" is becoming increasingly important for passing on balls which rebound from the backboard or the ring as well as balls which are passed on directly and often while jumping. This type of pass requires not only good jumping power and a quick reaction but also efficient wrist and finger work. The most frequent mistake is that it is performed too vigorously and the ball rebounds uncontrollably.

Defence against one-handed passes

On the whole the advice given in the previous chapters applies: In defending against one-handed passes the defender must bear in mind that he should not overreact to feints to one side because in most cases this leads to an unhindered breakthrough on the other side. When the player with the ball has finished dribbling with a close defence any mistake he makes in handling the ball or swinging it back can be exploited by the defender by disturbing deflecting or even intercepting the pass. When the ball is passed in jumping the defender should also jump but the jump should be timed to achieve maximum harassment.

Dribbling

Dribbling is a basic element of the basketball technique. By dribbling the player with the ball is able to cover any distance on the court without being restricted to a specified number of steps.

Technical perfection and the skilful use of the dribble in appropriate situations are essential factors for team success. Based on the rules we distinguish between rolling and floor dribble. Rolling dribble is of minor importance and is therefore given only little consideration in training. However mastery of the floor dribble with all its variations is important.

In floor dribbling the leading hand is on the ball, with fingers spread out. The ball is bounced against the floor in such a manner that the player gains space with each dribble. Maintaining the right relationship between the angle of incidence and his own movement ensures that he is not separated from the ball. This means that wish slow movements the ball must hit the floor at a steeper angle, and in the case of a quick movement it must hit the floor more obliquely.

The movement is performed with a slightly bent arm and with strong wrist and finger action. The ball must not be hit. It is received with a cushioning movement and is pushed back towards the floor. The angle of impact the height and frequency of the dribble as well as the whole body posture are determined by the position and activity of the nearest opponent. The dribbling hand should always be further away from the opponent, so that the dribbler's body is between the ball and the opponent. The dribble should be generally low and fast. This facilities a good reaction to the opponent's defensive move-hands. The eyes should

The dribble

not be directed exclusively at the ball. The ball should be controlled more by sense and feeling and peripheral vision to enable the dribbler to survey the situation on the court Changing hand's is one of the most important elements of dribbling. It can be performed in front of and behind the body as well as through the legs in order to remove the ball from the opponents defence line. The change of tempo and direction often facilities a successful it is necessary to be able to dribble equally well with either hand.

Dribbling is an integral part of the other elements of basketball technique and by combining them skilfully a wide variety of movements can be made.

These elements precede or follow the dribble (running, jumping, receiving, the ball stopping, pivoting passing shooting).

The one-handed pass applied directly after the dribble (underarm pass or swing pass) is of special importance for the quick and concealed utilization of a good situation. The following errors should be pointed out for correcting mistakes in the technique of dribbling the ball is led i.e., it is not pushed down but is taken along while running (infringement of the rules double dribble); the ball is hit and "bounded" too forcefully and not cushioned (loss of ball control); the eyes are fixed on the ball; the ball is dribbled with the wrong hand and in the wrong rhythm; the change of hands is not combined with a change of pace and is performed without gaining space.

Defence against the dribble

Because of the importance of dribbling as an element of attack special attention must be paid to the defence against dribbling. Due to a trend towards increasing active defence the player who is dribbling the ball is very are to drive the opponent aside to stop him, achieve a held ball, to hit the ball away and gain possession. An important prerequisite for success is a low, bent posture (low centre of gravity). The defender should not hit the opponent's hand but reach the ball when it is on its upward path. Such possibilities arise especially when the attacker changes his hands in front of his body. When a defender has been out-dribbled he can still continue active defence play by attacking the dribbler once again from behind. This often surprises the dribbler. In driving the opponent aside it should be borne in mind that the only remaining possibility is towards the edge of the court. Often a dribbler can also be stopped and forced to take up the ball by means of defensive feints.

Short medium and long one handed shots at the basket

Besides the technical elements already mentioned the shot at the basket is one of the most important and at the same time, most difficult elements; it represents the find phase of each action of attack. The speed of the movements of play should be combined with an accurate and harmonious shooting movement at the basket. This is also the main difference between basketball and other games where the offensive actions end with powerful throws shots or strikes. This is one of the reasons why players of other team games do not impress in basketball at the beginning because of their poor shooting ability. On the other hand, the good neuro-muscular coordination of a good account of themselves in other team games.

In international basketball literature one can find different aspects of systematization. We have decided to classify the subject matter into one-handed and two handed types of throws. And within these two categories we distinguish between short, medium and long distance shots. Previously one used to distinguish also between the various throws at the basket from low positions from the chest, from head level and from above head level. Today, in modern basketball the aim as regards throws is to train the players to shoot from the highest possible level. i.e., from above the head. The only exception are of course underhand shots. Before we explain the various about using the backboard and about the trajectory. With indirect shots at the basket (throws against the backboard a relatively flat ball trajectory can be chosen.

Experience shows that the indirect shot is more advantageous from a short distance, whereas from medium and long ranges as well as from the corner the direct shots the player therefore trains his sights at the front rim of the ring and chooses a medium height of trajectory as high trajectory makes it more difficult to calculate the distance and a flat trajectory reduce the area of the window through which the ball has to pass. With in indirect shots, the player must take into account the angle of rebound the elasticity of the backboard the hardness of the ball and its spin. A player shooting indirectly must aim at a certain point on the backboard in order to ensure the correct rebound of the ball into the basket. It is quite obvious that it is easier to aim at a ring which is clearly visible than at a white area the aiming point of which can easily become blurred. The marked square on the backboard is a help for the indirect shot.

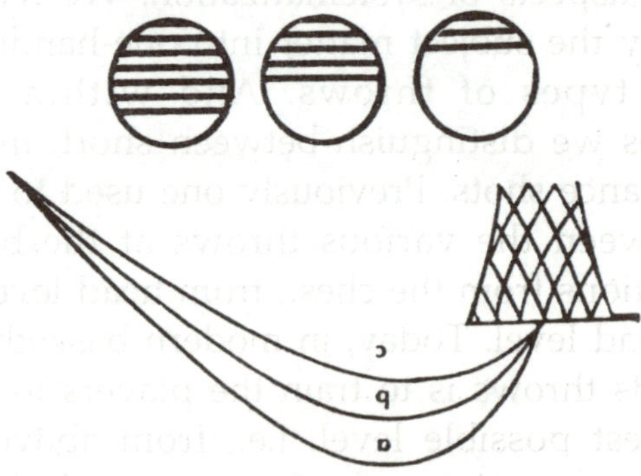

Trajectories of basket shots

In the following the various types of shots are explained for learning the shooting technique, the order in which they are listed having been picked at random.

Short one-handed shots

In modern basketball it is becoming increasingly characteristic for short shots to be mode from extremely fast running or jumping movements as well as when under intense harassment by an opponent. The basic forms described here are therefore applied with numerous variations by top class players in order to avoid the defender's arms and to be able to shoot despite body positions which are difficult to control during running and especially while jumping. The more important it is to pay attention to harmonious and smooth wrist and finger actions in the final phase of the shot. In modern basketball one-handed shots are becoming increasingly important. They are characterized by numerous variations.

It is important to try to learn and make short one-handed shots with either hand. A player who masters the technique of shooting equally well either hands has a tremendous tactical advantage.

The one-handed lay-up is executed with a forceful, in most cases one-legged take off (right-handed shooters take off with the left foot, left-handed shooters with the right foot). While jumping the ball is brought up above the head with both hands and only in the final phase it is town with one hand into the basket, with the usually touching the backboard. The ball must be protected from the defender who usually comes from the side, in such a manner that the arm opposite the shooting arm is moved outwards with the elbows slightly bent and directed towards the defender. This type of a shot is executed close to the basket, either from the side or from the front when the defender has already been slightly outplayed or if there is a some what wider space between him and the basket.

The lay-up

The one-handed overhead shot backwards is executed after taking the ball under the basket. This type of shot is mainly played against the backboard. It is suitable for a shot with the right hand after going under the basket from right to left or with the left hand after going under the basket from left to right it is applied mainly in situations where the defender respects a shot from in front and the attacker lengthens the last step within the two count rhythm thus managing to go under the basket. This type of shot can also be used as a surprise from a dribble along the base line.

The one-handed overhead shot backwards

The one-handed downward shot from above (one-hand dunk) is one of the attractions in modern basketball. The execution with one hand has the advantage that the player, when he is fully stretched can reach up higher than with both hands.

The one-handed "dunk"

The one-handed underhand shot is in principle performed in the some way as the two-handed shot which will be described later on. The one-handed type is also performed as a " lay in" and thus has the advantage over the two-handed shot that more space can be gained and the ball can be protected by the other arm.

The one-handed underhand shot

The hook shot from a short distance after going under the basket is executed mainly by using the backboard. The ball is taken from the side of the body and brought up above the head in a curve. It is suitable for a shot with the right hand after and vice versa for a shot with the left hand. This type of shot is also used when the attacker comes from the front and is driven aside by the defender or if he gets too for under the basket.

The hook shot close to the basket

The tip is used with one hand and also with two hands during offensive rebounding. In the case of failure, it is also done several times in a row. Modern basketball would be unthinkable without it when tussling for the ball near the basket. As has already been explained in the chapter on passing on volley play, during the tip the ball is held longer than in volleyball and it is gently pushed in the direction of the basket with wrist and finger snap.

One-handed shots from medium and long distances.

In modern basketball one-hand shots also from longer distances are becoming increasingly popular. The accuracy of one-handed shots has increased enormously in recent years. Many experts in basketball believe that it is not only due to the continuously improving training methods but also thanks to the fact there is less disproportionate application of force and fewer discrepancies in arm movement than with two-handed shots.

The one-handed shot from a standing position

This type of shot heads the list as a free throw and as a set shot from a long distance in terms of its frequency and effectiveness.

The player should prepare before receiving the ball so that the act of receiving of the ball fuses with the preparatory phase of the shot. This applies especially to the bent body posture and the position of the legs and feet. The feet are kept parallel and two widths of a hand apart, or the foot on the same side as the shooting arm is placed slightly in front. The knees are slightly bent. The ball is held with both hands the shooting hand being already somewhat under the ball whereas the other hand supports the ball from the side. The ball must not be held with the whole hand but it must rest on the roots of the spread fingers. The starting position can be at different levels. It is advisable to hold the ball above and in front of the head so that aiming at the basket is done from under the ball. The ball can also be held at shoulder height in front of the head. If a player's wrist is not insufficiently supple the ball can also be held at the side of the head the starting position may be high or low. The stretching phase begins with the legs and continues via the trunk to the arm so that a harmonious stretching movement of the entire body as well as a co-ordinated and appropriate power transmission is achieved. At the same time, both heels are lifted. A slight take-off from the ground is also allowed. The shooting arm is stretched forwards and the elbow which points slightly outwards is lifted at the same time. The other hand leaves the ball shortly after the start of the stretching movement. The ball receives the last impulse from the wrist and fingers, it rolls of the fingers with the hand following and the tips of the fingers of the shooting hand pointing forwards and obliquely downwards. A shorter finger movement with incomplete follow-up of the hand is also possible.

The one-handed shot from standing position (set shot)

As with the description of the two-handed shots from medium and long distances we would also like to mention some major deviations both permitted and faulty, which were established in scientific experiments in addition to the wealth of experience gathered by coaches.

Permitted deviations:

— stride position-feet a bit too for apart from each other;

— slight upward push-off which is associated with an insignificant gain in ground.

— bending the upper part of the body slightly back;

— taking the ball slightly behind the head.

— adopting a slightly slanting position of the shooting hand and exaggerating the tips of the thumb and index and middle fingers (ring finger and little finger only accompany this movement):

— no spreading of the fingers in the follow-up movement after the ball has left the hand (fingers closed when following the ball).

Faulty decisions:

— stride position- feet are too far apart resulting in a considerable gain in ground.

— too little bending of the knees and thus the body's movements are not harmonious.

— slight twisting of the body round the longitudinal axis due to wrong positioning of the legs (torsion);

— faulty stretching and lifting of the elbow;

— wrist movement with slight twisting to the right or left;

— faulty spreading of the fingers on the ball (the guiding area is too small);

— moving the shooting arm back too early;

— counter or wobbling movements of the hip;

— holding the ball in an oblique position and moving the elbow out to the side;

— pushing the ball in the final phase without finger and wrist action.

— finger action in the final phase by "snapping" into the final position, thus forming a first without any wrist action.

The one-handed jump shot

The one-handed jump shot is used most frequently from medium and long distances. Men shoot from a distance of up to 8 m and women from a distance of up to 5 m

The importance of anticipation in making one-handed shots from standing position has already been pointed out. This also applies to the jump shot. In addition, it should be emphasized that the position of the feet is of major importance for a good take-off. This is especially the case when bringing the rear foot next to the front foot as during the initial phase (right handed shooter-right foot left handed shooter-left foot) and when stopping from a run. All other points regarding the starting position have already been described in connection with the shot from a standing position.

The player executes a powerful take-off and lifts the ball at the same time above the head or if he receives the ball on this level, he keeps it there (he does not bring it down to a lower level). The shooting movement is the same as that used with the one-handed shot from standing position. Here the difficulties arise in obtaining good co-ordination between the jump and the relatively fast shooting movement. Individual tactical methods of attack bring about some *variations* of this shooting technique which are:

— The ball is thrown at the basket simultaneously with the jump, i.e. in the ascending phase. This requires powerful take-off;

— The entire movement is separated into two clearly distinct phases sot that the stretching of the arm is begun at the end of the jump and the player "stands" in the air so to speak. Thereby the jump and the shot from two distinct phases.

— The shot is performed with a delay so that the distinction between the two phases is even more marked. The arms are stretched only when the player starts his landing. This delayed ball release mostly from a medium distance is of ten attended by a backward bending of the upper part of the body.

The one-handed jump shot

Permitted deviations:

— slight forward jump without gaining much ground;

— slight backward jump without gaining much ground.

— taking the ball slightly backwards behind the head before shooting;

— relaxed jump (incomplete take-off reaching approx. 60 to 80 per cent of individual maximum height).

Faulty deviations:

— forward jump with a gain in ground.

— jump backwards gaining ground and losing balance;

— slanted posture to the side after take-off;

— poor take-off which impairs the movements that follow in such away that they are performed without harmony and too hastily;

— counter-movements of the hip and trunk in the one-legged of the jump.

The one-handed jump shot what is also called the "rising jump shot" is also used from a medium distance. After one-legged take-off (right-handed) shooter-left; left-handed shooter-right) the knee is lifted upwards and forwards-with vigorous action of the swinging leg and then the one-handed shooting movement is executed as already described. In case of an approach to the basket from the side this "rising jump shot" is associated with a 1/8 or 1/4 turn.

In principle the same technique applies to this shot as the one described for the one-handed jump shot.

The hook shot from medium distance

The hook shot one of the shots which determine performance especially for pivot and utility players from medium distances. It is performed either on the run or with an initial step and then take-off after pivoting or from a counter-move (body feint). The player stands with his back to the basket or he is positioned dragenally in relation to the basket. The ball is held in both hands to the side of or in front of the body at chest or shoulder level depending on the opponent's position. The knees are slightly flexed. While taking the initial step (right-hand shooter with the left leg and vice versa) the player takes the ball outside by stretching both arms and turns his trunk towards the basket so that the opposite shoulder to the shooting arm points to the basket. The ball lies on the speared out fingers of the shooting hand. The shooting arm which is now completely extended side ways is taken directly above the head in the direction of the opposite shoulder and the heel of the standing leg is lifted or the player takes off. At the same time the knee of the swinging leg is bent and lifted, thus supporting the harmonies movement of the entire body. The ball leaves the hand with a flick of the wrist and the fingers when the arm is at an angle of between 60 and 70 degrees. This angle depends on the distance to the basket. In any case a medium trajectory parabola must be achieved.

The hook shot from medium distance

Permitted deviations:

-execution of the hook shot movement slightly in front or behind the head;

-the shooting hand on the ball is held at a slight angle with a slight spin round the vertical axis.

-slight inclination of the body in the final phase of the stretching towards the basket;

-slight turn of the body towards the basket in the final phase so that the throwing arm is somewhat behind the body axis.

Faulty deviations:

— starting point for the shot is too low the consequence is a hanging throwing arm and holding the ball at hip height;

— the other hand is released too early;

— the ball is released too late too early;

— the wrist is held too stiffly resulting in insufficient finger action;

— the head is turned too late in the direction of the basket;

— the throwing arm is held a too far in front of or behind the head;

— the no stretching of the throwing arm (bent elbow joint);

— uncontrolled twisting of the upper part of the body which is transferred to the throwing arm (Skidding movement);

— falling of the body when releasing the ball in the direction of the basket (Excessive leading towards the basket);

Two-handed shots from short medium and long distances

In modern basketball two-hand shots and the part they play in training are no longer as important as they used to be.

Two-handed short shots

The two-handed shot is still occasionally used in elementary training in various forms. Near the basket the player takes up a basic position placing his feet in a slight stride position or in parallel arrangement. With the arms nearly stretched the ball is taken up above the head. With a brief knee thrust and stretching of the elbow the ball is pushed forwards and towards the basket mainly by flicking the wrist and fingers. We distinguish between two phases. During the first phase the player takes off powerfully from a position and the ball is taken explosively upwards. After the upward movement of the ball, at the highest point of the jump it stops for a short moment the second phase begins. This phase is similar to the above mentioned shooting movement from standing position. The execution of the shots after a one-legged take off and also after going under the basket with a backward shooting movement is nearly identical to the type described earlier.

The two and one handed putting of the ball into the basket (From above) is increasingly becoming the "spice of the game" in basketball. Besides being of great attraction to spectators and fellow players this shot is above all useful because it can hardly be blocked. Tall players and those who jump well should master and apply this so-called "dunk" in different variations especially after a successful drive in the final phase of a fast break in centre court situations and in rebounds. With a powerful take-off the ball is lifted above the head until the arms are completely stretched wrist and finger flick.

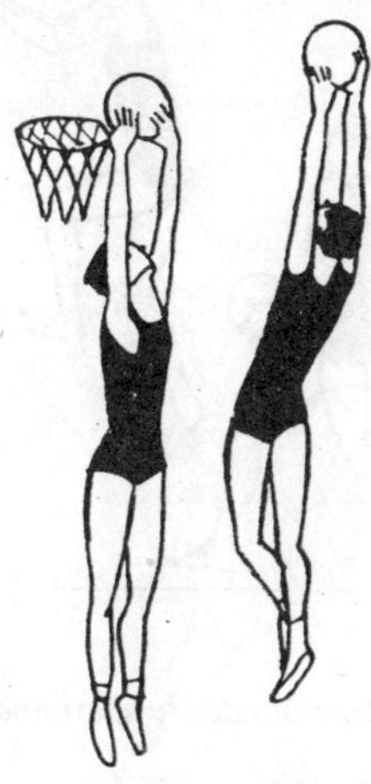

The two-handed "dunk"

The two handed underhand shot is used to outplay an opponent by passing the ball through under the opponent's arms or by evading them. This shot is also executed as what they calls " lay in". This shot is made after the attacker has outplayed the defender by a marked stretching and can no longer be harassed. With both types of execution the player while protecting the ball with his body completes the two-count rhythm. After take-off towards the basket the ball is held low. Then the arms are brought into a horizontal and then nearly to vertical position. By means of wrist and finger action the player then "lays" the ball into the basket. There are numerous variations of this shot. Repeated swinging movements of the arms while jumping towards the basket for instance are especially effective in order to deceive the opponent by feinting passes or to provoke fouls.

The two-handed underhand shot

Two-handed shots from medium and long distances

In modern basketball it is nowadays almost unthinkable for a team not to have several outstanding shooters from medium and long distances. Previously the shot from longer distances was an art mastered only by a few players. In the rapid development of basketball it became necessary however, mainly for tactical reasons to increasingly situations and hence try to bring the defence into disarray by shooting from short and long distances. A high and reliable rote of accuracy can be achieved with two-handed shots from medium and long distances. Very often women's teams prefer such two handed shots which in principle do not differ from one-handed shots with regard to their sequence of movement. Only the method of holding the ball requires special attention.

The technical mistakes and defects in aiming at the basket mentioned in connection with the description of the various types of shots have been subdivided by us into two categories:

1. Permitted deviations from the movements described which do not detract from the quality of the shot and are regarded as individual peculiarities and which in general can be easily corrected.

2. Faulty deviations which impede performance and can be corrected to some extent without major difficulties but which in some cases can only be eliminated by switching to a different type of shot or by curing underlying causes. The procedure for doing this differs from person to person.

The two-handed shot from chest level

The ball is held in both hands at chest or head level and lies on spread out fingers and the roots of the fingers. The thumps point towards each other. The index fingers are parallel or slightly to wards each other. The elbows point downwards and slightly outwards. The trunk in bent slightly forwards and the legs are in stride position with a slight flexion of the knees. The shooting movement starts from this position. The legs are stretched and at the some time the arms are pushed forwards and upwards in the direction of the arms in the final phase of the shooting movement the ball is thrown with a wrist and finger snap in such a way that after the ball has been released the palms point outwards. The body weight is transferred to the other leg which moves slightly forward with the shot. The continuity of movement of both arms harmoniously co-ordinated with the movement of the rest of the body is of special importance. The two-handed "chest shot" is used mainly as a free throw and as set shot in a standing position from longer distance.

The two-handed shot from chest level

Permitted deviations:

— light one-legged or two-legged take-off in the final phase of the shot;

— parallel position of the feet and foot push-off during the shot;

— no full elbow extension (in most cases because of shorter distance to the basket);

— slightly modified finger position on the ball, and finger and wrist action more downwards than outwards.

— the forward step and take-off are exaggerated;

— exaggerated preliminary movement;

— elbow point too much outwards;
— uneven movements of arms hands and fingers (if the becomes too prominent the player should switch to one-handed types of shots).

The two-handed overhead shot

This type of shot is performed from a standing position or while jumping. The ball is held above the head with bent arms. The position of the hands and fingers on the ball is similar to that of the "chest shot". The elbows point forwards the knees and trunk are slightly bent and the feet are parallel or in a slight stride position. The ball is shot forward and up by a harmonious stretching movement of the legs, the trunk and the arms. Wrist and finger action do not differ from the two-handed chest shot.

The two-handed overhead shot

When performing the shot as a jump shot the preliminary phase is somewhat more emphasized than with the stationary shot. With a powerful jump the ball is raised above the head and down at the basket at the highest point in the jump, with arm extension and wrist and finger movements.

The two-handed jump shot

Permitted deviations:

— taking the ball slightly behind the head;

— jumping slightly forwards or backwards;

— slight delay in releasing the ball after reaching the highest point during the jump;

Faulty deviations:

— excessive forward bending of the trunk resulting in a forward jump;

— counter-movement of the hip after take-off;

— sideways inclination during the jump;

— irregular hand and finger movements;

— the hands are withdrawn from the ball too early

(This results in the final thrust coming from the palm and not from the fingers).

The two-handed "swing shot" from below In modern basketball the two-handed shot from below in a standing position is only used as a free throw. The player stands with his legs a part and holds the ball with the hands either on the sides of or under the ball. The arms are relaxed. He assumes a squatting position and holds his arms between the knees. With the stretching of the legs the almost fully extended arms are simultaneously brought into a horizontal position and then up above the head. Hands and fingers accompany the ball with a relaxed but quick movement forward and up.

The two-handed "swing" shot from low down

Pivot shots

In the pivot actions were reserved mainly for all and extra tall players. In modern basketball they are mastered by utility players and tall outside players. The main characteristics of pivot shots are the player starting position is with his back turned to the basket many types of feints used in connection with pivoting; and variation of shots from a medium distance. The jump shot is also used with a body turn ranging from quarter to half, i.e., what is called the "turn jump shot". Besides the short shot techniques already described are used mainly from various starting positions at given for permitted and faulty deviations also apply to medium gauge shots taken by pivot players.

Defence against basket shots

The defence against basket shots is of utmost importance.

Whereas in the past a more passive from of defence, which was aimed at disturbing prevailed nowadays there are increasing tendencies that lead to active and ball-recovery defensive actions during shooting.

We have to distinguish not only between different kinds of defence shots but also medium and long distance shots but also between defensive actions against standing and jump shots. Constant readiness for action quick reaction jumping power, agility speed of movement and good concentration are important pre-requisites for successful defence. It is also important to keep a close watch on the player with the ball who is in a favourable shooting position to constantly adjust the defender's own position with the aim of frustrating the attacker's optimum shooting intention and anticipating the opponent's offensive actions without allowing himself to tempted into hasty actions by feints. Shots are parried almost exclusively while jumping. In this connect defender should not

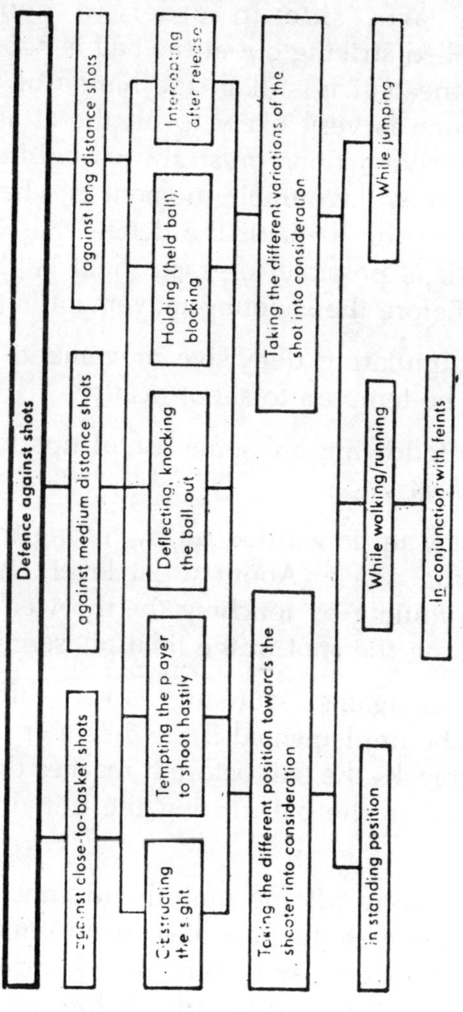
Defence against shots
against close-to-basket shots
against medium distance shots
against long distance shots
Obstructing the sight
Tempting the player to shoot hastily
Deflecting, knocking the ball out
Holding (held ball), blocking
Intercepting after release
Taking the different position towards the shooter into consideration
Taking the different variations of the shot into consideration
In standing position
While walking/running
In conjunction with feints
While jumping

take off too early and if the father away from the opponent he should not move directly towards the opponent but he should jump laterally past this shooting arm side in order to avoid a foul. Uncontrolled striking out at the ball is not advisable as long as the ball is still in the hands of the thrower because one is very likely to hit the attacker's (foul). The defensive actions must always be directed at the ball. The most favourable moment is when the ball is just leaving the hand. If the defender is closer to the thrower it is possible to grasp (held ball) or pull out the ball before the shooting movement is performed.

By simulating defensive movements the thrower can also be tempted to shoot rashly.

The following are some useful tips for the *defence against shots;*

- The lay up is warded off by hitting the ball in the starting phase (About waist level). Although one risks fouling by touching the thrower's arms or by blocking the shot in the final phase.
- Defence against "dunking" is very difficult and can only be implemented if the defender jumps in time and blocks the ball before it reaches the basket or if he strikes the ball during the initial phase of the shot.
- In warding off the underhand shot the defender has above all the possibility hand immediately after it is received or of blocking it during the final phase of the shot (Shortly before or after the ball has left the shooting hand). If the defence against the shot takes place during the relatively long shooting movement it is in most cases, unsuccessful

and invariably ends with a foul.

- Defence against the block shot is often possible during the initial phase of the shot as the attacker very often starts the movement rather low (waist height). For defensive players who are tall and jump well it is recommended that they block the ball in the final phase of the throwing movement of after it touches the backboard. If the defender has been outplayed and he is lagging behind the attacker when he (the attacker) prepares to shoot, it is possible to tip off the ball, which lies on the open shooting hand, from the side or from behind.
- The defence against medium and long distance shots is being extensively promoted in modern basketball. Therefore the blocking of the shot shortly before it is released is of great importance. In doing this the defender usually accepts the risk of an individual breakthrough as he can rely on the collective support of his team-mates. Although such defensive actions often do not parry a shot they disturb the thrower and this often results in an unsuccessful shot.

5

DEFENSIVE FUNDAMENTAL DRILLS

Before any team defense can be developed to its maximum potential individual defenders must become proficient at not only handling the attacker they are guarding (man defense) or the area they are responsible for (zone defense), but also at defending an unlimited number of recurrent offensive situations. Some of those repeated elements include stopping an open attacker who is driving for a basket, forcing a hurried jump shot, denying the pass to an inside cutter, and defending the stationary post. These components will appear and reappear whether your team is playing man to- man defense, or a zone, or a combination. They are called the fundamentals, of defensive basketball.

By drilling your players again and again on these fundamentals, you their coverage instinctive. When this coverage becomes involuntary, your defenders will always enjoy a step advantage, both mentally and physically on their attackers. So your first building block is to drill and further drill the pertinent sections of this chapter: those are, those drills relevant to your chosen team defense.

Drill 2: Held-ball drill

Objectives

1. To teach attackers to protect the ball by pivoting properly.
2. To teach the offensive step-through move to avoid double team pressure.
3. To teach defenders the proper techniques of gaining a held ball without fouling.

Procedure

1. Line up your team with one attacker and two defenders in each group.
2. Give the attacker a ball. The attacker has lost his dribble. The attacker must learn to pivot keeping the ball away from the two defenders.
3. The two defenders try to get one or two hands on the ball, trying to force a held-ball situation without fouling or trying to pry the ball out of the attacker's hands.
4. Let each attacker have the ball for 30 seconds. Total time of the drill, one and one-half minutes.

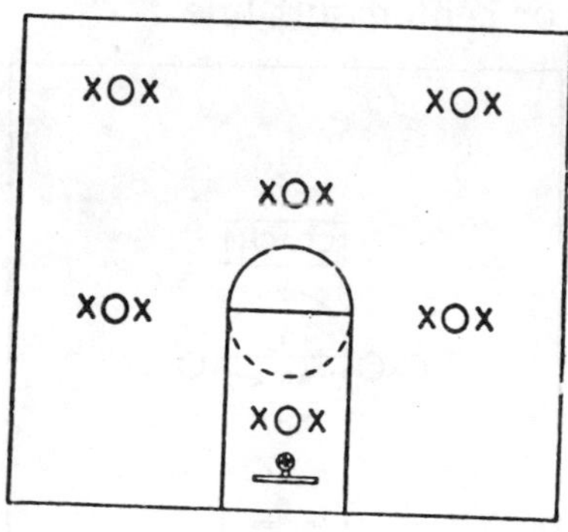

Diagram 1

5. After an attacker steps through for thirty seconds, one of the two defenders the next attacker. The player who began as an attacker becomes a defender.

Drill 3: Quick hands individual drill

Objectives

1. To teach quick aggressive hands.
2. To teach player how to slap at a loose ball for recovery.
3. To teach recovery of loose balls.
4. To teach one-on- one defensive and offensive techniques.
5. To teach instant conversion from offensive play to defensive play.
6. To teach hustling defense.

Procedure

1. Two lines should be formed near a line on the court.
2. Have first two players step out to the middle of the free throw or centercourt line.

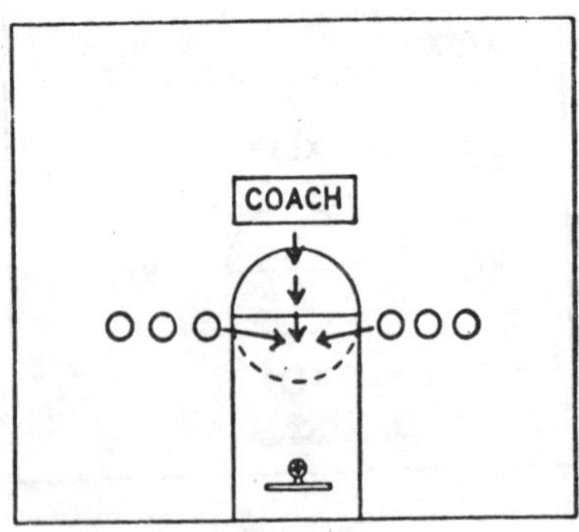

Diagram 2

3. Coach can require players to place hands on knees, hands in proper defensive position hands immediately in front of face, or any where the coach wants the defender's hands.
4. Coach tosses ball waist high between the defenders or he can bounce the ball off of the floor waist high. Two players try to recover the loose ball. Player recovering loose ball is on offense; the other player is on defense. They play a one-on-one game. After a source the players go to the end of the opposite line.
5. The next two players to the centre of the free throw or centercourt line and the drill continues.

Drill 4: Quick foot movement

Objectives

1. To teach defensive foot quickness.
2. To condition players to play in a crouched position for long periods of time.

Procedure

1. Three players place their feet on A and B: right foot on A, left foot on B.

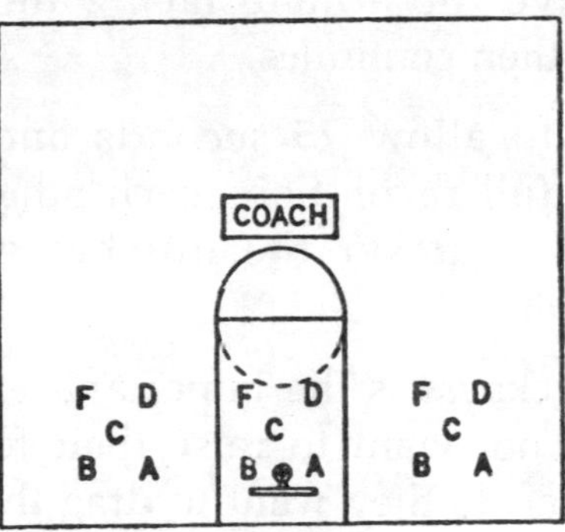

Diagram 3

2. Several different quickness drills begin from the above foot positions.

    a. Players jump in with right foot touching C; then out with right foot hitting D and left foot hitting. The player immediately makes a 180 degree turn putting his left foot on D and his right foot on F. Player puts right foot on C; then he jumps our with left foot hitting on A and B right foot on B. Then the player executes another 180 degree turn. This process continues.

    b. Instead of originally jumping into C with right foot, player could begin with left foot; and the same process continues.

    c. Instead of originally jumping into C with right foot, Player could jump into C with both feet.

    d. You could begin with player's left foot on A and right foot on B. The player's back is to the coach. The player jump in to the C block backward landing with both feet, with the right foot, or with left door (whichever you wish). Then the player jumps out with left foot on D and right foot on F. A 180 degree turn would then have the athlete facing the coach. The process then continues.

3. You want to allow 25 seconds and record the number of full revolutions each athlete manages. As they get quicker the number will increase immeasurably.

4. Because quickness is the important test on defense athletes do not want to raise their feet off of the floor. Neither do they want to drag their feet along

the floor-the friction between the shoe and floor would reduce quickness. Neither do you want the athlete to hop. You want him to glide quickly, lifting his feet ever so slightly. The athlete wants to have the sensation of his toes grabbing at the floor as he slides through the drill.

5. This drill is an excellent psychological defensive drill. It makes the athlete think quickness, an attribute seen in all great defenders.

Drill 5: The all important first-step drill (3,4,5)

Objectives

1. To teach stance.
2. To teach first-step movement the most important step in both offense and defense.
3. To teach concentration and anticipation prerequisites to quickness.

Procedure

1. You can use only one defender with a coach facing him, preferably at a line on the court, or you can begin the drill as a mass drill.

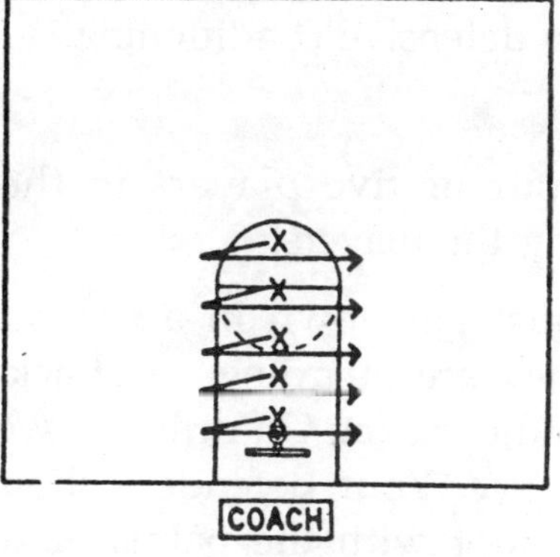

Diagram 4

2. The player moves only one step in the direction the coach moves. Coach should establish a pivot foot, and he should use a basketball.
3. The defender should take a long step. He wants to work on the advance step, the retreat step, and the swing step.
4. The player should be in a perfect defensive stance, and he must react quickly.
5. The coach must constantly check the stance and perfect it.
6. The coach steps forward, the defender retreats with the foot where the coach stepped (the retreat step). The coach brings his foot back to beginning position; the defender recovers to his beginning position(the advance step). The coach uses a cross over step; the defender answers with a swing step.

Drill 6: Quick lateral step defensive drill (3,4,5,6,7,8,9)

Objectives

1. To teach quick lateral foot movement needed for defense.
2. To develop defensive conditioning.

Procedure

1. Line up four or five players in the lane with a coach facing the players.
2. Players must get down in a defensive stance as through they are guarding an attacker who inters to drive to the basket. On dribbles, we advocate the parallel stance. Your defenders should be able to touch the floor with the palms of their hands as

they slide. This keeps them in a low defensive position.

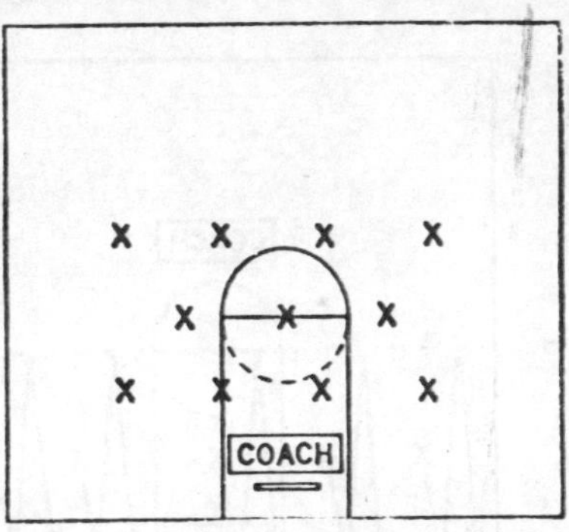

Diagram 5

3. Coach begins his timing with 60 seconds intending advance to 90 seconds.
4. Player must place their lead foot outside the lane as they slide from side to side.
5. Coach should record the number of completed revolutions by each player. This should improve with each work-out.
6. While defenders slide, they should not let their feet drag along the floor. Neither should they hop. Foot quickness is the important development.

Drill 7: Quick vertical-step defensive drill (3,4,5,6,7,8,9)

Objectives

1. To teach vertical defensive sliding quickness.
2. To develop defensive conditioning.

Procedure

1. Line up four or five players facing the coach.

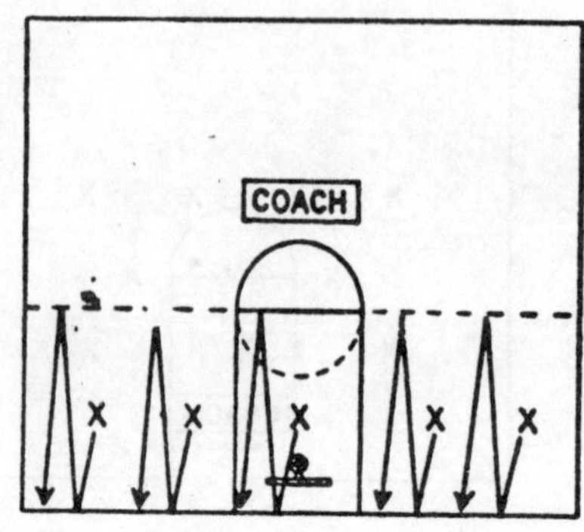

Diagram 6

2. Coach times the slides. Start with 60 seconds and work up to 90 seconds.

3. Record the number of complete revolutions by each player.

4. You could have your players run their slides in several different ways.

   a. *Backward:* You can have the players slide sideways as they retreat, simulating stopping a driving attacker; or you can have players slide backward as through they are trying to intercept a pass lobbed downcourt.

   b. *Forward:* You can have players race forward hard, trying to arrive to an attacker as the ball arrives; or you can have the players slide forward using the approach step.

5. Be sure players slide without hopping and without allowing shoes-floor friction.

6. You can extend the boundaries from baseline to top of the circle or to the 28-foot marker or to midcourt. What ever distance you choose, you want to put tape down or draw a line with chalk. You want to require the athletes lead foot to touch the line or go over it.

Drill 8: Mass-denial sliding drill (3,6,7,8)

Objectives

1. To condition legs in normal guarding (denial) position.
2. To teach defensive movement that must be used to deny inbounds passes, Vertical passes, and passes into the middle.
3. To teach visual reaction concentration.
4. To develop quickness of the feet.

Procedure

1. Players are to get down in normal fencing position. Feet are to be at right angles, hands out front as if the defenders are holding a foil.
2. Players are to use fence slides as though they are attacking.
3. On visual command the coach has the players advance, retreat, advance, retreat until they go the full length of the court.
4. Coach must be careful that players keep their body balanced (weight evenly distributed) and that their feet do not slide along the floor, creating friction that slows the defender. Defensive players should never let the knee of their front foot advance over

the toe of that foot. Start the drill slowly being sure that the proper balance is always kept.

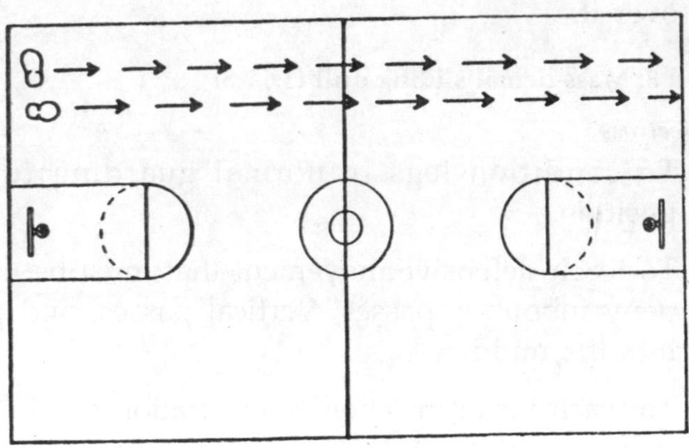

Diagram 7

Drill 9: Combination slide drill (3,4,5,6)

Objectives

1. To teach defenders to recognize which slide to use and to use it quickly.
2. To condition defensively.

Procedure

1. Line up three or four players facing a coach.
2. Coach has a basketball and establishes a pivot foot.
3. Coach steps forward, backward or dribble side ways. Players react with an advance step, a retreat step, or a lateral step.

4. Coach can require a player to immediately slide back to his original starting position, or the coach can continue his dribble and steps without having player return to starting position.

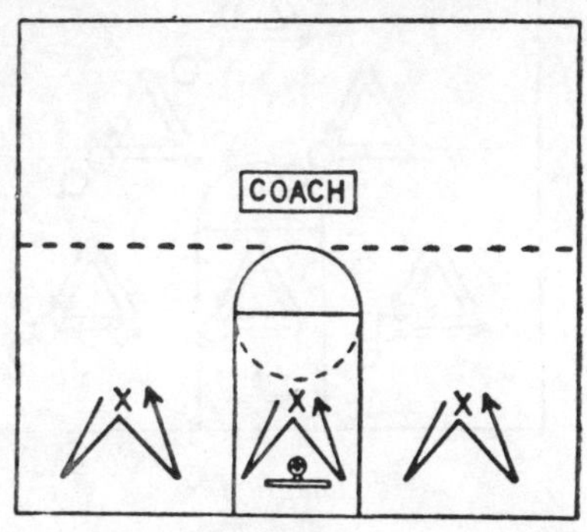

Diagram 8

5. Coach can cross over, requiring defenders to use swing step. Coach can turn his back to the defender (reverse dribble), requiring players to drop step preparing for their defense of the reverse dribble.

Drill 10: Triangle defensive Stance drill (3,4,5)

Objectives

1. To teach the lateral slide.
2. To teach the swing step.
3. To teach the approach step.
4. To teach the retreat step.
5. To condition the legs all-out defensive play.

Procedure

1. Line up players.

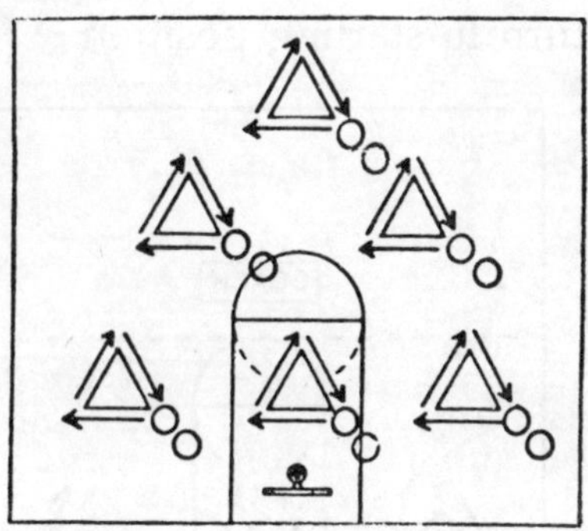

Diagram 9

2. Players slide for as long as you, the coach, desires.
3. You should do the completed triangle at least twice, hen reverse the directions.
4. Three players can be going on the triangle at one time. Start the second player when the first turns the corner.

Drill 11: Defensive circle drill (3,4,5)

Objectives

1. To teach defenders the approach step, the advance step, the retreat step, and the swing step.
2. To teach defenders the front-foot-to-pivot-foot stance.
3. To teach attackers the crossover the jab-step, the rocker steps and the reverse-pivot fakes.

Procedure

1. Line players up.

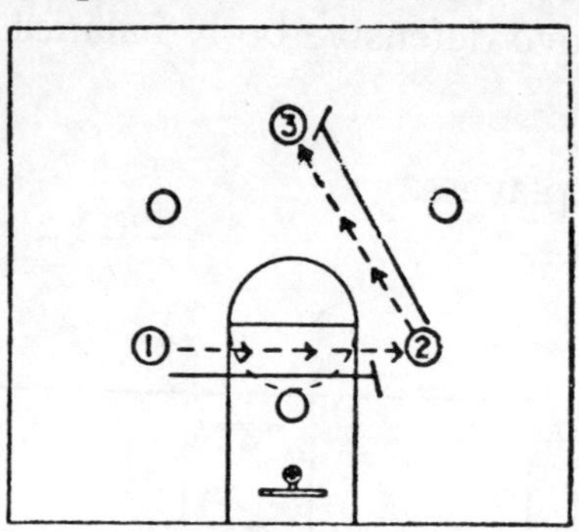

Diagram 10

2. Player 1 passes to 2. Player I goes to defend 2;2 chooses a pivot foot as I is on his way. Player 2 can jab step, crossover step, jab step then crossover, pivot into a reverse move, etc.
3. The steps by 2 require that I use the retreat step, the advance step, and the swing step. Player I also has to use the approach step when he approaches 2; I must make intelligent choices.
4. After 2 has tried the steps described above, 2 passes to 3. Player 2 goes to defend 3;3 then choose a pivot foot and the drill continues.
5. Player 1 stays at 2's location. When 3 passes, 3 goes to defend whomever he passes to. Player 2 will stay at 3's location.

Drill 12: Sliding drill-half court (6,7,9)

Objectives

1. To teach the backward slides for retreating defenders.

2. To condition the legs defensively.
3. To improve defensive body balance.

Procedure

1. Line up players.

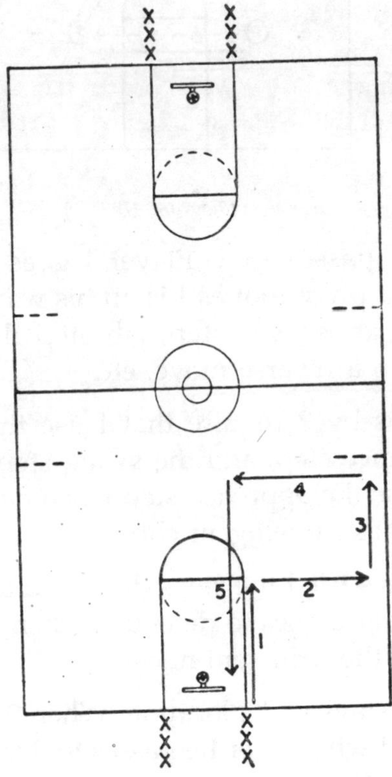

Diagram 11

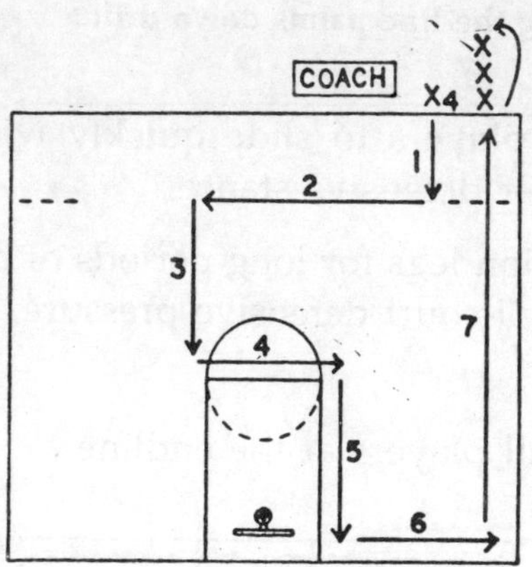

Diagram 12

2. Do the drill at both ends of the court as quickly as the defenders can correctly do them. You can do the drill several times before going to another drill.

3. In both diagrams, slide 1 is backward, slide 2 is a parallel slide, slide 3 is backward, slide 4 is a parallel slide, and slide 5 is a backward slide. Slides 6 and 7 are only in Diagram 2-a12: slide 6 is a parallel slide and slide 7 is an all-out sprint forward.

4. You can add talking on the second trip through the drill, and you can require sliding with the palms of the hands touching the floor on the third trip.

5. You can have players race hard backward on the back-ward slides, or you can have the players race sideways as though they are looking to intercept a long lob pass.

Drill 13: Sliding the line palms down drill

Objectives

1. To teach players to slide quickly without coming out of their defensive stance.
2. To condition legs for long periods of defensive play and for full-court defensive pressure.

Procedure

1. Line up all players at the endline.

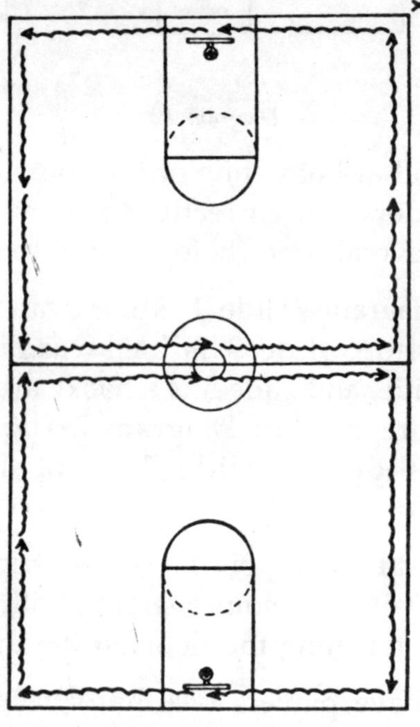

Diagram 13

2. Players first slide to their left as though in a parallel stance covering a non-penetrating dribbler.
3. Players then slide backward up the sideline to half court.

4. Players slide to their right using a parallel slide.
5. Players slide backward down the sideline (right).
6. Players slide left using a parallel slide along the near baseline.
7. Players slide forward up to midcourt using the approach step.
8. Players slide right using the parallel stance.
9. Players slide forward back to their beginning position using the approach step.
10. Begin by going once around the floor and work up to going four times around the floor without stopping. Between every slide players are to put their palms on the floor without bobbing. You could use the same route but require different slides.

Drill 14: Sliding drill-full court

Objectives

1. To teach the steps (retreat, advance, and swing) used in playing defensive basketball.
2. To condition the legs so the defenders can stay in a low defensive stance for an entire game.
3. To teach defensive communication.
4. To teach sliding backward, laterally, and forward using whichever technique the coach desires.

Procedure

1. Line up players.
2. You can go through the slides one, two, or three times.

3. Slide 1: retreat slide to the defender's right -swing step at the free throw line. Slide 2: retreat slide to defender's left with a swing step at midcourt line. Slide 3: retreat slide to the defender's right and a swing step at the free throw line. Slide 4: a left retreat slide with a swing step at the baseline. Slide 5: a parallel slide to the right. This drill continues with the defender always facing the baseline he began on. This should give the defender drills on all defensive slides.

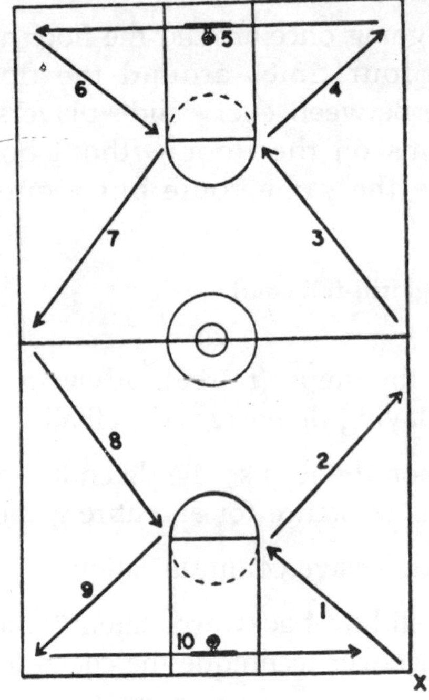

Diagram 14

4. Once through emphasizing the sliding step only. Then have the defender talk, not just talking but using terms used in your proposed defensive

structure. Then have the defender slide touching the floor with the palms of his hands as he slides.

Drill 15: Full-court talking drill

Objectives

1. To teach defensive communication.
2. To teach defensive sliding, staying low without bobbing heads.
3. To condition legs for pressing an entire game.

Procedure

1. Line up all players on end line.
2. First player in line races backward to the 28-foot line where he pivots facing out of bounds. He defensively slides to the free throw line extended (left sideline), hitting the palms of his hands on the floor with each slide. He again slides facing midcourt after his pivot. He slides defensively to the opposite sideline (right), then races backward to the point where the left sideline intersects the midcourt line. He slides across the midcourt line telling his team-mates what he sees in front of him, helping them avoid pile-ups. When he reaches the right sideline at midcourt, he races backward to the free throw line extend on the left sideline. He pivots, facing the end line, and slides defensively to the looking inward, and slides up to the 28-foot marker. From there he races backward to the end line. While racing through this maze, he constantly crosses the paths of his team-mates. Both he and his team-mates have their backs to each other. Only through talking will they circumvent contact. Defensive players should touch the palms of their

hands on the floor with every defensive slide. They should accomplish this without bobbing their heads.

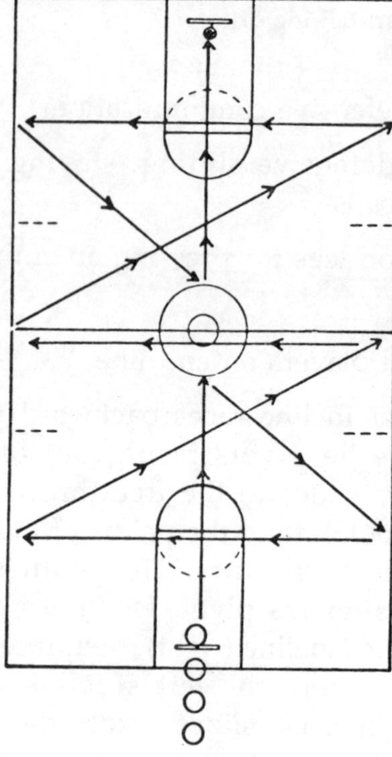

Diagram 15

3. Second player in the line begins racing backward when the first player reaches the first free throw line.

4. A trip downcourt and back by each player takes less than a minute. You can require one or more trips depending on the communication skills of the defenders.

5. You can alter what is said by having sports where defensive calls must be made. Calls should include terminology used in your team defense: "switch,"

"jump," "trap," "rotate," and so on. You choose the language and the spots on the floor where you want a particular term used.

Drill 16: Drawing the charge drill

Objectives

1. To teach drawing the charge under game conditions.
2. To teach hustling defense and recognizing when to draw the charge.
3. To teach an attacker to drive hard to the basket, not worrying about the contact of charging.

Procedure

1. Line up players.

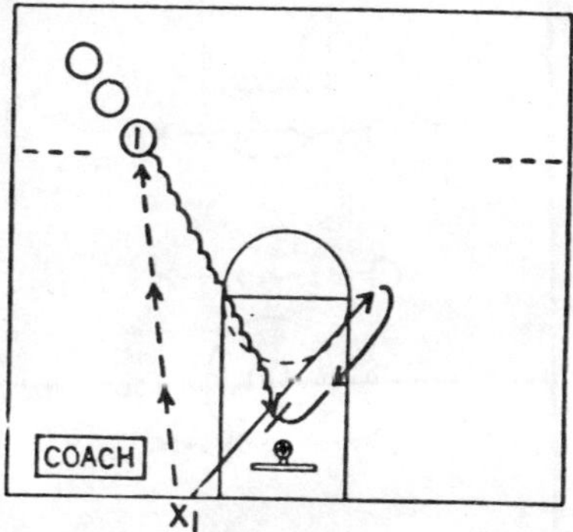

Diagram 16

2. Rotate from offense to defense to the end of the line. First man in line becomes the next 1.
3. XI rolls the ball to 1. Player 1 races hard to get the ball; then 1 begins to dribble, driving hard to the basket. Mean-while XI has touched the opposite free throw line, and XI must hurry back to get proper defensive position to draw the charge.

4. Coach calls whether it is a charge or a block.
5. You can alter the drill by requiring that I drive for the loose ball before getting up and driving hard to the basket. When using this phase of the drill, you should shorten I's distance or lengthen XI's.

Drill 17: Mass drawing-the-charge drill

Objective

1. To teach defenders how to draw the charge without getting hurt.

Procedure

1. Line up the entire squad about fifteen feet apart.

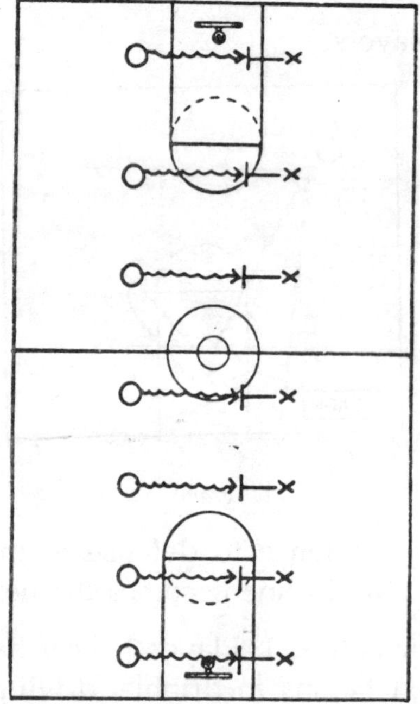

Diagram 17

2. On the whistle, the attackers begin driving hard straight across the court.

3. On the same whistle, the defenders take a step or two toward the driver and prepare for the contact. On contact, the defenders push off the balls of their feet and land on their buttocks. The defenders roll over to their sides after landing, raising their top leg. This should prevent injury except for the minor bruises and aches that come with contact and with falling on the floor.

Drill 18: One-on-one under control

Objectives

1. To teach your defensive stance on the ball handler (ours is front foot to pivot foot).

2. To teach defenders to cover a dribbler who may drive or shoot.

3. To teach good defense of the jump shot. Defender moves to cover his man when both hands of the dribbler touch the ball.

4. Your players can learn new offensive moves, and they learn to shoot under pressure.

5. To teach defense of the pump fakes.

Procedure

1. Player I begins with a basketball and may use any fake he desires.

2. When first teaching the drill, don't let I dribble. Then, advance him to one dribble, then two dribbles. Begin by letting I attack in only one direction. Then allow him both directions.

3. Player I may shoot when he gets XI off balance but never allow a forced shot.

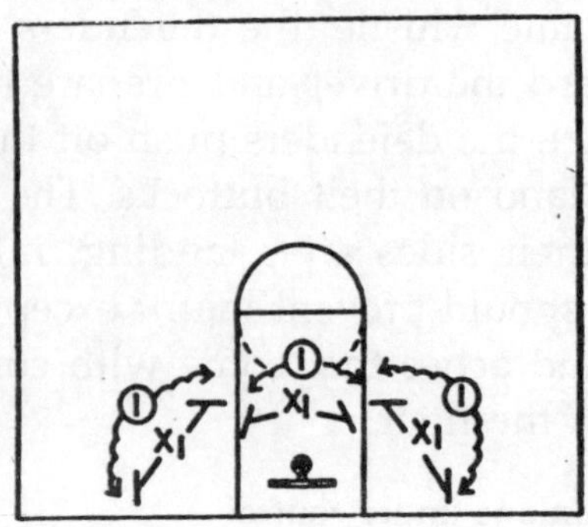

Diagram 18

4. Player XI begins in front-foot-to-pivot-foot stance (use your defensive stance on the ball).
5. Player XI must not leave his feet until I has left his.
6. Player XI must keep his hand extended, making his reach four inches longer.
7. Coach can stand where XI does not see him, hold up fingers to allow I that many dribbles. We limit it at first to dribbles in only one direction. We start out with no dribble, then move to one, then two.
8. You can require I to use his right foot as a pivot foot one time, then the left foot as the pivot foot the next time.
9. You can move I under the basket and let him use his pump fakes. Player XI must not allow I an uncontested shot. Player XI leaves his feet as I leaves his. Player XI extends himself, not trying to block the shot, but trying to force I to raise his shot.

Drill 19: Just one-on-one

Objectives

1. To teach XI and X3 how to control the driver, yet pressure the jump shot.
2. To teach 1 and 3 offensive moves from their positions.
3. To teach offensive and defensive rebounding.

Procedure

1. Line up players.

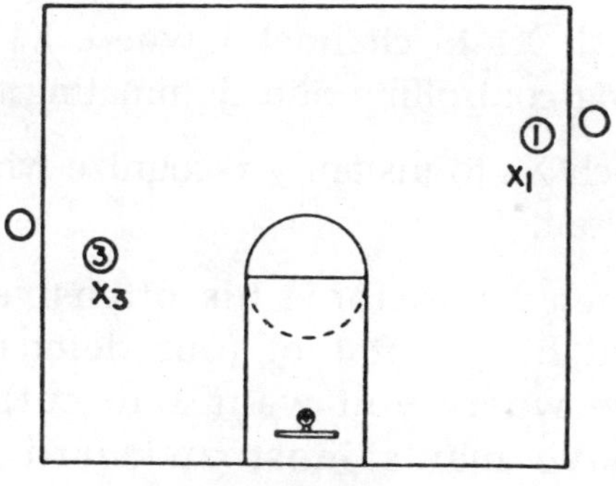

Diagram 19

2. Rotate from offense to defense to end of opposite line. First player in each line becomes the new offensive player.
3. Begin the drill by limiting the area 1 and 3 may use to score. Also, limit the number of dribbles the attackers may use.
4. Begin by alternating one-on-one plays by each line. After a few days let both lines go to the same time. This forces the defensive men to feel for any possible interference from the other line.
5. Begin by not letting the defense use their hands.

6. After X1 and X3 start controlling 1 and 3, let 1 and 3 have the entire court to operate and let X1 and X3 have the use of their hands.

Drill 20: Channelling drill

Objectives

1. To teach defenders the slowness of the bounce pass.
2. To teach X1 the approach step; to get to I without giving 1 the advantage.
3. To teach X1 to think defensively.
4. To teach X1 to channel 1 where X1 wants to go, teaching controlling and dominating the offense.
5. To teach X1 to instantly recognize which foot is 1's pivot foot.
6. To teach X1 to force his offensive man to cut toward his pivot foot (our defensive idea-you choose where you want 1 to cut). That is the offensive man's most awkward and slowest direction.

Procedure

1. X1 passes to, 1, then races to defend against him.

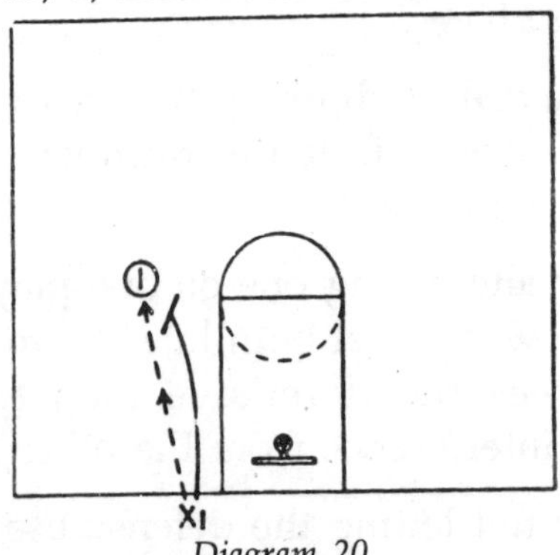

Diagram 20

2. X1 should use the bounce pass: it is slower. Player I cannot leave until he receives the pass. Player 1 chooses a pivot foot; X1 must recognize that pivot foot.

3. You could require X1 to alter his channelling route: one time cut 1 inside the next time cut 1 outside. To do we have to have 1 switch his pivot foot because of our front-foot-to-pivot-foot stance.

Drill 21: Cut inside or outside drill

Objectives

1. To teach stopping a driver on a fast break of after having broken a press.
2. To teach visual concentration.
3. To teach the defense how to prevent a driver from turning the corner.
4. To teach cutting inside or outside (your choice).
5. To teach full-speed ball handing.
6. To teach defense to stay in motion-use parallel stance until the defense decides which way to cut the offense, then slide with the trail foot as the advance foot in a staggered stance.
7. To teach defenders how to delay an offensive man who is advancing the ball on a fast break (this is used after the attackers are allowed to change directions).

Procedure

1. An offensive man begins at his defensive foul line and dribbles at full speed toward the opposite basket.

2. When the offense reaches half court the coach who is standing behind the dribbler, signals the defense which way to cut the offense.

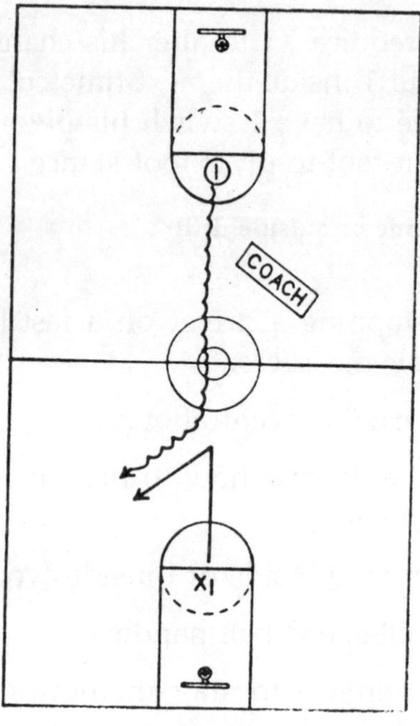

Diagram 21

3. The defender is in motion using the pat-the-floor motion.

4. The defender must cut the offensive man in the direction the coach has signaled.

5. The defender is to cur the offensive man out of bounds before he can turn the corner. The defender can do this by staying one-quarter a man's length behind the dribbler, using quick shuffle steps. The defender must also use the proper cushion so that

he will not get beaten. The proper cushion varies directly with the speed of the two men involved.

6. At first offensive man is not allowed to reverse his direction; but, when the defense becomes proficient we permit change of directions.

Drill 22: Covering the baseline-corner driver

Objectives

1. To teach the two methods of covering the baseline drive.
2. To teach the proper angle to cut off the offensive man.
3. To teach offensive men to drive the baseline correctly.
4. To teach drawing the charge.
5. To teach offensive men to jump back into the court without charging and still score.

Procedure

1. Line up players.

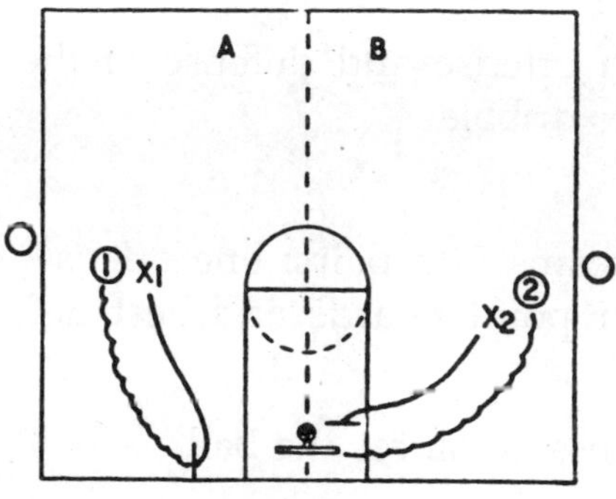

Diagram 22

2. Put a line on each side of the court-rotate from offense to defense to the end of the other line.
3. Player X1 cuts 1 baseline, then races and cuts off 1 by placing his left foot on the baseline.
4. Player X2 allows 2 to drive the baseline then tries to draw the charge as 2 jumps back into X2 on his scoring attempt; X2 must keep his shoulders to and directly underneath the backboard. Player X2's arms must be held straight up toward the ceiling eliminating any doubt in the official's mind.
5. Switch the side of the court from day to day for drills A and B.

Drill 23: Full-court zigzag drill

Objectives

1. To teach cutoffs by defensive overplays.
2. To teach pressure defense over the full-court.
3. To condition defensively.
4. To teach advancing the ball offensively under extreme pressure.
5. To teach offense and defense of the reverse and crossover dribbles.

Procedure

1. Divide teams into pairs: one offense, one defense. Put your point guards and best defenders in the middle lane.
2. The offense advances the ball.
3. The defense is to race back and turn the offense by use of an overlay.

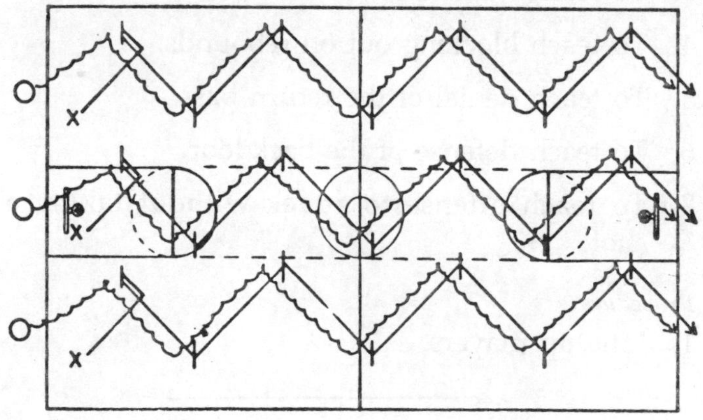

Diagram 23

4. We start the season without the use of hands, progressing to handwork after footwork is mastered.

5. Defenders must turn attacker at least three times in each half court.

6. We let offense go down and back; then we switch from offense to defense.

7. You can, in the early stages, require that the offense use only the reverse or only the crossover. You can then advance to allowing them the use of both.

Drill 24: One-on-one lane drill

Objectives

1. To teach one-on-one defensive footwork.
2. To teach defense of the crossover.
3. To teach defense of the reverse.
4. To teach blocking out on rebounds.
5. To teach denial of the return pass.
6. To teach defense of the backdoor.
7. To teach offense to attack without taking a bad shot.

Procedure

1. Line up players.

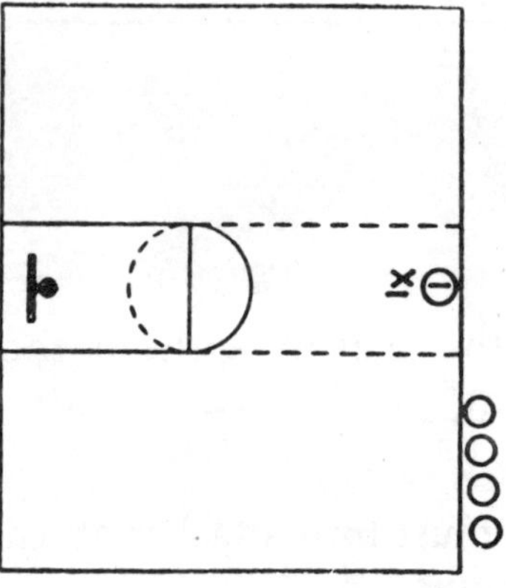

Diagram 24

2. Rotate from 1 to X1 to end of line. First player in line becomes the next 1.
3. Begin the drill by requiring X1 to lock his hands behind his back. He must use his feet and his head; otherwise I will score all night.

4. You can limit player 1 to two dribbles. This requires 1 to pass to the coach (who should move about outside the lane) and to get open to get a pass back from the coach. This means X1 will have plenty of opportunities to deny the pass back to 1, thereby perfecting his denial defense.

5. You can limit 1 to crossover moves only. You can limit him to reverses. You can give him both. To stop the crossover, X1 should slide in the direction of the dribble but use his trail hand swipe at the ball. To stop the reverse X1 would drop his foot in the direction of the reverse and recover to try to draw the charge.

6. Once 1 passes to the coach, X1 should contest the pass back to 1.

7. Player 1 can beaver get out of the lane-he must attack within the dotted lines.

8. Player X1 must box out when 1 shoots. Only I can rebound. Player X1 must let the carom hit the floor. When missed shots hit the floor, the drill is over and everyone rotates. You must make X1 stay on defense until he stops 1. Don't feel sorry for X1, or X1 will never be the defender you want him to be.

Drill 25: Defending the individual drive moves

Objectives

1. To teach attackers the dribble reverse, crossover, and other moves.

2. To teach defensive footwork against the dribbling reverse and the dribbling crossover.

3. To teach defense of the reverse the defender must

get a half step in front of the driver. If the driver continues, the defender draws the charge. When the defender sees the attacker square up sideways the defender quickly races to the opposite side, anticipating the reverse.

4. To teach drawing the charge.
5. To teach defensive overplays.

Procedure

1. Player I can use the dribbling reverse only (later add the crossover). He may use any other fake he would like, such as change of pace, head and shoulder fakes, etc. to try to free himself but the must reverse (later crossover) when he changes directions. After defending the reverse work on defending the crossover. Then give the attacker the right to use either or both.

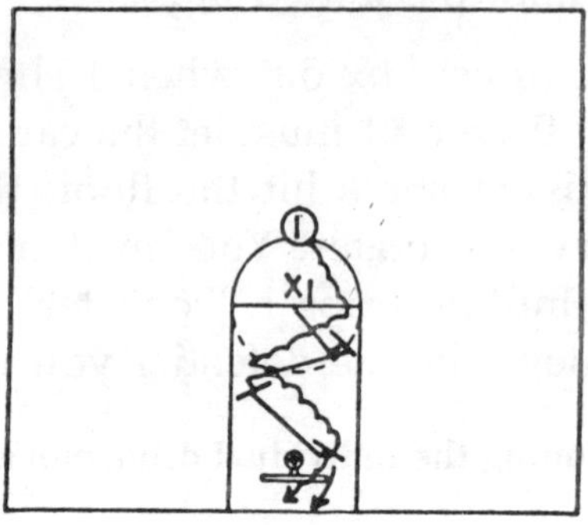

Diagram 25

2. To defend against the crossover the trail hand should swipe at the dribble as the defender slides in the direction of the dribbler. This coverage could result in forcing a turnover; it also prevents the

dribbler from gaining an advantage should the defender not deflect the ball.

3. Player I can change direction whenever he wishes, but he cannot go outside the free throw line and he must use the crossover or the reverse whichever is designated.
4. Player X1 must constantly hustle back into an overplay, causing 1 to reverse or crossover to change his direction.
5. Start the drill in the early season without letting X1 use his hands; progress to hand action in about one week (linger if defenders do not gain proficiency in foot movement).
6. Encourage X1 to draw the charge, using defensive hand fakes (when given hands), and head and shoulder fakes.
7. After mastering the defensive techniques give the offense more area in which to operate such as the entire left side of the half court.

Drill 26: Deny, deflect, and recover

Objectives

1. To teach defense of the flash pivot.
2. To teach defensive hustle and alterness.
3. To teach rccovery of loose balls.
4. To teach one-on-one play offensively and defensively.
5. To teach instant conversion from offense to defense.
6. To teach the offensive dip, change of pace and change of direction.

Procedure

1. Line players up.

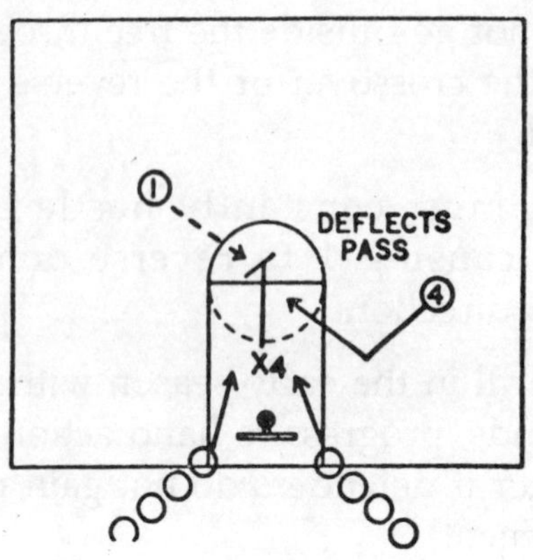

Diagram 26

2. Rotate from 1 to 4 to X4 to end of the left line to the end of the right line. First player in right line becomes the new 1.
3. Player 4 dips and breaks into the flash pivot; X4 cuts him off, beating him to the most favoured spot, and deflects the pass.
4. The two lines race for the deflected ball. They cannot leave until the defender (X4) touches the ball. The player who comes up with the loose ball is on offense; the other one is on defense in a one-on-one half-court game. You can designate the basket at the other end of the court as the area where the one-on-one game is to take place. This forces full-court decisions by your defenders.

Drill 27: Straight line tough-fight one-on-one

Objectives

1. To teach aggressive hustle to recover a loose ball.
2. To teach individual defense and individual offense.
3. To develop a competitive atmosphere among your defenders.

Procedure

1. Line up players.

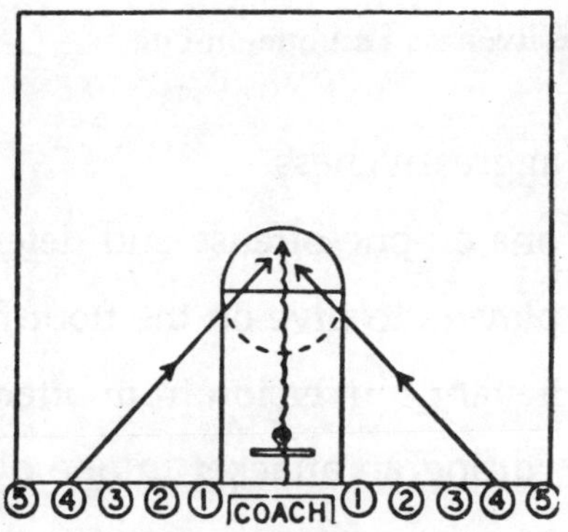

Diagram 27

2. Coach rolls ball down the middle of the floor. He should vary the speed and the distance.
3. Coach calls a number and those two race out to get the ball, diving if necessary to recover it.
4. The player who recovers the ball becomes the attacker and the other becomes the defender. They play one-on-one back to the basket, and then they return to their spot in the line.

5. Coach can make the drill highly competitive and keep score to a total number of baskets. He can put guards on one team and big men on the other, senors on one team and under-classmen on the other, or starters on one team and substitutes on the other.

6. Coach can make it a full-court transition drill by designating the basket at the opposite end of the court as the one-on-one basket after the recovery has been made.

Drill 28: Aggressiveness and one-on-one

Objectives

1. To teach aggressiveness.
2. To teach one-on-one offense and defense.
3. To teach players to dive on the floor for loose balls.
4. To teach instant conversion from offense to defense.
5. To teach cutting an attacker in one direction.

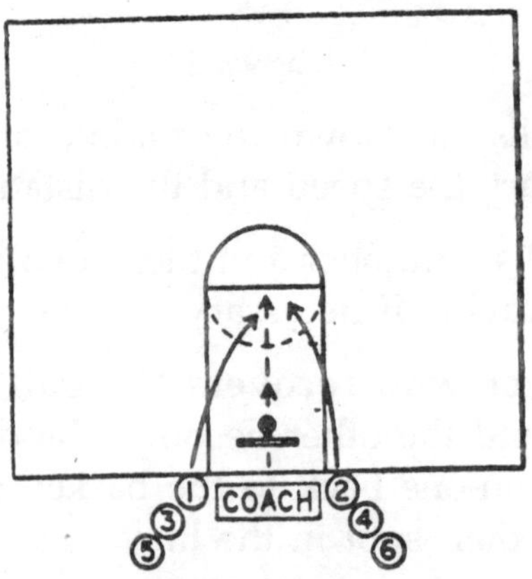

Diagram 28

Procedure

1. Line players up in two lines. Exhibits the lines at the intersection of the free throw and baselines. You can line up in the two corners or at midcourt or on the side lines. You can put the players at the opposite end of the court.
2. You can roll the ball down middle, or can bounce the ball high.
3. Players race to the ball. Player recovering the ball is on offense and the other is on defense.
4. You can play at only one basket. Or you can start at one basket and designate a different basket for the one-on-one play.

Drill 29: Quick feet-individual drill

Objectives

1. To teach the defensive lateral slide.
2. To teach hustling defense.
3. To teach instant conversion from offense to defense.
4. To teach one-on-one offensive and defensive techniques.
5. To teach recovery of loose balls.

Procedure

1. Line up players.
2. Roll the ball slowly up the floor. On signal, X1 and X2 slide to the corner around the ball and race to recover the loose ball.
3. Player who recovers the ball is on offense. The other player is on defense. They play one-on-one.

4. After those two play one-on-one they go to the end of the line. The first two players in the line prepare to chase down the next loose ball.

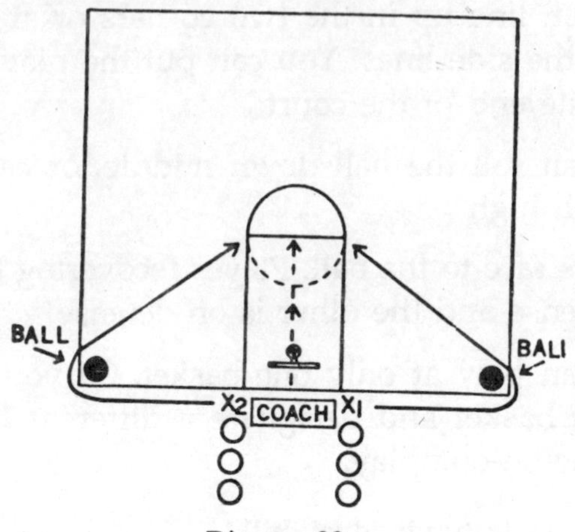

Diagram 29

5. You can have players play one-on-one at the beginning basket, or you can designate another basket for the one-on-one play.

Drill 30: Forward denial

Objectives

1. To drill on the fence slide by X2. He must keep 2 from receiving a pass below the free throw line extended.
2. To teach 2 the offensive dip to free himself for a pass or to teach 2 to reverse pivot and square out to receive a pass.
3. To teach 1 to pass under pressure.
4. To teach X1 the step-in-and-toward-every-pass principle.

5. To teach one-on-one defense including the stances.
6. To teach one-on-one offense.
7. To teach X1 to zone it (a basic man-to-man as well as zone principle).
8. To teach X1 to close the gap on inside drives.

Procedure

1. Line up players.

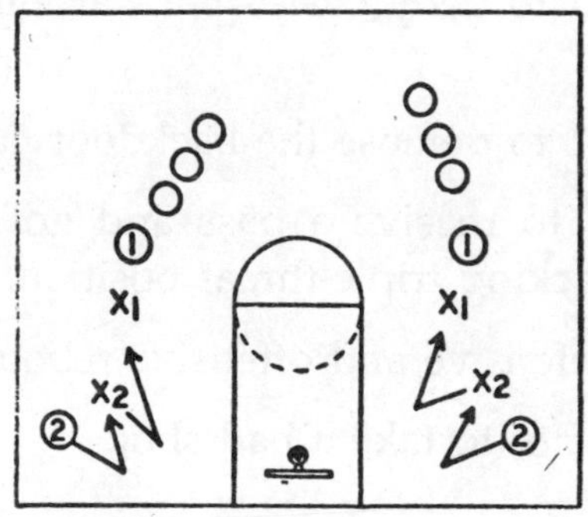

Diagram 30

2. Rotation would be from 1 to X1, X1 to 2, 2 to X2 to the end of the line. New 1 comes from front of the line.
3. Player 2 takes a deep dip and X2 fence slides trying to prevent 2 from receiving a pass from 1.
4. Player 1 must throw pass to 2 on the side away from the defense. Once I has completed the pass, X1 jumps one and a half steps toward 2 and one step in to the basket.
5. After 2 has received the pass, he goes one-on-one against X2 until 2 is stopped or scores.

6. Player X2 must be able to cover the baseline. He will have help, X1 on all inside drives. We start by not letting 1 move, then progress by giving 1 free rein in movement.

Drill 31: Deny ball reversal and defend

Objectives

1. To teach X1 to play one-on-one defense without allowing dribbling penetration.
2. To teach X1 to deny passes back around the top of the key.
3. To teach X1 to defense the backdoor cuts of 1.
4. To teach 1 to receive a pass and go immediately into an attacking triple-threat position.
5. To teach defensive and offensive rebounding.
6. To teach 1 not to take a bad shot.

Procedure

1. Line players up.

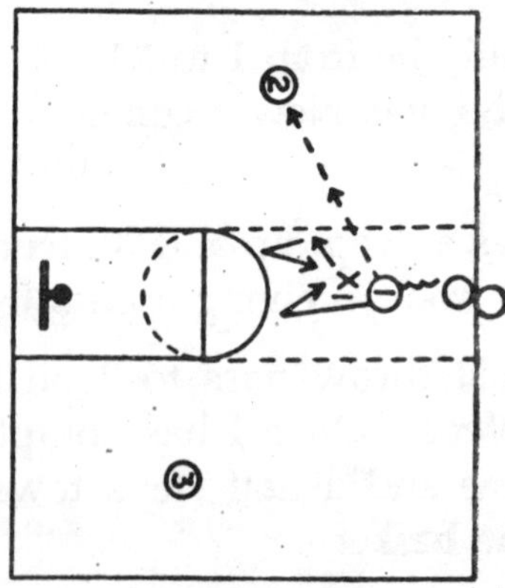

Diagram 31

2. Rotate from 1 to X1 to 2 to 3 to end of line. First player in line becomes the new 1.
3. Player 1 starts near midcourt and can only dribble inside the lane lines extended. We begin by giving 1 only two dribbles and we may extend the number of dribbles to an unlimited number when X1 has mastered controlling the dribbler.
4. In the beginning stages 1 can only shoot a lay-up. As the season progresses, we allow the jump short.
5. If I cannot score, he must take a bad shot; instead he passes to 2 or to 3. Then X1 jumps toward the pass and tries to deny a pass back to 1. This procedure continues until X1 steals the ball or scores.

Drill 32: Defending the side and low post

Objectives

1. To teach proper defensive footwork by side-pivot and low-post defenders.
2. To teach offensive and defensive one-on-one play from the side and the low-post positions.
3. To teach rebounding offensively and defensively.
4. To teach fronting playing behind and playing three quarter side positions.
5. To teach proper perimeter passing in order to get the ball inside.
6. To teach correct methods of passing into the pivot.
7. To teach 5 to post up properly: proper use of hand signals and use of the body are required to receive the pass.

8. To teach offensive moves, such as the drop step, upon receiving the pass inside.

Procedure

1. Line up players on side of the court.

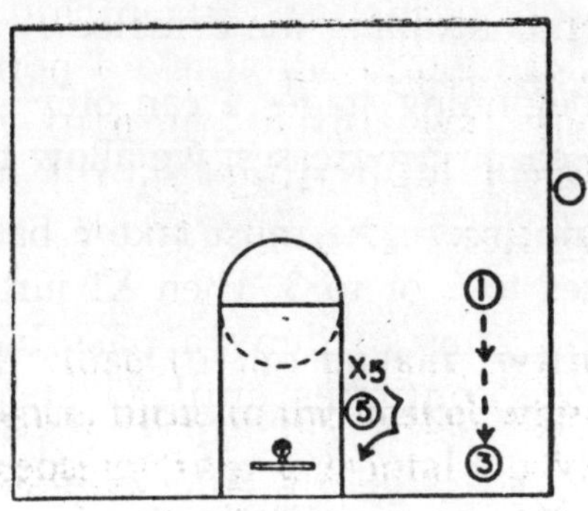

Diagram 32

2. Rotate from 1 to 3 to X5 to 5 to end of the line. First man in line takes the 1 position.
3. Players 1 and 3 drill on their passing techniques until they can pass to 5. No lob passes are permitted.
4. Player 5 must stand still at the beginning of the drill. After we are satisfied with X5's footwork, we allow 5 to slide up and down the lane.
5. Player 5 must learn to use his body to get into position to receive the pass.
6. Defender X5 uses proper footwork to prevent the reception of the pass.
7. If a pass is completed, 5 uses offensive moves to go one-on-one against X5.

8. We also progress the drill by allowing 1 and 3 to shoot, forcing X5 to box out and 5 to try offensive rebounding.
9. At intervals we either have X5 to front 5, or we have X5 play behind 5. If fronting is to be used, X5 plays tag to maintain his defensive position; if behind techniques are used, we go one-on-one when the pass goes inside.

Drill 33: Deny the flash pivot

Objectives

1. To teach X3 proper methods and techniques of defending a flash pivot.
2. To teach X3 progression from center to forward play, from weakside zoning responsibilities to strongside denial, from center to guard play.
3. To teach good one-on-one moves offensively and defensively.
4. To teach good guard, forward, and center defensing.
5. To teach defensive conditioning.
6. To help develop fast breaks after interceptions.
7. To ease conversion from offensive play to defensive play and from defensive play.
8. To teach 1 to make good passes to a moving pivot.
9. To teach 3 to receive the ball and be ready for instant fakes and drives on offense.

Procedure

1. Line players up as shown on the side of the court.

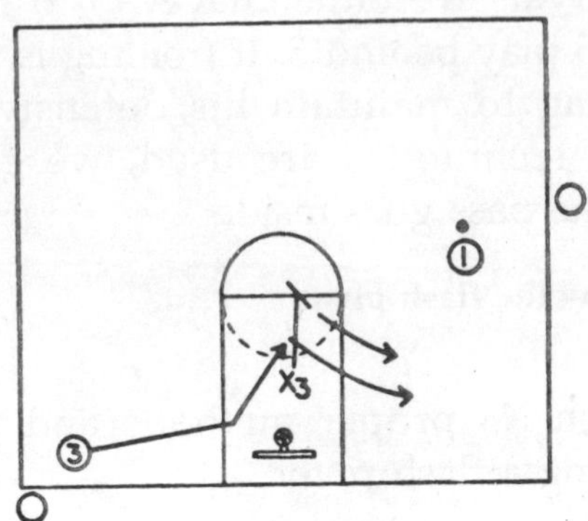

Diagram 33

2. Rotate from 1 to 3 to X3 to end of the line. First man in the line becomes the new 1.
3. Player X3 denies 3 the spot of the intended pass and forces 3 low. You should alter where I is stationed daily. X3 should always force 3 away from 1.
4. Player X3 denies 3 the pass in the flash pivot and on out into the corner. If 3 had turned up the court to become a guard, X3 denies pass until 3 gets above 1.
5. We begin the drill by walking through it. We then permit three-quarter speed and finally full speed. We would allow 3 to stop at the side post and manoeuvre for the ball, or we would allow him to come to guard position instead of cutting through the lane into the corner.

6. Now we progress by putting a defensive man on 1 and allowing a two-on-two game after 1 hits 3.
7. Any pass into the pivot should allow for one-on-one immediate manoeuvres.
8. After beginning the two-on-two phase, you can progress the drill to full court. If X1 and X3 rebound a missed short allow them to fast break. If a steal occurs, allow the defenders to fast break.

Drill 34: Center help, yet recover

Objectives

1. To teach helping to stop a free driving forward, yet recovering to play the defensive position. Defender X5 must not yell :rotate," X6 is hedging and recovering.
2. To teach recovering on one's own man after hedging. This action takes place in the paint.
3. To teach hustling on inside defense.
4. To teach difference between rotation (Drill No. 55) and hedging and recovering.
5. To teach driving toward the basket from the forward position and being able to pass off to a post player.

Procedure

1. Line up players.
2. Rotate from 3 to 5 to X5 to the line. First player in line becomes the new 3.
3. Player 3 fakes, then drives to the basket; X5 must stop him then race to cover 5, who is not permitted to move until after he has received the pass from 3.

4. X5 must rally move to get to 5 before he shoots; X5 must not foul 5.

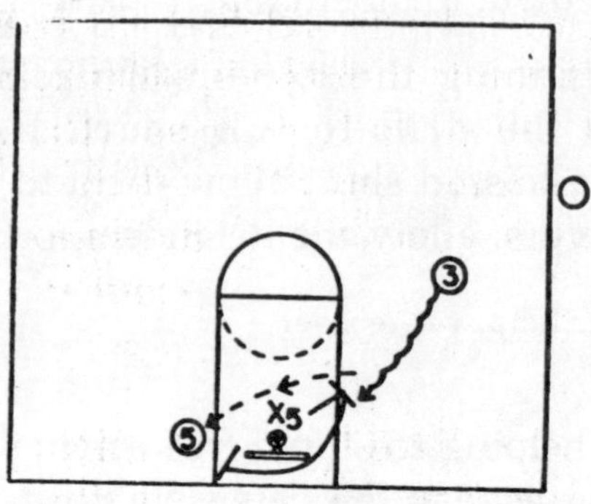

Diagram 34

5. We can program the drill for progression. You can give 3 a defender allowing rotation hedging or any of the run and- jump stunts to be called (this would make it a live two-on-two scrimmage). When you allow this two-on-two scrimmage, your defenders will not know the difference between the hedging and the recover techniques and the rotation techniques; between hedging and recovering and the run-and-jump stunts.

Drill 35: Helping on the lob

Objectives

1. This drill is good for both the zone and the man to man defense. Players must be more alter when playing man-to-man defense because the defender does not have a set area to cover.

2. To teach defense of the lob pass to inside positions.

3. To teach X1 to draw the charge.

4. To teach X1 to help the center (half-man principle) yet handle his own man (full- man principle) when playing man-to-man defense.
5. To teach lob-passing techniques.
6. To teach the center to receive the lob pass without charging.
7. To develop good hands and good inside moves against double-teaming pressure.

Procedure

1. Line up players.

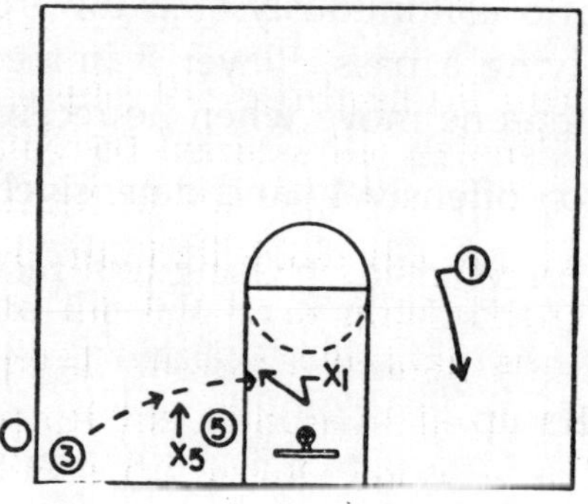

Diagram 35

2. Rotate from 3 to X5 to X1 to 1 to the end of the line. First main line becomes the new 3.
3. Player 3 throws lob pass away from defender X5. Player 5 goes to receive the pass while X5 and X1 go for the steal, or X1 draws the charge on 5.
4. Should the pass successful X5 must cover 5 and X1 drops back towards the basket to try to stop pass to 1 on backdoor cut-I does not have to cut backdoor

but he ;logically would. Defender X1 could stay and double team X5 if that is part of your team defensive plans.

5. Alternative 3's spot on the floor daily. This forces X1 to make a rationally sound judgment; it requires X1 to always see his man and the ball yet offer maximum help inside on 5.

Drill 36. One-on-one center in the paint

Objectives

1. To teach X5 to play continuously on defense inside. X5 must keep excellent defensive positioning.
2. To teach 5 to continuously step toward the passer when receiving a pass. Player 5 immediately goes into a one-on-one move when he receives a pass.
3. To condition offensively and defensively.
4. To teach correct inside passing and receiving.

Procedure

1. Line players up.

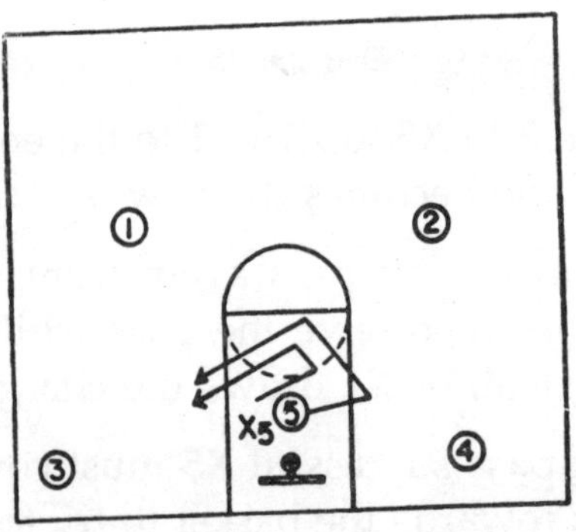

Diagram 36

2. Rotate from 1 to 2 to 3 to 4 to 5 to X5 to end of line. First player in line becomes the new 1.
3. Players 1,2,3, and 4 all have a basketball; 5 maneuvers toward either 1,2,3, or 4. X5 tries to prevent the inside pass, deflecting any pass he can, but keeping position should the ball be completed to 5.
4. When 5 receives a pass, he immediately explodes into a scoring move. X5 tries to prevent the score. Both 5 and X5 try to rebound the made or the missed shot.
5. Player 5 immediately moves towards either 1,2,3, or 4 for another passes and another move.
6. Station a manager under the goal to retrieve the made shot. The manager throws the ball back to 1,2,3, or 4 (whoever passed the ball inside to 5). This is a tremendous conditioning will when the balls are kept moving.
7. Allow each attacker and each defender one minute with the offense and one minute with the defense. These two minutes will certainly require stamina from your athletes.

Drill 37: Center defense with screeners cutters, posters and rollers

Objectives

1. To teach inside defense.
2. To teach helping out inside, yet recovering to your own assignment.
3. To teach one-on-one inside play, both offensively and defensively.

4. To teach avoiding screens to cover your own man.
5. To teach offensive and defensive rebounding.
6. To teach inside passing from the perimeter.
7. To condition defensively.

Procedure

1. Line up players.

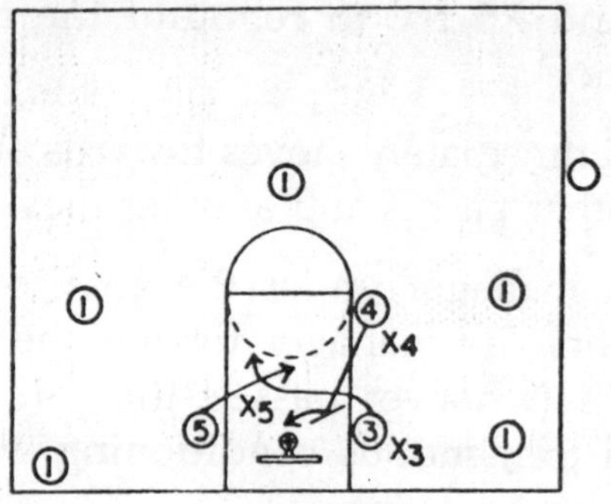

Diagram 37

2. Rotate from offense to end of the line. First three players in line become three new perimeter passers. Three perimeter passers become the new inside attackers.
3. The three inside players may move in any direction they choose. They can screen for each other, roll back to the ball, flash pivot, or make any move to get open. They cannot move more than a step outside the paint.
4. The defenders try to keep the attackers from receiving a pass. Once the attackers receive a pass,

the defenders must be ready to stop a shot or another penetrating pass.

5. If the attackers do not like their potential shot they back out to the perimeter and the movement continues.
6. As the ball is passed around the perimeter, each receiver must hold for a two count before passing again.
7. You should allow the defenders to stay on defense for about two minutes. After that, because of the demands of the drill, defensive play becomes weak.

Drill 38: Close the gap

Objectives

1. To teach closing the gap-a technique used in both man to-man and zone defense.
2. To teach drawing the charge, not blocking.
3. To teach the step-in-and-toward-each-pass helping principle.

Procedure

1. Line up players to teach them to close the gap from several court positions.
2. Put a defender on each attacker.
3. At the end of the drill, defensive men rotate to the end of the line, offensive men become defenders, and the next men in line become the new attackers.
4. Both defensive men are already in an overplay positions before the coach tosses the ball. Cut your attackers inside; you can cut them outside if that is your preference.

5. Coach tosses the ball to either offensive man. The attacker immediately begins his drive.

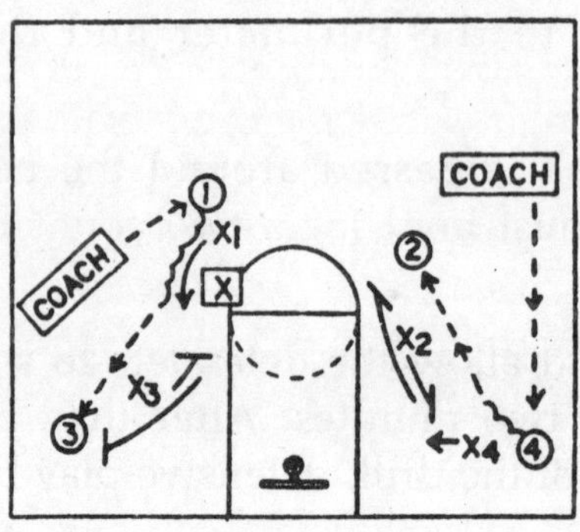

Diagram 38

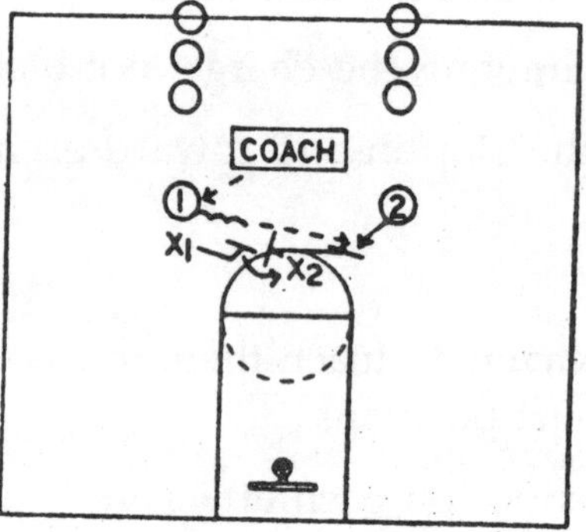

Diagram 39

6. The nearest offside defender must get in position to stop the drive. This defender gets both feet on the floor ready to draw the charge. The driver can immediately pass to the open man. Now the defender who closed the gap must use the

approach step to recover on his original man. This defender who closed the gap wants to cut the new assignment where there is help (man to-man) or in a predetermined direction (if you are in a zone). The drill continues until the attacker can drive through the hole for a lay-up. By demanding only lay-ups you several closing the gaps maneuvers in on drill sequence.

Drill 39: Point-wing defense

Objectives

1. To teach X1 and X3 to teach on passes. Defender X3 denies when playing man-to-man X3 could start at lane position when playing a zone.
2. To teach X1 proper method of covering a vertical flash-pivot cutter.
3. To teach 1 to become a vertical cutter.
4. To teach 1 and 3 good passing techniques.
5. To teach proper backdoor coverage when X3 is denying.

Procedure

1. Line up player on side of the court.
2. Rotate from 1 to X1 to 3 to X3 to end of line. First man in line becomes the new 1.
3. Player 1 passes to 3, and X3 and X1 react. 3 is a high wingman not a corner player.
4. Player 1 cuts vertically, hoping to get a give and go (A) or a backdoor (B), 1 is not to cut behind 3.
5. Player 1 becomes a flash pivot from out front. If I chooses the give-and-go route he is a side pivot. If

goes the backdoor route, he can rebreak into the flash pivot area from the side opposite the ball; X1 should in and toward each pass as indicated by (A) and (B).

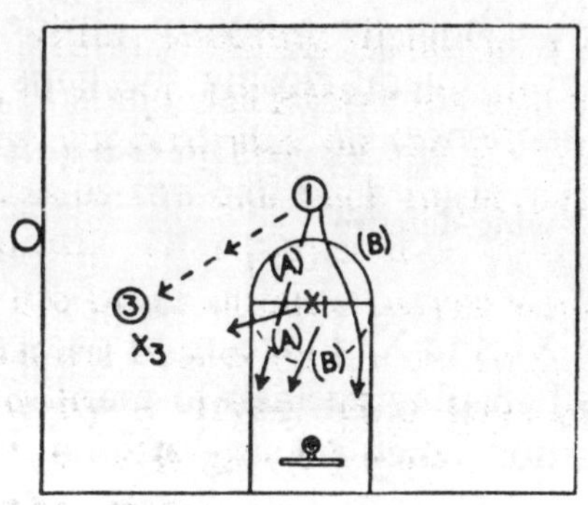

Diagram 40

Drill 40: Getting over the top

Objectives

1. To teach X1 to avoid picks and to fight over the top of screens when the ball is involved.
2. To teach 1 to dribble his man into a pick or a screen.
3. To teach 1 to jump shoot over a screen.
4. To teach 2 and 3 how to roll without taking their eyes off of the ball yet be aware of charging.

Procedure

1. Line up all players in one line on the side of court.
2. Rotate 1 to X1, X1 to 2, 2 to 3 and 3 to the end of the line. The new 1 comes from the front of the line.

3. Player 1 is to dribble until he runs X1 into 2 or 3. Player 1 can go in either direction; it keeps X1 honest.

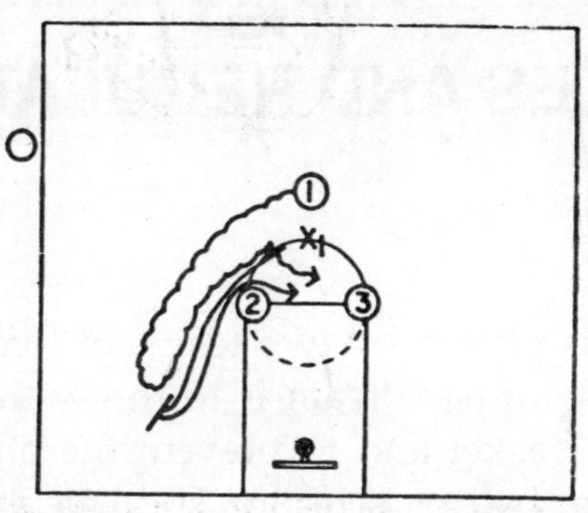

Diagram 41

4. If X1 goes behind 2 or 3, 1 shoots a jump shot over the screen.
5. If X1 gets rubbed off on 2 or 3, 1 can drive to the basket or pass to 2 or 3 on a screen and roll play for a lay-up.
6. Players 2 and 3 are not allowed to move to set picks.
7. You could put defenders on 2 and 3; then you could allow switching jump switching and so on. Defenders could learn to defense the screen-and-roll manoeuvre.

6

RULES AND REGULATIONS 

The game

Basketball is played by two teams of five players each. The purpose of each team is to throw the ball into the opponents' basket and to prevent the other team from securing the ball or scoring. The ball may be passed, thrown, tapped, rolled or dribbled in any direction, subject to the restrictions laid down in the following Rules.

Equipment

The playing court shall be a rectangular, flat, hard surface tree from obstructions. For the Olympic Tournaments and World Championships, the dimensions shall be 28 m in length by 15 m in width, measured from the inside edge of the boundary line.

For all other events, the appropriate entity of FIBA, such as the Zone Commission in the case of Zone or continental competitions, or the National Federation for all domestic competitions, has the authority to approve existing playing courts with dimensions which fall within the following limits: minus 4 m on the length and minus 2 m on the width, provided that the variations are proportional to each other. All new court shall be constructed in accordance with the requirements specified for the main official competitions of FIBA, that is: 28 m by 15m. The height of the ceiling or the lowest obstruction should be at least 7.00 m. The playing surface should be uniformly and adequately lighted. The light units should be placed where they will not hinder the vision of the players. The playing court shall be marked by well-defined lines which shall be at every point at least 2 m from the spectators, advertising boards or any other obstruction. The lines of the long sides of the court shall be termed the side lines, those of the short sides, the end lines.

The lines mentioned in this and in the following articles must be drawn so as to be perfectly visible and be 0.05 m in width. The centre circle shall have a radius of 1.80 m and shall be marked in the centre of the court. The radius shall be measured to the outer edge of the circumstance. A centre line shall be drawn parallel to the end lines from the midpoints of the side lines and shall extend 0.15 m beyond each side line.

A team's Front Court is that part of the court between the end line behind the opponents' basket and the nearer edge of the centre line. The other part of the court, including the centre line, is the team's Back Court. Three-Point filed goal areas shall be the floor areas marked on the court limited by the lines forming two arcs, each constructed as a semicircle with a radius of 6.25 m to the outer edge, taking as its centre the point on the floor directly perpendicular to the exact centre of the basket and, continuing parallel to the side lines, terminating at the end lines. The distance from the inside edge of the mid-point of the end line to the centre point from which the arc is constructed is 1.575 m. The restricted areas shall be the floor area marked on the court limited by the end lines, the free throw lines and the lines which originate at the end lines, their outer edges being 3 m from the mid-points of the end lines and terminating at the outer edge of the free throw lines.

The free throw lane are the restricted areas extended in the playing court by semi-circles with a radius of 1.80 m, their centres at the mid-points of the free throw lines. Similar semi-circles shall be drawn with a broken line within the restricted areas. Lane places along the free two lanes to be used by players during free throws shall be marked as follows: the first line shall be marked 1.75 m from the inside edge of the end line, measured along the line at the side of the free throw lane. The first lane place shall be limited by a line 0.85 m in width. All lines used to mark these lane places shall be 0.10 m long and 0.05 m wide, perpendicular to the side line of the free throw lane and shall be drawn outside the places they are delimiting.

A free throw line shall be drawn parallel to each end line. It shall have its further edge 5.80 m from the inner edge of the end line and shall be 3.60 m long and its mid-point shall lie on the line joining the mid-points of the end lines. Teem bench areas shall be marked outside the court on the same sides as the Score's Table and the Team Benches. Each areas shall be limited by a line 2 m in length, extending from the end line, and by another line 2 m in length, drawn 5 m from the centre line and perpendicular to the side line. The lines, 2 m in length, shall be of contrasting colour to that of the side and end lines. Each of the two backboards shall be made of hard wood, 0.03 m thick, or suitable transparent material (made in one piece and of the same degree of rigidity as those made of wood). For the Olympic Tournaments and World Championship, the dimensions shall be 1.80 m horizontally and 1.05 m vertically with the lower edges 2.90 m above the floor.

For all other events, the appropriate entity of FIBA such as Zone Commission in the case of Zone or continental competitions, or the National Federation for all domestic competitions, has the authority to approve backboard dimensions of either 1.80 m horizontally and 1.20 m vertically, with their lower edges 2.75 m above the floor, or 1.80 m horizontally, 1.05 m vertically, with their lower edges 2.90 m above the floor. All new backboards constructed shall be the same as those described for the Olympic Tournaments and World Championships, that is, 1.80 m by 1.05 m.

The front surface shall be flat and, unless it is transparent shall be white. This surface shall be marked as follows: a rectangle shall be drawn behind the ring and marked by a line 0.05 m in width. The rectangle shall have outside dimensions of 0.59 m horizontally and 0.45 m vertically. The top edge of its base line shall be level with the ring. The borders of the backboards shall be marked with a line 0.05 m in width. If the backboard is transparent, it shall be marked in white; in other cases, in black. The edges of the backboards and the rectangles marked on them should be of the same colour.

The backboard Shall be firmly mounted in a position at each end of the court at right angles to the floor, parallel to the end lines. Their centres shall lie in the perpendiculars erected at the points on the court 1.20 m from the inner edge of the mid-point of each end line. The uprights supporting the backboard shall be at a distance of at least 1.00 m from the outer edge of the end lines and shall be of a bright colour in contrast with the background in such a manner that they will be clearly visible to the players.

Both backboards shall be padded as follows:

For the bottom and sides of the backboards, the padding shall cover the bottom surface of the board and the side surface to a distance of a minimum of 0.35 m from the bottom. The front and back surface shall be covered to a minimum of 0.02 m from the bottom and the padding shall be of a minimum thickness of 0.02 m from the bottom and the padding shall be of a minimum thickness of 0.02 m. The padding of the bottom edge of the backboard shall be of a minimum thickness of 0.05 m.

The supports shall be padded as follows:

Any backboard support behind the backboard and at height of less than 2.75 m above the floor shall be padded on the bottom surface to a distance of 0.60 m from the face of the backboard. All portable backboards must have the bases padded to a height of 2.15 m on the court surface.

The baskets shall comprise the rings and the nets.

The rings shall be constructed of solid iron, With a 0.45 m inside diameter, painted orange. The metal of the rings shall be of a minimum diameter of 0.017 m and of a maximum diameter of 0.020 m with the possible addition of small gauge loops on the under edge Or Similar device for attaching the nets. They should be rigidly attached to the backboards and should hang horizontally 3.05 m above the floor, equidistant from the two vertical edges of the backboard. The nearest point of the inside edge of the rings shall be 0.15 m from the faces of the backboards.

The nets shall be of white cord suspended from the rings and constructed in such a way so that they check the ball momentarily as it passes through the basket. They shall be 0.40 m in length.

Pressure release rings shall meet the following specifications:

1. They shall have rebound characteristics identical to those of a nonmovable ring. The pressure release mechanism shall ensure these characteristics, as well as protect both ring and backboard. The design of the ring and its construction should be such as to ensure player safety.
2. For those rings with a positive-lock mechanism, the Pressure-release mechanism must not disengage until a static load of 105 kg has been applied to the top of the ring at the most distant point from the backboard.
3. When released, the ring shall not rotate more than 30 degrees below the original horizontal position.
4. After release and with the load no longer applied, the ring shall return automatically and instantly to the original position.

The ball shall be spherical and of an approved orange shade in colour; it shall be made with an outer surface of leather, rubber or synthetic material; it shall not be less than 0.749 m and not more than 0.780 m in circumference; it shall weight not less than 567 gr nor more than 650 gr.; it shall be inflated to an air pressure such that when it is dropped onto a solid wooden floor or the playing surface from a height of about 1.80 m measured the bottom of the ball, it will rebound to a height, measured at the top of the ball of not less than about 1.20 m nor more than about 1.40 m. The width of the seams and/or channels of the ball shall not exceed 0.635 cm. The home team shall provide at least one used ball that meets the above specifications. The Referee shall be the sole judge of the legality of the ball and he may select for use a ball provided by the visiting team. The following technical equipment shall be provided by the home team and shall be at the disposal of the Officials and their assistants:

a. The Game Clock and the Time-Out Watch; the Timekeeper shall be provided with at least a Game Clock and a stop-watch. The clock used for timing periods of play and the intervals between them and the stop-watch used for timing time-outs shall be placed so that they may be clearly seen by both the Timekeeper and Scorer.

b. A suitable device, visible to all players and spectators, shall be provided for the administration of the 30-second Rule and shall be operated by the 30-second Operator.

c. The official Score Sheet shall be the one approved by the International Basketball Federation and shall be filled in by the Scorer before and during the game as provided for in these Rules.

d. There shall be equipment for at least the three signals provided for in these Rules. In addition, there shall be a Scored Board visible to players, spectators and Table Officials.

e. Markers numbered 1 to 5 shall be at the disposal of the Scorer, Every time a players commits a foul, the Scorer shall raise, in a manner visible to both Coaches, the marker with the number corresponding to the number of fouls committed by that player. The markers shall be white with numbers of a minimum size of 0.2 m in length and 0.1 m in width, numbered from 1 to 4 in black, with the number 5 in red.

f. The Scorer shall be provided with two team foul markers. These shall be red, constructed in such a way that when positioned on the Scorer's Table they are clearly visible to players, Coaches and Officials. The moment the ball goes into play following the seventh player foul by a team, a marker shall be positioned on the Scorer's Table at the end nearer the bench of the team that has committed the seventh player foul.

g. A suitable device to indicate team fouls.

The facilities and equipment required for the following international competitions are subject to FIBA approval: Olympic Tournaments, World Champioships for Men, Women, Boys, Girls, and fro Men "22 and under.

a. The seating capacity of the playing hall shall be a minimum of 6,000 places for the World Championships for Junior Men, Junior Women and for Men "22 and Under', and a minimum of 12,500 places for the Olympic Tournaments and World Championships for Men and Women.

b. The playing floor shall be made of wood, or other material with similar characteristics approved by

FIBA. The playing Court Shall be a rectangular, flat, hard surface with dimensions of 28 m in length by 15 m in width. When the playing court is not delimited by 0.05 m wide boundary lines but by contrasting colours for the playing area and for the out-of bounds area, the line separating the two colours shall be considered as equivalent to the inside edge of the boundary lines as specified in 2 of the Rules.

c. There shall be backboards made of a transparent material having the same rigidity as 0.03 m thick wood, and their dimensions shall be 1.80 m horizontally, 1.05 m vertically with their lower edges 2.90 m above the floor.

d. The backboard supports must be placed at least 2.00 m from the outer edge of the end lines in the out-of-bounds area. They shall be of a bright colour in contrast with the background in such a manner that they will be clearly visible to the players.

e. The ball shall be made of leather and of a make approved by FIBA. The organisers shall provide at least 1 2 balls of the same make for training purposes during the warm-up period before the beginning of the game.

f. The lighting of the playing court shall have a minim of 1,500 lux; this level shall be measured 1 m above the playing court. The lighting shall meet the requirements of television.

g. The playing court shall equipped with the following electronic instruments which must be clearly visible from the Scorer's Table, the playing court and the team benches:

i. Two large scoreboards, each containing a clearly visible digital countdown type of clock, with a very loud automatic signal sounding at the end of each half and extra in the game throughout, and at least in the last 60 seconds of each half and extra period indicate this to one-tenth of a second. One of these clocks shall be designated by the Referee as the game clock. The Scoreboards shall also indicate the points scored by each team and shall likewise indicate the fouls committed by each player on the team. The does not eliminate the necessity of the markers used by the Scorer to indicate the number of fouls.

ii. Automatic 30-second devices, digital countdown in type, indicating the time in seconds. There shall be 2 such devices if located directly above the backboard, or 4 in the event that they are placed suitably near the corners of the playing court. The 30-second device shall be connected to the main game clock so that when the 30 second device reaches 'zero' and the signal sounds, the main game clock automatically stops as well.

iii. A lighted device indicating the number of fouls committed by each team; it should have numbers from 1 to 7.

iv. Three separate signals are required with distinctly different sounds: one for the Timekeeper, which sounds automatically at the end of each half of period to indicate the end of game, one for the Scorer and one for the 30-second Operator. All three signals shall be sufficiently powerful to be easily heard under adverse or noisy conditions.

h. The restricted areas and the centre circle shall be of a colour contrasting with that of the playing floor.

The standards specified above are also recommended for other major competitions.

Players, substitutes and coaches

Each team shall consist of not more than ten players and a Coach. One of the players shall be the Captain. Each team may have an Assistant Coach. In tournaments in which a team has to play more than three games the number of players on each team may be increased to twelve.

Five players from each team shall be on the court during time and may be substituted in accordance with the provisions contained in these Rules.

A member of the team is player when he is on the court and is entitled to play. Otherwise he is a substitute. A substitute becomes a player when the Official beckons him to enter the court and a player becomes a substitute at the time when the Official beckons that the player's replacement onto the floor. Each player shall be numbered on the front and back of his shirt with plain numbers of a solid colour contrasting with the colour of the shirt. The numbers shall be clearly visible: those on the back at least 0.20 m high, those on the front at least 0.10 m high and made of material not less than 0.02 m wide. Teams shall use number from 4 to 15. Players on the same team shall not wear duplicate numbers.

The uniform of the players shall consist of:

— Shirts of the same, single, solid colour-on both the back and front shall be worn by all players of the same team. Striped shirts are not permitted.

— Shorts of the same, single, solid colour shall be worn by all players of the same team.

— T-shirts may be worn under the shirts. However, if T-shirts are worn, they must be of the same, single colour as the shirt.

— Undergarments that extend below the shorts may be worn provided they are of the same, single colour as the shorts.

A player may not leave the playing court to gain an unfair advantage. When necessary, the Captain shall be the representative of his team on the court. He may address an official on matters of interpretation or to obtain essential information. This shall be done in a courteous manner. Before leaving the playing court for any valid reason, the captain shall inform the Referee regarding the player who will replace him as Captain during his absence. At least 20 minutes before the game is scheduled to being, each Coach shall furnish the Scorer with the names and numbers of the players who are to play in the game, as well as the names of the Captain of the team, the Coach and the Assistant Coach. At least 10 minutes before the game the Coaches will confirm their agreement with the names and numbers of their players and Coaches inscribed by signing with the names and numbers of their players and Coaches inscribed by signing the Scoresheet an at the same time shall indicate the five players who are start the game. The Coach of Team 'A' will be the first to provide this information. If a player changes his number during the game he (the player) shall report the change to the Scorer and to the Referee. Requests for charged time-outs shall be made by the Coach or Assistant Coach. When a Coach or Assistant Coach requires a substitution to be affected, the substitute must report to the Scorer to make the request and be ready to play immediately. If there is an Assistant Coach his name must be inscribed on the Score Sheet before the beginning of the game. He shall assume the responsibilities of the Coach if for any reason the Coach is unable to continue. The team Captain may act as Coach. If he must leave the playing court for any valid reason, he may continue to act as Coach. However, if he must leave following a disqualifying foul, of if he is unable to act as Coach because of severe injury, his substitute as Captain shall also replace him as Coach.

A player who has been designated by the Coach to start the game may be replaced in the event of an injury, provided that the Referee is satisfied that the injury is genuine. Substitutes arriving late may play, provided that the Coach had included them on the list of players give to the Scorer prior to the start of the game. The Coach or Assistant Coach is the only representative of the team who may communicate with the Table Officials during the game. He may do so whenever it is necessary to seek information concerning the score, time, scoreboard or number of fouls as permitted to request a charged time-out. His contact with the Table Officials must at all times be calm, courteous and definitely not interfere with the normal progress of the game.

When the Coach wishes to make a substitution, he shall instruct the substitute to report to the Scorer to request the substitution. The Coach shall not approach the table to make this request.

Officials and their duties

The Officials shall be a Referee and an Umpire, who shall be assisted by a Timekeeper, a Scorer and a 30-second Operator. A Technical Commissioner may also be present. The Officials and their Assistants shall conduct the game in accordance with the Rules and official FIBA interpretations of such Rules. It cannot be too strongly emphasised that the Referee and the Umpire of a given game should not be connected in any way with either of the organisations represented on the court and that they should be thoroughly competent and impartial. The Officials, their Assistants or the Technical Commissioner have no authority to agree to changes to the Rules. Officials shall wear a uniform consisting of black basketball shoes, long gray trousers and gray shirt.

The Referee shall inspect and approve all equipment, including all the signals used by the Table Officials and their Assistants. He shall designate the official timepiece and recognise its operator and shall also recognise the Scorer and the 30-Second-Operator. He shall not permit any player to wear objects which, in his judgement, are dangerous. The Referee shall toss the ball at centre to start the game. He shall decide whether a goal shall count if the Officials disagree. He shall have the power to stop a game when conditions warrant it, and to determine that a team shall forfeit the game if it refuses to play after being instructed to do so by the Referee or if it, by its actions, prevents the game from being played. He shall decide matters upon which the Timekeeper and Scorer disagree. At the end of each half and of each extra period or at any time he feels it is necessary, he shall carefully examine the Score Sheet, approve the score and confirm the time that remains to be played. His approval at the end of the game terminates the connection of the Officials with the game. The Referee shall have the power to make decisions on any point not specifically covered in the Rules.

The Officials shall blow their whistles and simultaneously give the signal to stop the clock, followed by all the signals to make clear their decision. The Officials shall not blow their whistles after a goal from the field or resulting from a free throw, but shall clearly indicate that a goal has been scored busing signal No. 1 or No. 3. If verbal communication is necessary to make a decision clear, this must be done in English for all international games. After each foul or jump ball decision the Officials shall exchange their positions on the court.

The duty of the Technical Commissioner during the game is primarily to supervise the work of the Table Officials and to assist the Referee and Umpire in the smooth functioning of the game. The Officials shall have power to make decisions for infractions of the Rules committed either within or outside the boundary lines. These powers shall start when they arrive on the court, which shall be twenty minutes before the game is scheduled to begin, and shall terminate with the expiration of playing time as approved by the Referee.

Penalties for fouls committed during intervals of play shall be administered as described. If, during the period between the end of playing time and the signing of the Score Sheet, there is any unsportsman like behaviour by player, Coaches, Assistant Coaches or Team Followers, the Referee must record on the Score Sheet that an incident has occurred and ensure that a detailed report is submitted to the responsible authority which shall deal with the matter with appropriate severity. Neither Official shall have the authority to set aside or question decisions made by the other within the limits of his respective duties as outlined in these Rules. Officials shall determine the order in which fouls or violations occur and administer appropriate penalties accordingly.

The Scorer shall keep a chronological running summary of points scored and shall record the field goals made and the free throws made or missed. He shall record the personal and technical fouls called on each player and shall notify the Referee immediately when the fifth foul is called on any player. He shall record the time-outs charged to each team and shall notify a Coach through an Official when he has taken a second time-out in each half. He shall also indicate the number of fouls committed by each player by using the numbered markers as provided. The Scorer shall keep a record of the names and numbers of players who are to start the game and of all substitutes who enter the game. When there is an infraction of the Rules pertaining to submission of line-up, substitution or numbers of players, he shall notify the nearest Official as soon as possible when the infraction is discovered.

The sounding of the Scorer's signal does not stop the clock or the game, nor does it cause the ball to become dead. The Scorer should be careful to sound his signal only when the ball is dead and the game clock is stopped, and before the ball goes again into play. It is essential that the sound of the Scorer's signal be different from that of any other sounding signal.

The Timekeeper shall note when each half is to start and shall notify the Referee more than three minutes before this time so that he may notify the team, or cause them to be notified, at least three minutes before the half is to start. He shall keep a record of playing time and time of stoppage as provided in these Rules. The signal of the Timekeeper causes the ball to become dead and the game clock to be stopped. For a charged time-out the Timekeeper shall start a time-out watch and shall direct the Scorer to signal when 50 seconds have elapsed after the start of the time-out. The Timekeeper shall indicate with a very loud signal the expiration of playing time in each half or extra period. If the Timekeeper's signal fails to sound or if it is not heard, the Timekeeper shall use other means to notify the Referee immediately. If in the meantime a field goal has been scored or a foul has been called, the Referee, if in doubt whether to award the field goal or administer the foul penalty, shall consult the Umpire. If further consultation proves necessary, the Referee shall seek advice from the Technical Commissioner, if present, as well as the Timekeeper an Scorer. However, the Referee shall make the final decision.

The 30-second Operator shall operate the 30-second device or clock as provided in Art. 57 of these Rules. The signal of the 30-second Operator causes the ball to become dead and the game clock to be stopped. The 30-second device shall be started by the Operator as soon as a player gains control of a live ball on the court.

The device shall be stopped as soon as team control is ended when:

a. A shot for goal is attempted and the ball is no longer in contact with the and of the shooter, or

b. An opponent, secures control, or

c. The ball becomes dead.

The device shall be re-set to 30 seconds and restarted only when a new 30-second period begins as player control is next established on the court.

A new 30-second period, however, does not begin following a throwing from out-of-bounds at the side line when:

— The ball has gone out-of-bounds and the throw-in is taken by a player from the same team that was previously in control of the ball, or

— The Officials have suspended play to protect an injured player and the throw-in taken by a player from the same team as the injured player.

Under such circumstances the 30-second Operator will restart the device from the time it was stopped, when a player of the same team gains control of the ball on the court after the throw-in has been made.

If the team in control of the ball fails to shoot for goal within 30-seconds, this shall be indicated by the sounding of the 30-second signal. The operator shall start the 30-second device as soon as a player establishes control of a live ball on the court, according to the provisions.

Once team control has ended, the device shall be stopped and a new 30-second count begun only when player control is again established on the court.

The device shall be constructed in such a way that, when neither team is in control of the ball there is no display on the device and such that when stopped for an out-of-bounds decision and no re-setting of the device is to take place, the device can subsequently be continued from that time. If the 30-second signal is sounded, but not heard by the Officials, the game shall be stopped as soon as possible. The game clock, if it continued, shall be re-set to the time the signal sounded and any field goals of fouls (except in the case of a technical, intentional or disqualifying foul) shall be disregarded.

If the signal is sounded in error and the ball is in flight on a shot for goal, then the goal, if made, shall count. Under other circumstances, when neither team has control of the ball and the signal is sounded in error, the ball becomes dead immediately and the game shall be re-started at the nearest circle by a jump ball. If a team had control of the ball, any player of that team shall throw it in from the point out-of-bounds at the side line nearest the place where the ball became dead.

Playing regulations

The game shall consist of two halves of 20 minutes each, with an interval of 10 minutes between halves. If local conditions warrant it, the organisers may increase the half-time interval to 15 minutes. This decision must be made known to all concerned before the beginning of the game. In tournaments lasting several days, the decision must be taken and made known to all concerned at the latest one day before the tournament is due to start.

The appropriate division of FIBA, the national and local organisations are permitted to extend the length of a single game to four periods of 12 minute duration or two halves of 22 minute duration.

The games shall be started by a jump ball in the centre circle. The referee shall make the toss between any two opponents. The same procedure shall be followed at the beginning of the second half and, if necessary, of each extra period. The visiting team shall have its choice of basket and team benches. On neutral court the teams shall toss. For the second half the teams shall change baskets. The game cannot begin if one of the team is not on the court with five players ready to play. If, 15 minutes after the starting time, the defaulting team is not present or is not able to field five players, the other team wins the game by forfeit.

A jump ball takes place when the Official tosses the ball between two opposing players. During a jump ball the two jumpers shall stand with their feet inside that half of the circle which is nearer to their own baskets, with one foot near the centre of the line that is between them. The Official shall then toss the ball upward (vertically) between the jumpers to a height greater than either of them can reach by jumping and such that it will drop between them. The ball must be tapped by one or both of the jumpers after it reaches its highest point. If it touches the floor without being tapped by at least one of the jumpers, the jump ball shall be re-taken. Neither jumper shall tap the ball before it reaches its highest point, nor leave their positions until the ball has been tapped. Neither jumper may catch the ball or touch it more than twice until it has touched one of the eight non-jumpers, the floor, the basket or the backboard.

Under this provision four taps are possible, two by each jumper. When a jump ball takes place, the eight non-jumpers shall remain outside the circle (cylinder) until the ball has been tapped. Team mates may not occupy adjacent positions around the circle if an opponent desires one of the positions.

A player shall not violate the provisions governing a jump ball. If, before the ball is tapped, a jumper leaves the jumping position or, if a non-jumper enters the circle (cylinder), it is a violation which shall be called immediately by one of the Officials. If there is a violation by both teams, or if the Official makes a bad toss, the jump ball shall be retaken.

The ball is awarded to an opponent for a throw-in from the side line nearest the place where the violation occurred. A goal is made when a live ball enters the basket from above and remains within or passes through.

A goal from the field counts 2 points unless attempted from the 3-point field goal area, when it counts 3 points; a goal from a free throw counts 1 point. A goal from the field counts for the team attacking the basket into which the ball is thrown.

If the ball accidentally enters the basket from below, it shall become dead and the game shall be resumed by a jump ball at the nearest free throw line.

If, however, a player deliberately causes the ball to enter the basket from below, it is violation and the game shall be resumed by an opponent throwing the ball in from the side line out-of bounds at the point nearest to where the violation occurred.

A three point field goal attempt changes its status after the ball has touched the ring and is legally touched the ring and is legally touched by an offensive or defensive player. An offensive player may not touch the ball when it is on its downward flight an completely above the level of the ring and is directly above the restricted area, whether it is a shot for a field goal or a pass. This restriction applies only until the ball touches the ring.

An offensive player shall not touch his opponents' basket or backboard while the ball is on the ring during a shot for a field goal or during a pass. The ball becomes dead when the violation occurs. No point can be scored and the ball is awarded to opponents for a throw-in from out-of-bounds at a position on the side line nearest the place where the violation occurred.

A defensive player shall not touch the ball after it has started on its downward flight during an opponent's shot for a field goal and while the ball is completely above the level of the ring. The restriction applies only until the ball touches the ring or until it is apparent that it shall not touch it. A defensive player shall not touch his own basket or backboard while the ball is on the ring during a shot for a field goal, or touch the ball or basket while the ball is within such basket.

The ball become dead when the violation occurs. The shooter is awarded two point, unless the shot was attempted from three point field goal area when three points are awarded.

The game is restarted from out-of-bounds behind the end line as though the shot for goal has been successful and there had been no violation. After a field goal or successful last free throw, any opponent of the team credited with the score shall be entitled to throw the ball in from any point out-of-bounds at the end of the court where the goal was made. He may throw it from any point on or behind the end line or he may pass it to a team mate on or behind the end line. Not more than 5 seconds shall be taken when throwing the ball in, the count starting the instant the ball is at the disposal of the first player out-of-bounds.

The Official should not handle the ball unless, by so doing, the game can be resumed more quickly. Opponents of the player who is to throw the ball in shall not touch the ball. Allowance may be made for touching the ball accidentally or instinctively, but if a player delays the game by interfering with the ball, it is a technical foul.

Following a technical charged against the Coach, an intentional or disqualifying foul committed by a player, the ball shall be thrown in from out-of-bounds at mid-court, opposite the Scorer's table, whether or not the last free throw is successful.

A game shall be decided by the scoring of the greater number of points during the playing time. A team shall forfeit the game if it refused to play after being instructed to do so by the Referee or, by its actions, prevents the game from being played. When, during a game, the number of players of a team on the court is less than two, the game shall end and that team shall lose the game by forfeit. If the team to which the game is awarded is ahead, the score at the time of forfeiture shall stand. If the team is not ahead, the score shall be recorded as 2 to 0 in its favour. If the score is tied at the expiration of the second half, the game shall be continued for an extra period of 5 minutes or as many such periods of 5 minutes as are necessary to break the tie. Before the first extra period, the teams shall toss for baskets and shall change baskets at the beginning of each additional extra period. An interval of 2 minutes shall be allowed before each extra period. At the beginning of each extra period, the game shall be restarted with a jump ball at the centre circle.

The game shall terminate at the sounding of the Timekeeper's signal indicating the end of playing time. When a foul is committed simultaneously with or just prior to the Timekeeper's signal ending a half or an extra period, any eventual free throw or throws as a result of the foul shall be taken.

When a shot is taken near the end of playing time, the goal, if made, shall count if the ball was in the air before time expired. All provisions contained. 29 and 30 shall apply until the ball touches the ring. If the ball strikes the ring, rebounds and then enters the basket, the goal shall count. If, after the ball has touched the ring, a player of either team touches the ball, it is after the ball has touched the ring, a player of either team touches the ball, it is violation. If a defensive player commits such a violation, the goal shall count and either 2 or 3 points awarded. If an offensive player commits such a violation, the ball becomes dead and the goal, if scored, shall not count. These provisions apply until it is apparent the shot will not be successful. If, at the end of a game, there are doubts regarding the exact termination of playing time, the Referee shall immediately consult the Umpire to determine the exact time that remained to be played. If further consultation proves necessary, the Referee should seek advice from the Technical Commissioner, if present, as well as the Timekeeper and Scorer. However, it is the Referee who shall make the final decision. The Referee shall then clearly indicate on the Score Sheet the score at the moment the timekeeper's signal was sounded and shall order the game to be continued for the time remaining. The Referee shall then clearly indicate on the Score Sheet the score at the moment the timekeeper's signal was sounded and shall order the game to be continued for the time remaining. The Referee shall start the game as if nothing had occurred, by administering the violation, the jump ball or the foul. Should a protest be filed by one of the teams, he shall immediately report the incident to the competent authority.

In the event that an extra period or additional extra period is required upon completion of the free throw(s) taken following a foul committed simultaneously with or just prior to the end of the second half or extra period, then all fouls that are committed after the signal to end playing time and prior to the completion of the free throw(s) shall be considered as having occurred during an interval of play and penalised in accordance with.

Timing regulations

The game clock shall be started:

a. When the ball, after having reached its highest point on a toss during a jump ball, is tapped by the first player, or

b. If a free throw is not successful an the ball is to continue in play, when the ball touches a player on the court, or

c. If the game is resumed by a throw-in from out-of-bounds, when the ball touches a player on the court.

The game clock shall be stopped:

a. At the end of each half or extra period, or

b. When an Official blows his whistle, or

c. When the 30 second signal is sounded, or

d. When a field goal is scored against the team of a Coach who has requested a charged time-out prior to the ball being released from the hands of the shooter on a try for a field goal.

The ball goes into play when:

a. The Official enters the circle to administer a jump ball, or

b. The Official enters the free throw lane to administer a free throw, or

c. In an out-of-bounds situation, the ball is at the disposal of the player who is at the point of the throw-in.

The ball becomes alive when:

a. After having reached its highest point in a jump ball, it is tapped by the first player, or

b. The Official places it at the disposal of a free throw shooter, or

c. After a throw-in-from out-of-bounds, it touches a player on the court.

The ball becomes dead when:

a. Any goal is made or

b. An official's whistle is blown while the ball is alive or in play, or

c. It is apparent that the ball will not go into the basket, on a free throw for a technical foul by the Coach, Assistant Coach, substitute, or Team Follower, an intentional or disqualifying foul committed by a player, or a free throw which is to be followed by another free throw, or

d. The 30-second Operator's signal is sounded while the ball is alive, or

e. Time expires for half or an extra period, or

f. The ball already in flight on a shot for goal is touched by a player or either team after time has expired for a half or extra period, or after a foul has been called. The provisions of Articles 29, 30 and 35 still apply.

The ball does not become dead at the time of the listed act and the field goal, if made, counts, if'

1. The ball is in flight on a free throw or a shot for a field goal when b, d, or e, occurs, or
2. An opponent fouls while the ball is still in the control of a player who is in the act of shooting for foal and who finishes his shot with a continuous

motion which started before the foul occurred. The goal does not count if he makes an entirely new effort after the whistle blows.

This does not apply at the end of a period.

Two charged time-outs may be granted to each team during each half of playing time and one charged time-out for each extra period. Unused time-outs may not be carried over to the next half or extra period. A Coach or Assistant Coach has the right to request a charged timeout. He shall do so by going in person to the Scorer and asking clearly for a "time-out", making the proper conventional sign with his hands.

The Scorer shall indicate to the Officials that a request for a charged time-out has been made by sounding his single as soon as the ball is dead and the game clock is stopped but before the ball goes again into play. A Coach or Assistant Coach may also be granted a charged time-out if, after a request from him for a time-out, a field goal is scored by his opponents, provided that the request was made before the ball left the hand of the shooter. In this case, the Timekeeper shall immediately stop the game clock. The scorer shall the sound this signal and indicate to the officials that a charged time-out has been requested.

A charged time-out is not permitted from the moment the ball goes into play for the first or only free throw, until the ball become dead again after a clock running phase of the game, except:

a. When a foul occurs between free throws, in which case the free throws will be completed and the time-out taken before the ball goes into play for the new foul penalty, or

b. A violation is called before the clock starts, the penalty for which is a jump ball or a throw-in from out-of-bounds at the side line.

A time-out of one minute's duration shall be charged to a term under these provisions. If the team responsible for the time-out is ready to play before the end of the charged time-out, the Referee shall start the game immediately. During the time-out, the players are permitted to leave the playing court and sit on the team bench.

No time-out is charged if an injured player is ready to play immediately without receiving treatment, or is substituted as soon as possible, or if a disqualified player or a player who has committed his fifth foul is replaced within one minute, or if an Official permits a delay.

The following points, related to the administration of charged timeouts, are brought to the attention of Coaches and Scorer.

a. A time's request for a charged time-out may be withdrawn only before the Sector singles to the Officials that a request for a charged time-out has been made.

b. The Sector shall with hold his single to request a charged time-out when an official is about to enter the circle to administer a jump ball, the free throw lane to administer a free throw, or to hand the ball to the player or place it at the disposal of the player who is to take the throw-in from out-of-bounds.

c. The time out is charged to the Coach of the team who is first to make a request, unless the time-out is granted following a field goal scored by the opponents, and without a foul being called.

d. The Sector shall sound his single to the Official when 50 seconds have elapsed from the start of the time-out.

The Officials may stop the game in cause of injury occurs, the Officials shall withhold their wistles until the play has been completed, this is, the term in control of the ball has shot for goal, lost control of the ball, has withheld the ball from play, or the ball has become dead. When necessary to protect an injured player, the Officials may suspend play immediately.

If the injured player cannot continue to play immediately and receives treatment, he must be substitute within one minute, or as soon as possible should the injury prevent an earlier substitution. If free throws have been awarded to the injured player, they must be attempted by his substitute; in the event the last free throw is successful, the substitute for the injured player may not be substituted until the next substitution opportunity for his team. If an injured player is not substituted as set out in this article, his team shall be charged with a time-out, except in the case of a team having to continue with fewer than five players. If his team has no charged time-outs left, a technical foul shall be charged against the Coach.

In the case of injury to an Official, the other Official shall apply the same provisions as those indicated in the case of injury to a player. if an official cannot continue to fulfil his duties within 10 minutes of the incident, the game shall be resumed and the other Official will official by a qualified substitute Official.

After the ball has become dead for any reason, the game is resumed as follows:

a. If a team had control of the ball, any player of that team shall throw it in from the point out-of bounds at the side line nearest the place where the ball become dead,

b. If neither team had control, by a jump ball in the circle nearest the place where the ball became dead,

c. After a foul,

d. After the held ball.,

e. After the ending of a half or extra period,

f. After a field goal,

g. After a free throw,

h. After an out-of-bounds,

i. After a violation,

Players regulations

A substitute, before entering the court, shall report to the Scorer and must be ready to play immediately. The Scorer shall sound his signal as soon as the ball become dead and the game clock is stopped, but before the ball goes again into play.

Following a violation, only the non-violating team who is to make the throw in from out-of-bounds may effect a substitution. If such a situation occurs, the opponents may also then effect a substitution. The substitute shall remain outside the boundary line until an Official beckons him onto the court, where upon he shall enter immediately. Substitutions shall be completed as quickly as possible. If, in the opinion of the Official, there is an unreasonable delay, a time-out shall be charged against the offending team.

A player involved in a jump ball may not be substituted by another player. The player who has been substituted may not re-enter the court during the same period of substitution.

A substitution is not permitted.

a. After a field goal has been scored, unless a change time-out is granted or a foul has been called, or

b. From the moment the ball goes into play for the first or only free throw, until the ball become dead again after a clock-running phase of the game, or until a foul or a violation is called before the clock starts, the penalty for which is a free throw or throws, a jump ball or a throw-in from out of bounds on the side line.

In a event that a foul occurs between free throws, substitutions will be permitted, but only after the free throws for the earlier foul have been completed and before the ball goes into play for the new foul penalty. After a successful last or only free throw, only the player who was attempting the free throw may be substituted, provided that such substitution was requested before the ball went onto play for the first or only free throw, in which case the opponents may then be granted one substitution provided the request is made before the ball goes into play for the last or only free throw.

After the Scorer has sounded the signal for the substitution to be effected, it is no longer possible to cancel the request for substitution. However, a substitution request may be cancelled at any stage prior to the Scorer's signal being sounded. The location of a player is determined by where he is touching the floor. When he is the air from a leap, he retains the same status as when he last touched the floor as far as the boundary lines, the centre line, the 3-point line, the free throw line or the lines delimiting the free throw lanes are concerned.

The location of an Official is determined in the same manner as that of a player. When the ball touches an Official, it is the same as touching the floor at the Official's location. In basketball the ball is played with the hands. It is a violation to run with the ball, kick it or strike it with the first.

Kicking the ball or blocking it with any part of a player's leg is a violation only when it is done deliberately. To accidentally touch the ball with the foot or leg is not a violation.

A player is in control when he is holding or dribbling a live ball or in an out-of-bounds situation, when the ball is at his disposal for a throw-in. A term is in control when a player of that team is in control and also when the ball is being passed between team mates. Tram control continues until an opponent secure control, the ball become dead or on a shot for goal, when the ball is no longer in contact with the hand of the shooter.

A player is out-of-bounds when any part of his body is in contact with the floor on or outside the boundary lines.

The ball is out-of-bounds when it is touches:

(a) A player of any other person who is out of bounds, or

(b) The floor or any object on or outside a boundary line, or

(c) The supports or the back of the backboards.

The ball is caused to go out-of bounds by the last player to touch it before it goes out, even in the event of the ball going out-of-bounds by touching something other than a player. An Official shall clearly indicate the team which shall take the throw-in from Out-of-bounds. To case the ball to go out-of-bounds is a violation. For penalty. Officials should declare a held ball when they are in doubt as to which team caused the ball to go out-of-bounds.

A dribble is made when a player, having gained control of the ball, gives impetus to its by throwing, tapping or rolling or and touches it again before it touches another player. In a dribble the ball must come in contact with the floor. After giving impetus to the ball as described in the foregoing, the player completes his dribble the instant he touches the ball simultaneously with both hands or permits the ball to come to rest in one or both hands. There is no limit to the number of steps a player may take when the ball is not in contact with his hand. A player shall not dribble a second time after his first dribble has ended, unless it is after he has lost control because of:

a. A short for goal, or

b. A tap by an opponent, or

c. A pass of fumble that has then touched by another player.

A player who throw the ball against a backboard and touches it before it touches an other player commits a violation unless, in the option of the Official, it was a short.

The following are not dribbles

(a) Successive shots for goal,

(b) Accidentally losing and then regaining player control (fumble) at the beginning or at the end of a dribble,

(c) Attempts to gain control of the ball by tapping it from the vicinity of other players striving for it,

(d) Tapping it from the control of another player,

(e) Blocking a pass and recovering the ball, or

(f) Tossing the ball from hand(s) and permitting it to come to rest before touching the floor, provided he does not commit a progressing with the ball violation.

To make a second dribble is a violation.

The ball is awarded to an opponent for a throw-in from the side line nearest the place where the violation occurred.

A pivot takes place when a player who is holding the ball steps once or more than once in any direction with the same foot; the other foot, called the pivot foot, being kept at its points of contact with the floor. A player may progress with the ball in any direction within the following limits:

Item I-A player who receives the ball while standing stall may pivot, using either foot as the pivot foot.

Item II-A player who receives the ball while he is progressing or upon complétion of a dribble, may use a two-count rhythm in coming to a stop or in getting rid of the ball.

The first count occurs:

a. As he receives the ball if either foot is touching the floor at the time he receives it, or

b. As either foot touches the floor or as both feet touch the floor simultaneously after he receives the ball, if both feet are off the floor when he receives it.

The second count occurs when, after the count of one, either foot touches the floor or both feet touch the floor simultaneously.

A player who has come to a Stop at the first count of the two-count rhythm, is not entitled to a new movement within the second count.

When a player come to a legal stop, if one foot is in advance of the other, he may pivot, but the rear foot only may be used as the pivot foot. However, if neither foot is in advance of the other, he may use either foot as the pivot foot.

Item III-A player who receives the ball while standing still or who comes to legal stop while holding the ball:

a. May lift the pivot foot or jumps when he shoots for goal or passes, but the ball must leave his hands before one or both feet again touch the floor, even if a defensive player makes contact with the ball with one or both hands. If the hand or hands are so firmly on the ball that neither player can gain possession without undue roughness, a held ball shall be called, or

b. May not lift the pivot foot in starting a dribble before the ball leaves his hands.

To progress with the ball in excess of these limits is a violation.

The ball is awarded to an opponent for a throw-in from the side line nearest the place where the violation occurred. A held ball should not be called too quickly, thereby interrupting the continuity of the game and unjustly taking the ball from the player who has gained or is about to gain possession. It should only be called when one or more players of opposing teams have one or both hands firmly on the ball so that neither player could gain possession without undue roughness.

A held ball decision is not warranted merely on the grounds that the defensive player gets his hands on the ball. Usually such a decision is unfair to the player who has firm possession of the ball.

A jump ball shall take place

a. When held ball is called. If there are mire than two players involved, the ball shall be tosses up between two opposing players of approximately the same height.

b. If the ball goes out-of bounds and was last touched simultaneously by two opponents, or if the Official is in doubt as to who last touched the ball, or if the Officials disagree, the game shall be resumed by a jump ball between the two players involved at the nearest circle.

c. Whenever the ball lodges on the basket support the game shall be resumed by a jump ball between any two opponents on the bearer free throw line.

A player is in the act of shooting when, in the judgement of an Official, he has started an attempt to score by throwing, dunking or tapping the ball and the attempt continues until the ball has left the player's hand(s). Players who tap the ball towards the basket directly from a jump ball are not considered to be in the act of shooting. The criteria concerning progressing with the ball and the first and second count of the two-count rhythm are not the basis for determining whether or not a player is in the act of shooting. For a foul to be considered to have been committed on a player who was in the act of shooting, the foul must occur after the start of the action which normally precedes the release of the ball on the shot.

A player shall not remain for more than three consecutive seconds in that part of the opponent's restricted area, between the end line and the farther edge of the free throw line, while his team is in control of the ball. The 3-second restriction is in force in all out-of-bounds situations, and the count shall start at the moment the player taking the throw-in is out-of-bounds and has control of the ball. The lines bounding the restricted area are part of the restricted area and a player touching one of these lines is in the area. The 3-second restriction does not apply while the ball is in the air during a shot for goal, during a rebound, or is dead because neither team has control of the ball at such times. Allowance may be made for a player who, having been in the restricted area for less than 3 seconds, dribbles in to shoot for goal.

An infraction of this Rule is a violation. The ball is awarded to an opponent for a throw-in from the side line nearest the place where the violation occurred.

A violation shall be called when a closely guarded player who is holding the ball does not pass, shoot, roll or dribble the ball within five seconds.

The ball is awarded to an opponent for a throw-in from the side line nearest the place where the violation occurred.

When a player gains control of a live ball in his back court, his team must, within ten seconds, cause the ball to go into its front court. The ball goes into a team's front court when it touches the court beyond the centre line or touches a player of that team who has part of his body in contact with the court beyond the centre line.

An infraction of this Rule is a violation.

The ball is awarded to an opponent for a throw-in from the side line nearest the place where the violation occurred. When a player gains control of a live ball on the court, a shot for goal must be made by his teak within 30 seconds.

An infraction of this Rule is a violation occurred.

A new 30-second period, does not being following a throw-in from out-of bounds at the side line when:

a. The ball has gone out-of-bounds and the throw-in is taken by a player from the same team that was previously in control of the ball.

b. The Officials have suspended play to protect an injured player and the throw-in is taken by a player from the same team as the injured layer.

Under such circumstances, the 30-second Operator will re-start the device from too time. It was stopped when a player from the same team gains control of the ball on the count after the throw-in has been made.

All regulations concerning the end of playing time shall apply to violations of the 30-second Rule.

The mere touching of the ball by an opponent does not start a new 30-second period if the same team remains in control of the ball.

A player whose team is in control of the ball in the front court may not cause the ball to go into his back court. It is caused to go into the back court by the last player of the team in control to touch it before it goes into the back court. This restriction applies to all situation occurring in a team's front court, including a throw-in from out-of-bounds.

The ball goes into a team's back court when it touches a player of that team who has part of his body in contact with the centre line or with the court beyond the centre line, or is first touched by a player of that team after it has touched the back court. The ball is awarded to an opponent for a throw-in from the mid-point of a side line. He shall have one foot on either side of the extended centre line and be entitled to pass the ball to a player at any point on the playing court. A player in his front court who gains control of the ball directly from a jumps ball at the centre circle may not pass or dribble the ball into the back court.

It is not a violation when, during a jump ball at centre, a player jumps from his front court, gains control of the ball while in the air directly from a jump ball and lands with one or both feet in the back court.

Infractions and penalties

A violation of the Rules involving personal contact which is the loss of the ball by the term that committed the violation. A foul is an infraction of the Rules involving personal contact with an opponent or unsportsmanlike behaviour, charged against the offender and consequently penalised according to the provision of the relevant article of the Rules.

After the ball has become dead, following an infraction of the Rules, the game is resumed by:

a. A throw-in from out-of bounds, or

b. A jump ball at one of the circles, or

c. One or more free throws, or

d. One or more free throws followed by a throw-in from out-of-bounds at the mid-point of the side line opposite the Scorer's table.

Procedure when a violation is committed: When a violation is committed, the Official shall below his whistle and simultaneously, give the signal to stop the clock, causing the ball to become dead. The ball is awarded to an opponent for a throw-in from the side line nearest the place where the violation occurred. If the ball enters the basket while the ball is dead following a violation, no point can be scored.

When a personal foul is committed, the Official shall bellow his whistle and simultaneously, give the signal to stop the clock. He shall than indicate to the offender that a foul has been committed. The offending player is required to acknowledge this by raising his hand in the air only if requested to do so by the Official. The Official shall than move into a position to establish clear visual contact with the Scorer and signal the number of the offender, the nature of the offence, and the penalty that is to follow. When the foul has been acknowledged by the Scorer, inscribed on the score-sheet and the foul marker raised, the Officials shall exchange positions. The game shall be resumed by one of the Officials handing the ball to the player who is to take the throw-in from out-of-bounds at the side line or end line, or take the free throw(s) from the free throw line. If the act is flagrant, the Officials shall penalise the offender by disqualifying him from the game and banishing him from the proximity of the court.

When a technical foul is committed, the Official shall below his whistle and simultaneously, give the signal to top the clock.

The player who is to throw the ball in from out-of bounds shall stand out-of bounds at the side of line at the place nearest the point where the ball left the count, or where the violation occurred or the foul was committed. Within five seconds from the time the ball is at his disposal, he shall throw, bounce or roll the ball to another player within the court. While the ball is begin passed into the court, no other player shall have any part of his body over the boundary line. Whenever the ball is awarded to a team for a throw-in from out-of-bounds at the side line, an Official must hand the ball directly to the player, or place it at his disposal. The player who is to take the throw-in must do so from the place designated by the official.

When the margin of out-of-bounds territory, free from obstruction, is less than 2m, no player of either team shall be within 1 m of the player taking the throw-in. A player shall not violate provisions governing a throw-in from out-of-bounds. These provisions

Forbid that:

a. A player who has been awarded the ball, or had the ball placed at his disposal for a throw-in, to touch it in the court before it has touched another player, or to stop in the court while releasing the ball, or to consume more than 5 seconds before releasing the ball, in order to throw, bounce or roll it to another player on the court.

b. Any player who has been awarded the ball, or had the ball placed at his disposal for a throw-in, to take more than one normal step along the side line from the place designated by the Official before releasing the ball for the throw-in.

c. Any other player to have any part if his body over the boundary line before the ball has been throw across the line.

d. The ball touching out-of-bounds before contacting a player on the court following the release of the ball for the throw-in.

An infraction of this Rule is a violation.

The ball is awarded to the opponents for a throw-in from out-of-bounds at the side line at the point of the original throw-in. A free throw is an opportunity given to a player to score one point from an unhindered shot for goal from a position directly behind the free throw line.

When a personal foul is called and the penalty is the awarding of free throw(s), the player against whom the foul was committed shall be designated by the Official to attempt the free throw(s).

The player who is to attempt a free throw(s) has 5 seconds from the time the ball is placed at his disposal by one of the officials to release the ball in a shot for goal. The free throw shooter shall take a position immediately behind the free throw line and may use nay method to shoot for goal, provided he does not touch the free throw line or the playing court beyond the line until the ball has touched the ring. It is a violation by the free throw shooter to take a free throw.

In the event that a player by mistake executes a free towards the wrong basket, the free throw shall be annulled, whether successful or not, and a new attempt shall be granted at the correct basket.

In the event that the wrong player attempts a free throw(s), it shall not count whether successful or not, and the correct free thrower shall attempt the throw(s). If the designated player must leave the game because of injury, his substitute must attempt the free throw(s). When there is no substitute available, the free throw(s) may be attempted by the captain or by any player designed by him. If there is a request for the player who has been fouled to be substituted, he must attempt the free throws before leaving. When a technical foul is called, the free throws may be attempted by any player of the opposing team.

Players may not attempt to disconcert the free throw shooter by their actions. Neither Official shall stand in the restricted area or behind the backboard.

During a free throw, the other player shall be entitled to take a position:

a. In one of the designated six lane places along both sides of the restricted area, provided they do not enter the restricted area or neutral zone until the ball has left the hand of the free throw shooter.

   Player who occupy the lane places shall take up alternate position, with the defensive team only having the privilege to occupy the first lane place, on both sides of the restricted area. The lane places are considered to be one meter in depth and shall only be occupied by a player of the term entitled to that place, otherwise they shall remain unoccupied.

b. Anywhere else on the court, except in the free throw lane and between the end line and first lane place, and in such a way that they do not disturb the free throw shooter. They are entitled to move into the restricted area or neutral zone after the ball has touched the ring following the free throw.

During free throws which are to be followed by a throw-in from out-of-bounds at mid-court on the side line, the player shall not be entitled to occupy the lane places, and all players are required to be behind the free throw line extended and not in the free throw lanes.

In all other situations, the game shall be re-started following the last free throw:

a. By a throw-in from the end line by the opponents, if the free throw is successful, or

b. By continuing play, if the free throw is unsuccessful and no violation has occurred, or

c. In accordance with the procedure, in case of a violation of the free throw provisions.

After the ball has been placed at the disposal of the free throw shooter:

a. He shall shoot for goal within 5 seconds and in such a way that the ball enters the basket or touches the ring before it is touched by a player.

b i. Neither he nor any other player shall touch the ball while it is on its way to the basket, nor touch the ball, the basket or the backboard while the ball is on the ring during a free throw. An opponent shall not touch the ball or the basket while the ball is within such basket.

ii. On the first free throw, to be followed by a further free throw(s), the restriction on touching the ball is applicable as long as the ball has an opportunity to enter the basket.

iii. During the first of a one-and one or the last or only free throw, neither he nor any other player shall touch the ball until such time as it has touched the ring and rebounded from it.

c. i. He shall not touch the floor on or across the free throw line, until the ball touches the ring, nor purposely fake a free throw.

ii. No player from either team along the free throw lane may enter the restricted area until the ball has left the hand of the free throw shooter.

iii. No other player from either team may enter the restricted area until the ball has touched the ring following the free throw or it is apparent it will not touch it.

iv. No opponent may disconcert the free throw shooter.

During the first of a one or the last or only free throw, the attempt changes its status after the ball has touched the ring, rebounded from it and is legally touched by an offensive or defensive player.

1. If the violation is by the free throw shooter only, no point can be scored. The ball becomes dead when the violation occurs. The ball awarded to the opponents for a throw-in from out-of-bounds at the side line opposite the free throw line, except after a technical foul charged against the Coach, Assistant Coach, substitute or Team Follower, an intentional or disqualifying foul committed by a player, when the throw-in-from out-of-bounds at the mid-court of the side line opposite the Scorer's table by the free throw shooters team.

2. If the violation of 'b' is by a team mate of the free throw shooter, no point can be scored and the violation shall be penalised as above. If the violation of 'b' is by both teams, no point can be scored and the game is resumed by a jump ball at the free throw line.

If the violation of "bi" or "bii" is by the opponents of the free throw shooter, the free throw will be considered successful and one point awarded. If the violation of 'biii' is by the opponents of the free throw shooter, the free throw will be considered successful, one point awarded and a technical foul shall be charged to the player who has committed the violation.

3. If the violation of 'c' is by a team mate of the free throw shooter and the free throw is successful, the goal shall count and the violation disregarded. If the free throw is not successful or if the ball misses the ring, goes out-of-bounds or falls within bounds the violation shall be penalised by awarding the ball to the opponents for a throw-in from out-of-bounds at the sideline opposite the free throw line.

4. If the violation of 'c' is by the opponents of the free throw shooter only and the shot for goal is successful, the goal shall count and the violation disregarded; if it is not successful, a substitute free throw shall be attempted by the free throw shooter.

5. If there is a violation of 'c' by both teams and the free throw is successful, the goal shall count and the violation disregarded. If the free throw is not successful, the game shall be resumed by a jump ball at the free throw line.

If more than one free throw is taken, the out-of-bounds and jump ball provision apply only to a violation during the last free throw.

Officials may correct an error if a rule is inadvertently set aside and results in only the following situation:

a. Failure to award a merited free throw(s) or

b. Awarding an unmerited free throw(s), or

c. Permitting a wrong player to attempt a free throw(s), or

d. Attempting a free throw(s) at the wrong basket, or

e. Erroneously counting or cancelling a score.

To be correctable, errors listed in items a., b., c., d. and e. must be discovered by an official before the ball become alive following the first dead ball after the clock has started following the error.

If the error is a free throw by the wrong player or at the wrong basket or the awarding of an unmerited free throw, the free throw and all the activity accompanying it shall be cancelled, unless there is unsportsmanlike conduct or disqualifying, intentional or technical fouls. However, other points scored, consumed time and additional activity, which may occur prior to the recognition of a mistake, shall not be nullified. Errors because of free throw attempts by the wrong player or at the wrong basket shall be corrected according. After the correction of an error, the game shall be restarted at the point at which it was interrupted to correct the error. The ball will be awarded to the team entitled to the ball at the time the error was discovered.

An Official may stop the game immediately upon discovering a correctable error, as long as it does not place either team at a disadvantage. Other error or mistakes shall be dealt with according to the appropriate Rule or protest procedure.

Rules of conduct

The proper conduct of the Game demands the full and loyal cooperation of members of both teams, including Coaches and substitutes, with the Officials and their assistants. Both teams are entitled to do their best to secure victory, but this must be done in a spirit of sportsmanship and fair play.

An infringement of this cooperation or of this spirit, when deliberate or repeated, should be considered as a Technical Foul and penalised as provided in the following article of these Rules. Acts of a violent nature may occur during a basketball game, contrary to the spirit of sportsmanship and fair play. These should be immediately stopped at the very first alarming sign, first of all by the floor officials and, if necessary, by the forces responsible for maintaining public order.

The playing court and the adjacent out-of-bounds areas including the Scorer's table, the teams' benches and the areas immediately behind the end lines are fully and exclusively under the jurisdiction of the Officials, who are the Referee and the Umpire. Whenever acts of violence occur between players, substitutes, Coaches and Team Followers, the Officials shall take the necessary action to stop them. The forces of public order may enter the court only if requested to do so by the Officials. Should spectators enter the court with the obvious intention of committing acts of violence, the force of public order must immediately intervene to protect players and officials.

All other areas, including ways of access and dressing rooms, come under the jurisdiction of the organiser and of the forces responsible for the maintenance of public order. In a basketball game, personal contact could be considered as a form of organised violence, limited and controlled by very strict rules with relevant penalties applied impartially on the court by the Officials.

The two Officials continually change their positions on the court, thereby producing more uniform and objective officiating. During the game, they must call the infractions of the Rules, violations and fouls, and administer the relevant penalties. In close partnership with the Table Officials, they must ensure the correct and efficient administration of the game. The decision of the Officials are final and cannot be contested or disregarded. The Officials must have authority. They must also be tactful; a friendly smile may, at times, be helpful, but the same smile at another time may be considered a provocation. An Official should never touch a player, unless it is to help him get up from the floor.

Acts of violence between opponents are generally the consequence of an escalation in the roughness of personal contact. These may being with mere occasional touching or hand guarding, followed by more intentional forms of holding or pushing, with the illegal use of elbows, shoulders, hips or knees, finally culminating with rough holding or pushing or even hitting with the first. All such contact is illegal and should be promptly called and penalised by the Officials. But the threshold of personal contact demanding a penalty is not always easy to determine: Officials should warm players guilty of touching an opponent that a personal foul could be called if they persist in doing so. Players who are guilty of flagrant acts of aggression against opponents should be promptly disqualified for the rest of the game, and the Officials should report the incident to the body responsible for the competition.

A player shall not disregard admonitions by Officials or use unsportsmanlike tactics, such as: disrespectfully addressing or contacting an Official. Or using language or gestures likely to give offence, or baiting an opponent or obstructing his vision by waving his hands near his eyes, or delaying the game by preventing the throw-in from being taken promptly, or not raising his hand properly after being requested to do so by an Official when a foul is called on him, or changing his playing number without reporting to the Scorer and Referee, or entering the court as a substitute without reporting to the Sector, or leaving the court to gain an unfair advantage, or grasping the ring in such a way that the weight of the player is supported by the ring. However, a player may grasp the ring if, in the judgement of the Official, the player is trying to prevent injury to himself or to another player.

Technical infractions, which are obviously unintentional and have no effect on the game or are of an administrative character, are not considered technical fouls, unless there is repetition of the same infraction after a warning by an Official to the offending player and to his Captain.

Technical infractions, which are deliberate or unsportsmanlike or give the offender an unfair advantage, should be penalised promptly with a technical foul.

i. A foul shall be charged and recorded for each offence and two free throws awarded to the opponents. The Captain shall designate the free throw shooter.

ii. For flagrant or persistent information of this

Article, a player shall be disqualified, removed from the game, and the same penalty as in Art. 76 applied.

If the discovery of such a foul is made after the ball is in play following the foul, the penalty should be administered as if the foul had occurred at the time of discovery. Whatever occurred in the interval between the foul and its discovery shall be valid. All player fouls which involve contact with an opponent are personal fouls, even when committed during a dead ball or when the clock was stopped. However, all fouls committed by substitutes and all player fouls which do not involve contact with an opponent are technical fouls. An Official may prevent technical fouls by warning players when they are about to make some minor infraction, such as failing to report to the Scorer or to an Official when entering the game as a substitute. It is good judgement for him to forestall and, in some cases, overlook minor technical infractions which are obviously unintentional and have no effect on the game. On the other hand, technical fouls which are deliberate or unsportsmanlike or give the offender an unfair advantage should be penalised promptly.

The Coaches, Assistant Coaches, Substitutes and Team Followers must stay with in their team bench area, except:

- A Coach, Assistant Coach or Team Follower may enter the playing court to attend to an injured player after receiving permission from an Official to do so.
- A substitute may request a substitution at the Scorer's table.

- A Coach or Assistant Coach may request a charged time-out.
- When the clock is stopped, courteously and without interfering with the normal progress of the game, he may seek information from the Scorer's table concerning the score, time, scoreboard or number of fouls.

A Coach, Assistant Coach, Substitute or Team Follower shall not disrespectfully address Officials (including Technical Commissioner if present), Scorer, Timekeeper, 30-second Operator or opponents. A Coach, or Assistant Coach, may address his players during the game and during a charged time-out providing he is within the team bench area.

A foul by a player who has previously committed his fifth foul is inscribed against the Coach and penalised accordingly. A foul be charged and inscribed against the Coach and two free throws awarded. The opposing Captain shall designate the free throw shooter. During the free throws, players shall not line up along the free throw lanes. After the free throws, the ball shall be thrown in by any player of the free throw shooter's team from out-of-bounds at mid-court on the side line opposite the Scorer's table, whether or not the free throws are successful.

The player taking the throw-in shall have one foot on either side of extended centre line and be entitled to pass the ball to a player at any point on the playing court. For a flagrant infraction of this Article, or when a Coach is charged with three technical fouls as a result of unsportsmanlike conduct by the Coach, Assistant Coach, substitute or Team Follower, the

Coach shall be disqualified and banished from the proximity of the court, which include the team bencharea and the area surrounding the playing court, and may no longer be in communication, in any way, with his team.

He shall be replaced by the Assistant Coach inscribed on the score sheet or, in the event of there not being an Assistant Coach, by the Captain.

For a flagrant infraction of this Article by the Assistant Coach, Substitutes or Team Followers, they may also be disqualified and banished from the proximity of the court. Technical fouls may be called during an interval of play. An interval of play is the period prior to the start of the game, the half-time interval and the interval prior to all extra periods.

If the foul is called against a player or substitute, it is inscribed against his name and the penalty shall be two free throws. If the foul is called against a Coach, Assistant Coach or Team Follower, it is inscribed against the Coach and the penalty shall be two free throws. After the two free throws have been attempted, the game shall be started or resumed with a jump ball in the centre circle.

A charged time-out is not considered to be an interval of play.
Physical actions of players, Coaches and team followers which could lead to damage of playing equipment-grasping the ring and violent dunking are only example-should not be permitted by Officials. The possibility of personal injury, delay of the game, and spectator inconvenience are features to be taken into consideration.

When conduct of this nature is observed by the Officials, the Coach of the offending team shall be warned immediately that this action is unsportsmanlike and will not be tolerated. Should the action be repeated, a technical foul will be called immediately. The game shall start with a jump ball at the centre circle after the free throws have been attempted.

Although Basketball is, theoretically, a no-contact game, it is obvious that personal contact be avoided entirely when ten players are moving with great rapidity over a limited space. If personal contact results from a 'bona fide' attempt to play the ball, provided the players are in such positions that they could reasonably expect to obtain possession of the ball without contact and if they use due care to avoid contact, such contact may be considered incidental and need not be penalised, unless it put the player who has been contacted at a disadvantage. On the other hand, if a player is about to catch the ball and an opponent behind him jumps in an attempt to get the ball and contacts him in the back, the opponent commits a foul, even though he is playing the ball. In such cases, the player behind is usually responsible for the contact because of his unfavourable position in relation to the ball and his opponent.

Many decision related to personal contact must result from a judgement which must be exercised with the following basic principles in mind: it is the duty of each player to avoid contact in any possible way; any player is entitled to a normal floor position not occupied by an opponent, provided he does not cause personal contact in taking up such a position; if a contact foul occurs, the foul is caused by the player responsible for the contact.

A personal foul is a player foul which involves contact with an opponent, whether the ball is in play, alive or dead. A player shall not block, hold, push, charge, trip, impede the progress of an opponent by extending his arm, shoulder, hip or knee, or by bending his body into other than a normal position, nor use any rough tactics.

Definitions

Blocking is personal contact which impedes the progress of an opponent.

Charging is personal contact, with or without the ball, by pushing or moving into an opponent's torso.

Guarding from the rear which results in personal contact is a personal foul. Official should give special attention to this tape of infraction. The mere fact that the defensive player is attempting to play the ball does not justify him in making contact with an opponent who controls the ball.

Handchecking is the action by a defensive player in a guarding situation where the hand(s) are used to contact an opponent to either impede his progress or to assist the defensive player in guarding his opponent. Such contact is illegal as it gives an unfair advantage to the defensive player.

Holding is personal contact with an opponent that interferes with his freedom of movement.

Illegal use of hand(s) occurs when a player contacts an opponents with his hand(s) in an attempt to play the ball, unless such contact is only with the opponent's hand while it is on the ball and is incidental.

Pushing is personal contact that takes place when a player forcibly moves or attempts to move an opponent. Contact with a player holding the ball by an opponent approaching from the rear may be a form of pushing.

Screening is an attempt to prevent an opponent who does not control the ball from reaching a desired position.

A dribbler shall not charge into or contact an opponent in his path, nor attempts to dribble between opponents or between an opponent and a boundary line, unless there is a reasonable chance for him to go through without contact. If a dribbler, without causing contact, passes on opponent sufficiently to have head and shoulders in advance of him, the greater responsibility for subsequent contact is on the opponent. If a dribbler has established a straight line path, he may not be forced out of that path, but if an opponent is able to by stopping or changing direction.

If a player disregards the ball, faces an opponent and shifts his position as the opponent shifts, such player is primarily responsible for any contact that ensues, unless other factors are involved.

The expression, "unless other factors are involved" in the foregoing statement refers to deliberate pushing, charging or holding of the player who is being screened. This player must make a reasonable effort to avoid contact, and any deliberate act on his part which causes contact should be penalised.

It is legal for one or more players to run down the court close to a team mate who has the ball with the apparent intention of preventing opponents from approaching the player with the ball. If, however, they run into an opponent who has taken a legal position in their path, and charging or blocking occurs, the greater responsibility is on the offensive team in case of contact in such a play.

It is legal for a player to extend his arm or elbow in taking position on the floor, but the arm or elbow must be lowered when an opponent attempts to go by, otherwise blocking or holding by that player usually occurs.

The principle of verticality: On the basketball court, players have a right to the space immediately above them. This principle of vertically protects the air space above the player but, as soon as he leaves his vertical position and body contact occurs, he is responsible and a foul may be called on him.

Thus, a defensive player cannot prevent an offensive player form jumping vertically and shooting for goal by placing his arms above the offensive player, unless, in doing so, he makes contact with the ball or the hand(s) of the offensive player which is (are) in contact with the ball. If body contact occurs, the dribbler is responsible. An offensive player may dribble the ball close to the end line under the opponents basket and then jump obliquely in order to attempt a shot to goal. If, in doing so, he lands in a place not already occupied by an opponent and no body contact occurs, this is legal play. But, if contact occurs, the dribbler is responsible.

An offensive player who, while in the act of shooting for goal, leans of an opponent who is legally guarding him from behind, thereby losing his vertical position and causing body contact, commits a foul. A legal guarding position may be considered as a vertical plane, rectangular in shape, with one short side on the floor limited by the two feet of the player, two long sides vertical from the location of his feet and the other short side in the air, higher than any player on the court can jump.

Screening-illegal Screening: Screening occurs when a player attempt to prevent an opponent who does not control the ball from reaching a desired position on the court. Screening may be legal or illegal. Legal screening occurs when the player who is attempting to screen an opponent is not in motion but standing still and has both feet on the floor. illegal screening occurs when the player who is attempting to screen an opponent is moving when contact occurs with the player who is being screened. If that occurs, the screener is guilty of blocking, and blocking is a foul.

If a player establishes a stationary legal screen in the direct field of vision (frontal or lateral) of the player who is being screened and who is in motion and contact occurs, the player who is being screened is responsible for it and a foul may be called on him. If the screen is set outside the field of vision of a stationary opponent, the screener must permit the opponent to take one normal step toward the screen without making contact.

When the player is taking a stationary screening position within the field of vision of a stationary opponent, he may establish it as close to him as he desires, short of contact. If the opponent is in motion, however, the screener must leave enough space so that the player who is being screened is able to avoid the screen by stopping or changing direction in order to go around him. A player who is legally screened is responsible for any contact with the player who has set up the screen.

Blocking: A player who is attempting to screen is blocking if contact occurs when he is moving and his opponent is stationary or retreating from him. In other cases of contact resulting from an attempt to screen when both players are in motion, the greater responsibility is on the player who is attempting to screen.

A player who screens has the greater responsibility if contact occurs when: he takes an illegal position so near an opponent and outside the field of vision that pushing or charging occurs when normal movements are made by the opponent, or he takes a position so quickly in a moving opponent's path that the opponent is not able to stop or change direction. A personal foul shall be changed to the offender in all cases. In addition: if the foul is committed on a player who is not in the act of shooting, the game shall be resumed by a throw-in by the non-offending team from out-of-bounds on the side line nearest the place of the foul.

After the foul is called and administered, the Official shall hand the ball to the opponents for a throw-in-from the side line.

If the foul is committed on a player who is in the act oi shooting:

i. If the goal is made, it shall count, and in addition, one free throw shall be awarded, or

ii. If the shot for goal for 2 points is unsuccessful, two free throws should be awarded, or

iii. If the shot for goal for 3 points is unsuccessful, three free throws shall be awarded.

After the foul is called and administered, the Official shall hand the ball to the free thrower for the appropriate number of shots as in i., ii. and iii above.

Legal guarding position

A defensive player has taken a legal guarding position when he is facing his opponent and has both feet on the floor in a normal straddle position. The distance between his feet is generally proportional to his height but he must not assume an abnormal straddle position. Furthermore, the legal guarding position extends vertically above him. He may raise his arms above his head but he must maintain them in a vertical position.

Guarding a Player who does not Control the Ball

A player who does not control the ball is entitled to move freely on the court and take any position not already occupied by another player. However, such a player and any opponent guarding him must take into account the elements of time and distance. This means that player who do not control the ball, either belonging to the defensive or offensive team, cannot take a position so near an opponent in motion (and the distance is directly proportional to the speed of the opponent, neither less than one nor more than two paces), or too quickly in the path of a moving opponent that the latter does not have sufficient time or distance to either stop or change his direction. If a player disregards the elements of time and distance in taking his position and body contact occurs, he is responsible for the contact and a foul may be called on him.

Once a defensive player has taken a legal guarding position, he may not prevent his opponent from passing him by extending his arms, shoulders, hips or legs in his path. He may, however, turn or place his arm in front of his body to avoid injury in case of a charge. Once a defensive player has taken a legal guarding position, he may shift or move laterally or backwards in order to remain in the path of his opponent. He may not move forward toward his opponent: if body contact occurs, he is responsible for it. He must respect the element of space, in this case the distance between himself and his opponent.

Guarding a player who controls the ball

In Guarding a player who control the ball, the elements of time and distance should be disregarded. The player with the ball must expect to be guarded and therefore must be prepared to stop or change his direction immediately when an opponent takes a legal guarding position in front of him, even if this was done within a fraction of a second. Of course, the guarding player must do so with out causing body contact prior to taking his position, otherwise a foul may be called on him. Once the defensive player has taken a legal guarding position, he must not extend his arms, shoulders, hips or legs to prevent the dribble from passing by him.

Position of players with respect to the ball

When two or more players of both teams try to reach for the ball and body contact occurs, the Official in calling the foul must take into consideration the relative position of players with respect to the ball. If a player tried to reach for the ball from a position at the side or rear of an opponent who is in a more favourable position to catch the ball and body contact occurs, that player is responsible and a foul may be called on him. Such a situation occurs very often two or more players of both teams try to catch a rebound. The player who is in a less favourable position (behind an opponent) may in deep try to reach the ball without causing contact with his arms or hands but, generally, he contacts his opponent with his chest or hips. One must not overlook the fact that, in a rebound situation, both players are not in control of the ball and that the player who is behind, therefore, must leave a certain space between his body and that of his opponent.

If both player face one another and both are in a favourable position to catch the ball and contact occurs, it may be disregarded unless one of the player uses his arm, shoulders, hips or legs to push the opponent out of his position, in which case a foul may be called on him. If the contact is particularly violent and both players are involved, a double foul may be called. The principle described above in a rebound situation is of course also valid elsewhere on the court, whenever two or more opponents try to reach for the ball simultaneously.

If a dribble is closely guarded by an opponent and, without causing body contact, passes his guard and has his head and shoulders past him and contact occurs, the defensive player is generally responsible and a foul may be called on him. However, if the offensive player contacts the guard on the chest or shoulders, then the offensive player is responsible for the contact and a charging foul may be called on him. This, of course, assumes that the guard was in a legal guarding position and was not moving forward toward the dribbler.

A player who has jumped in the air from a spot on the court is entitled to land again at the same spot without hindrance by opponents. He may also land at another spot on the court provided the landing spot was not already occupied by an opponent at the time of the take-off and that the direct path between the take-off and landing spot was not already occupied by opponents. A player may not move in the path of an opponent after the latter has jumped into the air. Moving under a player who is the air is always an intentional foul and in certain cases it may be disqualifying foul.

However, if a player has taken off and landed but his momentum causes him to contact an opponent who has taken a legal guarding position near the landing spot, then the jumper is responsible for the contact, and a foul may be called on him.

The touching of an opponent with a hand or hands, in itself, is not necessarily an infraction. However, if the contact in any way restricts the freedom of movement of an opponent, such contact is a foul. Likewise, a dribbler may not use an extended forearm or hand to prevent an opponent from securing the ball. Situation of this nature can result in an advantage not intended by the Rules and should be discouraged as it will lead to increased contact between opponents.

Some players have a tendency to touch an opponent while they are moving on the court. This is generally done in order to identify the position of a opponent. When the opponent is in the field of vision of a player, there is no justification in touching with the hands and such action should be considered illegal personal contact.

The principle of verticality also applies to post play. Both the player in the post position and an opponent guarding him must respect each other's vertical right. The pivot player should not be allowed to shoulder or hip his opponent out of position, nor interfere with the latter's freedom of movement by the use of extended elbows or arms. On the other hand, the defensive player should not allowed to interfere with the pivot player's freedom of movement by the illegal use of arms, knees or other parts of the body.

An intentional foul is a personal foul in a player with or without the ball which, in the opinion of the Official, was deliberately committed by a player against an opponent. It is not determined by the severity of the act, but is the contact which appears to be premeditated or designed. A player who repeatedly commits intentional fouls may be disqualified. A person foul shall be changed to the offender. Free throw(s) shall be awarded to the non-offending team, followed by possession of the ball for a throw-in from out-of-bounds at the mid-point of the side line opposite the Scorer's table.

The number of free throw to be awarded shall be as follows:

i. If the foul is committed on a player not in the act of shooting, 2 free throws shall be awarded.

ii. If the foul is committed on a player who is in the act of shooting, the goal, if made, shall count and in addition one free throw shall be awarded.

iii. If the foul is committed on a player in the act of shooting who fails to score, two or three free throws shall be awarded, according to the place from where the shot for goal was attempted.

During the free throw(s), players shall not line up along the free throw lanes. After the free throw(s), the ball shall be throw in by any player of the free throw shooter's team from out-of-bounds at mid-court on the side line opposite the Scorer's table, whether or not the free throw(s) are successful. The player takes the throw -in shall have one foot on either side of the extended centre line, and be entitled to pass the ball to a player at any point on the playing court.

Officials should call intentional fouls in accordance with the spirit and intent of the rules, especially at the end of a game when intentional fouls can be committed to gain a tactical advantage. If these intentional fouls are not recognised and penalised, the team committing the intentional foul can gain an unfair advantage. Furthermore, the control by the Officials could be weakened. If, in the opinion of the Official, any of the following criteria apply, then the foul should be called as intentional.

Fouls committed:

i. To stop the game clock, especially near the end of the game.

ii. Against an opponent who has an open path to the basket to prevent an opportunity to score.

iii. Against an opponent in control of the ball, that are not legitimate attempts to directly play the ball.

iv. When the game clock is stopped, such as prior to a throw-in or jump ball.

v. By player dangerously moving under an opponent who is in the air.

vi. By a player swinging an elbow.

vii. By a player holding or pushing a player who is away from the ball.

In applying the above criteria the personal foul must have been committed deliberately, i.e. on purpose. Any flagrantly unsportsmanlike infraction of 70 or 74 is a disqualifying foul. Two free throws and possession of the ball for a throw-in from out-of-bounds at the mid-point of the sideline opposite the Scorer's table. A player who commits such a foul must be charged with the foul, disqualified and banned form the proximity of the court, which includes the team bench and playing court areas, and may no longer, in any way, be in communication with his team.

A double foul is situation in which two opposing players commit fouls against each other at the same time. In case of a double foul, no free throws are awarded but a personal foul shall be charged against each offending player.

The game shall be resumed at the nearest circle by a jump ball between the two players involved, unless a valid field goal is scored at the same time, in which case the ball shall be put into play from the end line.

Whenever a foul is committed against a player after he has started his shooting action, the goal shall count if made, even if the ball leaves the player's hand after the whistle has blown. The goal does not count if he makes an entirely new effort after the whistle has blown. This does not apply at the end of a period.

Each Official has the power to call fouls independently from the other, at any time during the game, whether the ball is in play, alive or dead.

Any number of fouls may be called at the same time against one or both teams. irrespective of the penalty, a foul shall be inscribed on the Score Sheet against the offender for each foul. A player who has committed five fouls either personal or technical, must automatically leave the game. After a team has committed seven player fouls, personal or technical, in a half, all subsequent player fouls shall be penalised by the one and one rule, unless a penalty of greater severity is involved.

In the event that the foul is committed by a player while his team is in control of the ball, Art. 84 is applied. All fouls occurring before the game are considered to be part of the first half. All fouls that take place in the interval of play before the second half or during extra periods are considered to be part of the second half. When a player commits a subsequent personal foul after his team has committed seven player fouls, personal or technical, in a half, the one and one rule comes into effect, whereby the player against whom the foul has been committed is given the opportunity to shoot one free throw.

If this free throw is successful, it is followed by a further free throw taken by the same player. If, however, the first free throw is unsuccessful, the game shall continue in accordance with.

A foul committed by a player while his team is in control of the ball shall always be penalised by recording the foul against the offender and awarding the ball for a throw-in to an opponent at the nearest point out-of bounds at a side line. Situations other than those foreseen in these Rules may occur when fouls are committed at approximately the same time or during the dead ball period which follows a foul or a double foul. In such situations, the following principles shall be applied.

a. A foul shall be charged for each offence.

b. Fouls against both teams that involve the same penalties shall not be penalised by awarding free throws or possession of the ball for a throw-in from the side line. For this purpose, the one and one and the two free throws penalties shall be regarded as being the same. The game shall be re-started by a jump ball at the nearest circle unless a field goal has been scored, in which case the game shall be re-started by a throw-in from out-of-bounds on or behind the end line.

c. Fouls against both teams that do not involve the same penalties shall be penalised and administered according to the order in which they occurred. If fouls are called against both teams at approximately the same time, the Officials must determine the order in which the fouls occurred.

d. The right to possession of the ball for a throw-in as the result of a previous foul penalty shall be forfeited in the event that another foul is called before the throw-in is taken.

Any bench personnel who leaves the confines of the team bench area during a fight or during any situation which may lead to fight, shall be disqualified from the game and shall be banned from the proximity of the court, which included the team bench area and the playing court area and may no longer, in any way, be in communication with his team.

In addition, for any incident of this nature, a single technical foul shall be charged against the Coach. However, The Coach may leave the confines of the team bench area during a fight or during any situation which may lead to a fight in order to assist the Officials to maintain or restore order.

If a Coach leaves the confines of the team bench area and fails to assist, in any way, in maintaining or restoring order, he shall be disqualified and shall be banned from the proximity of the court, which includes the team bench area and the playing court area and may no longer, in any way, be communication with his team. The disqualifying foul(s) under this Article will not be recorded as team fouls.

Choice of baskets and team benches

The decision by the visiting team or the toss for baskets shall take place at least twenty minutes before the game is scheduled to being in the presence of the Referee and the Captain or Coach of each team.

a. The visiting team, or on neutral courts, the team winning the toss shall have the choice of basket and team benches.

b. Before each half and each extra period, the team are entitled to practise in that half of the court in which their opponent's basket is situated.

Team bench

During the game, the only persons permitted to sit on a team bench are the Coach, the Assistant Coach, the substitutes and a maximum of five Team Followers with special responsibilities.

To be a Team Follower is a privilege, and this involves a responsibility. Therefore a' Team Follower's behaviour comes under the jurisdiction of the Officials.

No other person may sit within two metres of a team bench. The referee may, where conditions warrant it:

a. Reduce the number of Team Followers that can sit on the bench.

b. Permit the Assistant Coach or one of the accredited Team Followers to sit as a representative of his team at or near the Scorer's Table. However, if his behaviour interferes with the work of the Table Officials, the Referee may have him removed from that place.

Procedure for substitution

The Coach should send the substitute-who must be ready to play-to sit on the seat provided until the Scorer sounds his signal. He should then stand up and indicate to the nearer Official that he wishes to enter the court. He should not enter the court until beckoned to do so by an Official. If a substitution is required during a charged time-out, the substitute must report to the Scorer and the nearer Official before entering the court.

It a team believes, its interests have been adversely affected by a decision of an Official or by any event whatever that took place during a game, it must proceed in the following manner:

a. At the moment when the incident takes place, either immediately when the ball is dead and the clock is stopped, or at the first time-out that follows, the Captain of the team shall make his observations to the Referee, provided this is done in a calm and courteous manner. The Referee may explain his decision or, if necessary, may examine the Score Sheet and check the score and the playing time. If this interruption of the game exceeds 30 seconds, it shall be changed as a time-out to the team in question, unless the Referee decides otherwise, recognising the validity of the observation.

b. if, at the end of the game, the team in question should deem to have been put at a disadvantage by what has happened, its Captain shall immediately report to the Scorer's Table and inform the Scorer that his team is protesting against the result of the game. He shall then sign the Score Sheet in the space marked "To be signed by Captain in case of Protest". In order to make this declaration valid, it shall be necessary that the official representative of the team on the court (either its Coach or the representative of the national federation) give confirmation of this protest in writing with in 20 minutes following the end of the game, without however giving detailed explanations (for instance: "The national federation of X protests against the result of the game between the teams of X and of Y"), then deposition with the representative of FIBA or of the Technical Committee, as security, a sum equivalent to DM 200.

c. The national federation of the team in question

must submit to the President of the Technical Committee the text of its protest within the hour that follows the end of the game. If the protest is accepted, the security shall be refunded.

d. Should the national federation of the team in question, or that of the opposing team, not be in agreement with the decision of the Technical Committee, it may then address an appeal to the jury of Appeal. To make this valid, the appeal must be made immediately and accompanied by a deposit, as security, equivalent to DM 400. The jury of Appeal shall judge the appeal in the last instance, and its decision shall be final.

Classification of team

The classification of teams shall be made on points according to their win-loss records, namely 2 points for each game won, 1 point for each game lost, and 0 points for a game lost by forfeit.

i. If there are two teams equal in this classification, the result(s) of the game(s) between the two teams involved will be determine the placing. In the event that the total points scored and conceded are the same in the games between the two teams, the classification will be determined by both teams.

ii. If more than two teams are equal in the placing, a second classification will be established, taking into account only the result of the games between the teams that are tied.

In the event that there are still teams tied after the second classification, then goal average, taking into account only the results of the games between the teams still tied, will be used to determine the placing.

INDEX